THE NORT

# POCKET BOOK

# OF WRITING

# BY STUDENTS

Melissa A. Goldthwaite

ST. JOSEPH'S UNIVERSITY

W. W. NORTON & COMPANY   New York   London

W. W. Norton & Company has been independent since its founding in 1923, when William Warder Norton and Mary D. Herter Norton first published lectures delivered at the People's Institute, the adult education division of New York City's Cooper Union. The firm soon expanded its program beyond the Institute, publishing books by celebrated academics from America and abroad. By mid-century, the two major pillars of Norton's publishing program—trade books and college texts—were firmly established. In the 1950s, the Norton family transferred control of the company to its employees, and today—with a staff of four hundred and a comparable number of trade, college, and professional titles published each year—W. W. Norton & Company stands as the largest and oldest publishing house owned wholly by its employees.

Composition by TexTech, Inc.
Manufacturing by Worldcolor
Book design by Joanne Metsch
Production manager: Eric Pier-Hocking

Library of Congress Cataloging-in-Publication Data

   The Norton pocket book of writing by students / [edited by] Melissa A. Goldthwaite. —1st ed.
      p. cm.
   **ISBN: 978-0-393-93230-0 (pbk.)**
   1. College students' writings, American.   I. Goldthwaite, Melissa A., 1972–
   PS508.C6N67  2010
   810.8' 09235—dc22

                                                    2009054283

W. W. Norton & Company, Inc., 500 Fifth Avenue, New York, NY 10110
wwnorton.com

W. W. Norton & Company Ltd., Castle House, 75/76 Wells Street, London
WIT 3QT

1 2 3 4 5 6 7 8 9 0

In memory of
Wendy Bishop (1953–2003)
and
David Citino (1947–2005)

Friends, writers, teachers
who believed in learning from students

# Contents

## Contents

# Contents

# LOOKING BACK, LOOKING FORWARD
## A Preface for Students and Teachers

Remember those old composition books, with marbled covers and lined paper inside? Remember when the rules of grammar and "good" writing were as black and white as those covers? When the readings in composition books were by E. B. White and Annie Dillard and other famous authors, and a textbook author wouldn't dream of using contractions, much less sentence fragments? Simpler times, perhaps.

The times and the rules were probably never that simple, but they're surely not simple now. And so *The Norton Pocket Book of Writing by Students* reflects—and celebrates—how the times have changed in writing classrooms. Its black binding and generic white label might suggest something of the past, but the black marbling has given way to watercolors—and the writing inside has come a long way from the five-paragraph essays of the past. The forty-two selections include thesis-driven essays and mixed-genre pieces, research reports and poetry—and a poem Barack Obama wrote when he was a college student. But all have one thing in common: each is an example of excellent writing, here to celebrate and inspire.

### TO CELEBRATE, TO INSPIRE

Writing programs across the country publish collections of their students' work. Many schools do so annually, with committees reading and vetting sometimes hundreds of pieces of student writing, to celebrate the finest and to use these pieces as pedagogical models in class.

The purpose of this collection is similar: to celebrate excellent student writing and to honor the kinds of teaching and assignments that help students produce such writing. Students spend a great deal of time writing in response to these assignments—honing their attention to their rhetorical situations and producing strong writing for a small audience: sometimes an entire class but just as often only a few peers and the teacher. For most students there is little opportunity to celebrate such work and little chance for other students and teachers to enjoy, appreciate, and learn from such writing. Like the many teachers and writing program administrators who organize contests and readings and publish their students' work, I believe that student writing deserves careful attention and a wider audience—not only for the purposes of celebration but also for teaching and learning.

Students, like professional writers, learn by example, and profit from reading and studying exemplary writing by their peers. Teachers benefit from seeing new assignments—or different approaches to familiar assignments, perhaps finding a way to include a research assignment in a creative writing class or poetry in a composition class.

Each selection opens with a headnote, with information about the author and assignment. In addition, it includes information about why the piece was nominated for the anthology, helping students to recognize what other readers value in specific written texts and perhaps to think about their own criteria for what distinguishes excellent writing from good writing. And each selection is followed by several "reading to write" questions, helping students to see some of the techniques and elements of craft demonstrated in each piece, and prompting them to try those techniques out in their own writing.

## HOW THE WRITING WAS CHOSEN AND EDITED

In autumn of 2007, I sent a call for submissions of excellent student writing to the Writing Program Administrators listserv. I provided suggestions for genres (literacy narratives, textual and literary analyses, reports, arguments, memoir and other autobiographical essays, profiles, short stories, poems, mixed-genre pieces) but emphasized that any exemplary writing would be considered. I asked teachers to nominate individual pieces but also to send whole collections published by their writing programs or to invite students to nominate their own work. Four months after that initial call for papers, I had received more than eighty individual submissions (from both teachers and students) and stacks of custom-published readers from writing programs across the country. The response from that initial call provided the framework for this collection. In spring of 2008, another call for papers—this time in print form—was distributed at the Conference on College Composition and Communications, and the submissions sent in response (supplemented by requests to individual teachers and students) rounded out the collection.

The initial batch of individual submissions included work from schools in twenty different states; from large research universities, small liberal arts colleges, medium-sized comprehensive universities, schools with religious affiliations, and Ivy League schools. The topics represented in the writing ranged widely: disability, health, finances, government, art, sexuality, voice, memory, ethics, social spaces, literature, holidays, advertising, gender, popular culture—and more. The submissions, too, were written for different kinds of classes: first-year composition, freshman seminars, poetry workshops, literature classes, and many different "themed" classes.

Still, there were absences: no submissions of writing from students at two-year or community colleges, no submissions from more than half the states in the country (although every region of the country was represented). And there were other puzzling statistics: 74 percent of those first individual submissions were from female students, and 74 percent of those pieces of writing were done in classes taught by women (though many female instructors submitted work by male students and many male instructors submitted work by females). My editor at Norton and I puzzled over these statistics, particularly the ones related to gender, which didn't compare with other published anthologies.

In the initial round of selections, I did not consider geography, types of schools represented, or gender. I simply read each submission, noted its genre, made comments about its strengths and weaknesses, and then assigned a number: 1–10. I put any piece that scored an 8 or higher in a separate pile and started with those as the foundation for the book, arranging them generically, even as some genres overlap. Other selection considerations included length (I wanted there to be strong examples of both shorter and longer pieces in each chapter), and, when possible, I sought two excellent pieces in answer to the same assignment—or a similar assignment—to show that there can be more than one outstanding response to the same assignment and to provide teachers and students an opportunity to discuss the qualities these pieces have in common as well as how they differ.

And then there was the question of editing. To what extent should we edit the writing? The writing included in this book looks very much like it did when it was submitted. That is, it has been edited lightly, perhaps less so than most writing done by professional authors. Although these pieces were submitted as "final" drafts and some teachers encouraged revision before submitting them, several teachers recognized that there still might be room for improvement, even in writing deemed exemplary. The appendix includes an example of one writer's drafting process and her teacher's comments. Although such a process is made invisible by including only final drafts in the rest of the book, most of the writers in this collection have gone through a similar process, one that involved not only their own efforts but also the contributions of their peers and teachers. Excellent writing rarely, if ever, happens on the first try.

## WHAT MAKES WRITING EXCELLENT?

A significant question for both teachers and students—and one at the very foundation of this book: *What makes writing excellent?* It's a question teachers ask when composing assignments, reading and commenting on drafts, developing rubrics or other standards for evaluation, and determining grades. It's a question students ask as they write, revise, and receive feedback. I've seen answers to this question in reading nominations and in reading students' reflections on what they've learned through revising. Some of the headnotes in this book include quotations from teachers about why they nominated a particular piece; others contain reflections from students about what they learned through the process of writing and revising their work. And in the questions that follow each selection, I encourage readers to focus on some of the elements that make the writing successful.

Answers to this question about "excellence" are always genre- and audience-specific, but some common themes emerge: in thesis-driven writing, readers value clarity, organization, development, an effective use of sources and evidence, and some new contribution in terms of ideas. More than once in these submissions, an instructor commented that the work was publishable for its unique contribution. No matter the genre, nominators valued engagement with complexity, attention to voice and detail, and a level of personal interest in the topic that led to deeper intellectual exploration.

Although these themes and patterns emerged, the difficulty with defining excellence remains. Is it possible to list all the qualities of the writing that make teachers forget they are evaluating or grading and let them simply enjoy and often learn something new? I experienced many such moments of enjoyment and learning while reading these submissions, and will offer just three examples: I identified with Tess Bird's "The Shadow That the Apple Casts: Thoughts on Exposure," having myself considered the difficult ethical issues involved in writing about, and potentially "exposing," oneself and others. In reading "Freeing the Caged Bird: My Conversations with Maya Angelou," I was impressed by Kristin Taylor's facility in bringing together different generic conventions as she seamlessly wove the personal, literary, and scholarly in her braided essay. And after reading Jonathan Payne's "Xenakis, Cage, and the Architecture of Music," I purchased a copy of John Cage's

*Silence,* and as I read this book outside on a cool June afternoon, I became aware—thanks, in part, to Payne's charting of sounds and the description of his own research—of the ways in which the practice of "silent reading" is immersed in sound (wind in the leaves of the birch, protective robins, pages turning, my dog's breathing).

If there is a message for students in this collection, it is this: when you care about what you write and take the time to hone and revise in response to readers' questions and concerns, you can learn about and clarify ideas for yourself even as you do so for others. The message for teachers, I hope, is this: the assignments you craft, the many hours you spend commenting on drafts and engaging in conferences, and the discussions you lead in class make a difference in the lives and work of individual students and can have a broader impact, a wider audience. This collection celebrates and honors the hard work, talent, and thoughtfulness of students and teachers. I trust it will spark new ideas for assignments and approaches to those assignments—and that you, students and teachers alike, will share your successes, your excellent work, with others.

## LOOKING BACK, LOOKING FORWARD

There is value in looking back—in seeing a writer's development over time. Whether this is your first year of college or you've been teaching for thirty years, you've had many writing experiences that have shaped you. Maybe you wrote books in elementary school and "published" them for parents' night. When I was in the first and fourth grades, our revised stories and essays were bound with wallpaper samples and cardboard and displayed in the school cafeteria. Several decades later, I still have these books and recognize in them themes and concerns similar to those in the writing I do now.

This collection opens with a chapter of literacy narratives, of writing about writing. The readings in this chapter encourage writers to look back, to think about formative events that have shaped you as a writer. Such reflection might also encourage you to look ahead, to think about where you'd like to be in the future, for who you are as a writer reflects something of who you are as a person.

Even the most famous and eloquent writers and speakers have had formative experiences that have shaped their writing. Much has been made, for example, of President Barack Obama's ability as a writer and speaker. He's known for his eloquence and delivery. He, too, was once a student writer, and a couple of his poems—including the one printed below—were published in the literary magazine at Occidental College when he was a student there.

# Pop

## Barack Obama

Sitting in his seat, a seat broad and broken
In, sprinkled with ashes,
Pop switches channels, takes another
Shot of Seagrams, neat, and asks
5     What to do with me, a green young man
Who fails to consider the
Flim and flam of the world, since
Things have been easy for me;
I stare hard at his face, a stare
10    That deflects off his brow;
I'm sure he's unaware of his
Dark, watery eyes, that
Glance in different directions,
And his slow, unwelcome twitches,
15    Fail to pass.
I listen, nod,
Listen, open, till I cling to his pale,
Beige T-shirt, yelling,
Yelling in his ears, that hang
20    With heavy lobes, but he's still telling
His joke, so I ask why
He's so unhappy, to which he replies . . .
But I don't care anymore, cause
He took too damn long, and from
25    Under my seat, I pull out the
Mirror I've been saving; I'm laughing,
Laughing loud, the blood rushing from his face

To mine, as he grows small;
A spot in my brain, something
That may be squeezed out, like a                                    30
Watermelon seed between
Two fingers.
Pop takes another shot, neat,
Points out the same amber
Stain on his shorts that I've got on mine, and                      35
Makes me smell his smell, coming
From me; he switches channels, recites an old poem
He wrote before his mother died,
Stands, shouts, and asks
For a hug, as I shink,* my                                          40
Arms barely reaching around
His thick, oily neck, and his broad back; 'cause
I see my face, framed within
Pop's black-framed glasses
And know he's laughing too.                                         45

* "Shink" may be a typo, but the poem is reproduced as published.


This poem, likely based on an experience Barack Obama had with his maternal grandfather, includes many of the same elements of his more recent writing: repetition, simile, attention to detail, reflection on how familial relationships have shaped him. More than a decade after this poem was first published, Obama wrote his first book, later republished as *Dreams of My Father*, in which he also considers the significance of family relationships. His book first appeared in 1995, when Obama was in his early thirties. Nine years later, in a new edition of that book, Obama reflected on his earlier writing:

> For the first time in many years, I've pulled out a copy and read a few chapters to see how much my voice may have changed over time. I confess to wincing every so often at a poorly chosen word, a

mangled sentence, an expression of emotion that seems indulgent or overly practiced. I have the urge to cut the book by fifty pages or so, possessed as I am with a keener appreciation for brevity. I cannot honestly say, however, that the voice in this book is not mine—that I would tell the story much differently today than I did ten years ago.

Thus does President Obama reflect on his development as a writer and something of who he is as a person. Whether you're a college student publishing your first poems in a literary magazine, in your early thirties publishing your first book, in your early forties looking back on your early writing, or speaking and writing to the world as president of the United States, there's value in looking back and forward.

I hope *The Norton Pocket Book of Writing by Students* will help you reflect on your own development as a writer—and to see that development as a lifelong process with certain milestones worth celebrating along the way, to recognize your own successes and those of your peers and students, and to continue to reach toward excellence.

MELISSA A. GOLDTHWAITE

# Acknowledgments

Every book that makes it to print is a deeply collaborative effort, and *The Norton Pocket Book of Writing by Students* is especially so. The creation of this book was dependent on the hard work of multiple people at W. W. Norton & Company; the contributions of numerous students, teachers, and writing program administrators; and the support of many colleagues and friends.

I am especially grateful to Marilyn Moller—an extraordinary and remarkably supportive editor—for her knowledge, her enthusiasm for this project, her hard work, and her collaborative spirit. I also had the good fortune of working with Elizabeth Mullaney, whose editorial skills, patience, kindness, and attention to detail cannot be overestimated. Thanks, also, to Debra Morton Hoyt for her cover design; Jennifer Cantelmi for proofreading the manuscript; and Eric Pier-Hocking for managing the production process.

I am grateful to the teachers who design assignments, comment on drafts, and make the kinds of final comments that motivate students to continue working on their writing even after they have received grades. The teachers, too numerous to name individually, who sent in individual nominations showed both respect and enthusiasm for their students' work. I am also indebted to the writing program administrators and other teachers who distributed the call for papers and who sent custom-published volumes from their schools. And I wish to thank my colleagues at Saint Joseph's University, especially those who enthusiastically shared their students' work: April Lindner, Tenaya Darlington, Joseph Feeney, S.J., and Peter Norberg.

Two friends in particular provided assistance and support: Tricia Sadd's patience and technological skills made it possible for me to do

## Acknowledgments

much of the work on this book from afar; she helped make me comfortable in a world of PDFs and skydrives so I could take advantage of the quiet and space provided by a much less technologically advanced world of pine trees and fields. And Jody Ziegler—especially in the final months of this project—"listened to" numerous email updates and provided an artistic eye on more than one occasion.

This book is dedicated to Wendy Bishop and David Citino—friends, teachers, writers. David was one of my teachers. Wendy provided some of my earliest opportunities for publication when I was still a student. Both valued their students' writing immensely, and their care for students went far beyond the walls of the classroom. Both wrote, responded to student writing, and encouraged young writers more in their too-short lives than most can imagine.

Finally, I offer my deepest thanks both to the students whose writing is the body of this text and to the exceptional students in my classes, past and present. Their hard work and enthusiasm for learning have made and continue to make my work a pleasure.

THE NORTON

POCKET BOOK

OF WRITING

BY STUDENTS

# 1

## WRITING ABOUT WRITING
### Literacy Narratives and Reflections

What are your earliest memories of writing? What experiences have shaped the way you approach writing and your understanding of yourself as a writer? What aspect of writing challenges you most? These are some of the questions that guide the literacy narratives and reflections in this chapter, and they're questions that might help you reflect upon the role writing plays in your own life. Whether you're thinking about certain stylistic features of your writing (as Madeline Kelly does in "The Voice from the Window") or considering how much you want to reveal about yourself or others (as Tess Bird does in "The Shadow That the Apple Casts: Thoughts on Exposure"), literacy narratives and reflections can help you think hard about your own approach to writing.

A literacy narrative, like any other story, calls for attention to detail, pacing, scene, character, dialogue, and setting. Tess Bird's essay includes all of these elements, allowing the scenes to unfold and the significance of her topic ("exposure") to emerge. Some literacy narratives include explicit reflections on the significance of the events described, but generally the significance is revealed through the story, and writers avoid overt analysis.

Some of the selections in this chapter provide more reflection than story, and in that sense they're more direct about the significance of particular literacy experiences. For example, Emily Vallowe's reflective essay "Write or Wrong Identity" recounts memories of some of her early experiences related to writing, yet she spends more time

1

reflecting upon *how* she came to see herself as a writer—and the anxiety that label can cause.

The balance between story and reflection in your own writing about writing will depend upon your purpose and your assignment. The headnotes introducing the essays in this book provide information about the assignment to which each student responded; note the differences and similarities between the various assignments, and be attentive to the particulars of any assignments your teacher gives.

As you read the selections in this chapter, consider your own relationship to writing. Why do you write? When is writing particularly difficult or easy? How has your identity as a writer been affected by your experiences with parents, teachers, friends, classmates, reading, early attempts at writing, or other experiences? How do you develop your own voice as a writer? What do you choose to expose of yourself and others in your work? Literacy narratives and reflections can help you explore these questions and consider how the answers might shape your writing now and in the future.

# You Ask Me Why I Write

## *Laura Buenzle*

*Laura Buenzle wrote this poem in a poetry workshop at Saint Joseph's University in Philadelphia. Her assignment was to respond to the prompt "Why do you write?" She says that she chose "images that spelled color and vibrancy, and conveyed a sense of giving and of life," and she reflects further: "I even put some of the lines in parentheses, as if the poem itself were full, just as the poet's heart is full. It seemed fitting to address the reader as a 'dear friend' because for me, a poem comes alive when it is shared. The joy of writing poetry is twofold: first, being moved in life to create art, and second, viewing the poem as a gift."*

Don't you know
that even the shy one
cannot keep all the world
enclosed in her
heart?                                                            5
I tell you—
it is only a matter of time
before it quivers
then bursts
and out come the poems                                            10
(like so many butterflies
hovering in the pasture,
like the pure white cranes
that flew over Kyoto
in the moonlight                                                  15
in my dreams)
tumbling

(the way the Dutchman laughed
as if so many windmills were spinning
20      throwing off tulips
like sparks!)
continually
(like a fountain in that park—
even in frozen January
25      it was tossing out streams of water).
The poems, they never seem to cease—
the way the sun peeks through stained glass
day after day . . .
                the way the tabernacle candle
30                          has an eternal flame.


Friend,
you ask me why I write.
I tell you how I love.

---

### Reading to Write

1. Laura Buenzle writes a poem of direct address, to "you" and "friend." What is the effect of this directness? As a reader, do you identify more with the person being addressed or with the speaker? Why?

2. Buenzle uses several similes to describe her writing process and why she writes. For example, she compares her poetry writing to hovering butterflies and flying cranes. What do these similes communicate to you about her process and reason for writing?

3. Write a poem or 2- to 4-page essay reflecting on why you write. Like Buenzle does, use similes in your reflection. As you prepare to write this piece, make a list of five similes, using the following prompt as a starting place: writing, for me, is like . . .

4

# On Philosophy and Writing

## Julie Green

*Julie Green wrote this reflection for the Writing for Publication course at George Fox University, a Quaker college in Oregon. Her teacher, Melanie Springer Mock, nominated Green's essay, saying that it shows both "the angst that some students have about writing" and how many adult learners, returning to school after years of parenting, work, and other life experiences, sometimes feel, and "how working through a difficult assignment gave her new insight into her own identity as a writer."*

T he past two weeks of this semester have been a veritable wrestling match with dread and self-deprecation. I literally cannot wait for classes to be over.

It's not that my courses have been unusually difficult, but some of the reading material has been challenging—and from this reading must come a significant final paper for my philosophy class. It's due in two days and I don't even have a coherent rough draft.

Writing, to me, is like breathing: it is necessary, it makes me feel good, and it's pretty much automatic. Most of the time, first drafts are easy. The thoughts seem to slide from my mind and through my hands onto the paper as if they were greased. Even editing is a pleasure—shaping the lumps of clay into something graceful and profound gives me a tremendous sense of satisfaction. The entire process of writing has been one of the truest joys I have ever known—that is, up until now.

This philosophy paper is the first writing assignment that's caused me to panic, in a very concrete way. Just thinking about it causes a sort of anxiety that is mostly foreign to me. I actually burst into tears the other night while trying to massage some life into a few lifeless para-graphs I'd assembled, and no one in my house knew what to do for me, especially my youngest son. It must have been an extreme mystery to him how using the computer could cause his mommy almost to have a nervous breakdown. After all, he *loves* to be on the computer.

5    But perhaps it's not the writing that is the problem.

For a while now, as an older student with nearly twenty years of marriage and three kids, I've had a certain self-perception that is turn-ing out to be a bit inaccurate. Quite simply: I'm not as good a writer as I've always thought myself to be. Much of my work has been mined from a wealth of life experience; I smugly assumed this gave me story-telling skills my younger and less "life-savvy" classmates couldn't touch. However, these young students have consistently offered constructive and insightful criticism of my writing. There is plenty to learn from those whose writing lives have been more consistent than mine—and dues to pay if I am ever going to be published.

My philosophy class this semester has taught me something simi-lar, despite all the ruckus with the final paper: I am a very small part of a very big and complicated universe. Things I've always thought were facts maybe aren't that, and like writing, philosophical wisdom has a way of informing one's perception of "place" in the cosmos. My aca-demic advisor told me a while back that studying philosophy is quite beneficial for those who want to be writers, since it teaches the art of deep reflection. He was right.

What is now patently obvious is that the façade of superior intel-lectualism I've built over the years needs to go. Struggling to write my paper has been a good catalyst for getting the process started, but I expect it to be more long-term than not. Fear, it turns out, is an unfor-tunate side effect of dealing with the assumptions that create false self-confidence. And *that*, I suspect, is what made me cry the night I sat defeated in front of my computer, panicking about a writing assign-ment that previously would never have created such anxiety.

The true beauty of writing is that, like life, you can almost always return to the page and change course if you must. I will finish my philosophy paper, and I will be okay. Different, perhaps, but okay nonetheless.

Thank God I love to write. 10

---

## Reading to Write

1. In paragraph 3, Julie Green uses simile and metaphor to describe her usual writing process, saying that writing is "like breathing" and comparing editing to shaping lumps of clay. What similes and metaphors would you use to describe your approach to writing?

2. Reflection often leads writers to make discoveries about themselves. What discoveries does Green make about herself as a writer?

3. Write a 2- to 3-page reflection about a time when writing was particularly difficult for you. Describe the situation and also reflect on *why* writing was especially hard at that time. In thinking and writing about that experience, you may—like Green—also discover something about yourself, something worth sharing with readers.

# Write or Wrong Identity

## Emily Vallowe

*Emily Vallowe wrote this literacy narrative for a class on the Writing Process at the University of Mary Washington in Virginia. Her teacher, Sarah Allen, asked students to write a narrative about a pivotal or transformative moment in their writing life and to "reflect on the event's implication(s): on what issues it brings up for you, on what conflict it instigates/propagates, on what it means to you, personally." Allen nominated Vallowe's essay, calling it "provocative and challenging" and lauding its "rigorous analysis."*

I'm sitting in the woods with a bunch of Catholic people I just met yesterday. Suddenly, they ask me to name one of the talents God has given me. I panic for a split second and then breathe an internal sigh of relief. I tell them I'm a writer. As the group leaders move on to question someone else, I sit trying to mentally catch my breath. It will take a moment before the terror leaves my forearms, chest, and stomach, but I tell myself that I have nothing to fear. I am a writer. Yes, I most definitely am a writer. *Now breathe,* I tell myself . . . *and suppress that horrifying suspicion that you are actually not a writer at all.*

The retreat that prepared me for my eighth grade confirmation was not the first time I found myself pulling out the old "I'm a writer" card and wondering whether I was worthy enough to carry this sacred card in the wallet of my identity. Such things happen to people with identity crises.

In kindergarten I wrote about thirty books. They were each about five pages long, with one sentence and a picture on each page. They were held together with three staples on the left side or top and had construction paper covers with the book's title and the phrase "By Emily Vallowe" written out in neat kindergarten-teacher handwriting. My mom still has all of these books in a box at the bottom of her closet.

One day at the very end of the school year, my kindergarten teacher took me to meet my future first-grade teacher, Mrs. Meadows. I got to make a special trip to meet her because I had been absent on the day the rest of the kindergarteners had gone to meet their future teachers. Mrs. Meadows' classroom was big and blue and different from the kindergarten class, complete with bigger, different kids (I think Mrs. Meadows had been teaching third or fourth graders that year, so her students were much older than I was). During this visit, Mrs. Meadows showed me a special writing desk, complete with a small, old-fashioned desk lamp (with a lamp shade and everything). I'm not sure if I understood why she was showing me this writing area. She may have said that she'd heard good things about me.

This handful of images is all I can remember about the most significant event in my writing life. I'm not sure why I connect the memory of my kindergarten books with the image of me sitting in Mrs. Meadows' old classroom (for by the time I had her she was in a room on the opposite side of the school). I guess I don't even know exactly when this major event happened. Was it kindergarten? First grade? Somewhere in between? All I know is that some event occurred in early elementary school that made me want to be a writer. I don't even clearly remember what this event was, but it is something that has actively affected me for the fourteen years since then.

I have wanted to be a writer my entire life—or at least that's what I tell people. Looking back, I don't know if I ever *wanted* to be a writer. The idea might never have even occurred to me. Yet, somehow I was marked as a writer. My teachers must have seen something in my writing that impressed them and clued me in on it. Teachers like to recognize kids for their strengths, and at the age of five, I probably started to notice that different kids were good at different things: Bobby was good at t-ball; Sally was good at drawing; Jenny could run really fast. I was probably starting to panic at the thought that I might not be good at

5

anything—and then a teacher came along and told me I was good at writing. Someone gave me a compliment, and I ran with it. I declared myself to be a writer and have clung to this writer identity ever since.

There are certain drawbacks to clinging to one unchanging identity since the age of five. Constant panic is one of these drawbacks. It is a strange feeling to grow up defining yourself as something when you don't know if that something is actually true. By the time I got to middle school, I could no longer remember having become a writer; I had just always been one—and had been one without any proof that I deserved to be called one. By the age of ten, I was facing a seasoned writer's terror of "am I any good?!" and this terror has followed me throughout my entire life since then. Every writing assignment I ever had was a test—a test to see if I was a real writer, to prove myself to teachers, to classmates, to myself. I approached every writing assignment thinking, "I am supposed to be good at this," not "I am going to try to make this good," and such an attitude is not a healthy way to approach anything.

It doesn't help that, if I am a writer, I am a very slow one. I can't sit down and instantly write something beautiful like some people I know can. I have been fortunate to go to school with some very smart classmates, some of whom can whip out a great piece of writing in minutes. I still find these people threatening. If they are faster than I am, does that make them better writers than I am? *I thought I was supposed to be "the writer"!*

My obsession with being "the" writer stems from my understanding of what it means to be "the" anything. My childhood was marked by a belief in many abstract absolutes that I am only now allowing to crumble. I was born in Chicago (and was thus the fourth generation of my family to live there), but I grew up in Northern Virginia. I came to look down on my Virginia surroundings because I had been taught to view Chicago as this great Mecca—the world's most amazing city to which I must someday return, and to which all other places on earth pale in comparison. Throughout my childhood, I gathered that Chicago is a real city in which average people live and which has an economy historically based in shipping and manufacturing; Washington, D.C., on the other hand, where my Dad works, has a population that includes a bizarre mix of impoverished people and the most influential leaders and diplomats in the world—and so manufactures nothing but political power. People in Chicago know how to deal with snow; Virginians panic at the *possibility* of snow. Chicago rests on soil that is so fertile it's *black*; Virginia does not even have soil—it has reddish clay suitable for growing nothing except tobacco. Even Chicago's tap water tastes amazing; D.C.'s tap water is poisoned with lead. I grew up thinking that every aspect of Chicago was perfect—so perfect that Chicago became glorious to the point of abstraction. No other city could compare, and after a while I forgot *why* no other city could compare. I just knew that Chicago was "the" city . . . and that if "the" city exists, there must also be an abstract "the" everything.

I grew up with this and many other abstract ideals that I would     10
defend against my friends' attacks . . . until I learned that they were just abstractions—and so was I. My writing identity was just another ideal, an absolute that I clung to without any basis in fact. I used to use writing as an easy way to define myself on those over-simplistic surveys teachers always asked us to fill out in elementary and middle school—the surveys that assumed that someone could know all about me simply by finding out my favorite color, my favorite T.V. show, or my hobbies. I used to casually throw out the "I'm a writer" card just to get these silly surveys over with. "I'm a writer" was just an easy answer to the complicated question, "Who are you?" I always thought the surveys avoided asking this question, but maybe I was the one avoiding it. For years, I had been defining myself as "the writer" without really pondering what this writer identity meant. Is a writer simply someone who writes all the time? Well, I often went through long stretches in which I did not write anything, so this definition did not seem to suit me. Is a writer someone who is good at writing? Well, I've already mentioned that I've been having "Am I any good?!" thoughts since elementary school, so this definition didn't seem to fit me, either. I was identifying myself as "the writer" as an abstraction, without any just cause to do so.

The funny thing is that I recognized my writing identity as an abstract ideal before I recognized any of the other ideals I was clinging to, but that didn't make the situation any better. It is one thing to learn that dead people have been voting in Chicago elections for decades, and so perhaps Chicago isn't the perfect city, but what happens when the absolute ideal is you? More importantly, what would happen if this absolute were to crumble? It was terrifying to think that I might discover that I was not a writer because to not be a writer was to suddenly be nothing. If a writer was the only thing that I had ever been, what would happen if writing was a lie? I would vanish. Looking back, the logical part of my brain tells me that, if I am not a writer, I am still plenty of other things: I am a Catholic; I am a Vallowe; people tell me that I have other good qualities. But when facing these horrifying spells of writer's doubt, my brain doesn't see these other things. I am driven only by the fear of nothingness, and the thought that I have to be a writer because I'm not good at anything else.

Am I really not good at anything else? I used to blame this entire writer's complex on whoever it was that told me I was a writer. If that person hadn't channeled this burdensome identity into me, I might never have expected great literary things from myself, and life would have been easier. I had these thoughts until one day in high school I mentioned something to my mom about the fact that I'd been writing since I was five years old. My mom corrected me by saying that I'd been writing since I was three years old. At the age of three I couldn't even physically form letters, but apparently I would dictate stories to my mom on a regular basis. My mom explained to me how I would run to her and say, "Mommy, Mommy, write my story for me!"

This new information was both comforting and unsettling. On one hand, it was a great relief to know that I had been a writer all along—that I would have been a writer even if no one had told me that I was one. On the other hand, the knowledge that I had been a writer all along drove me into an entirely new realm of panic.

I've been a writer my entire life?

WHAT?!

I've been a writer since I was three? *Three?* Three years old: How is that even possible? I didn't know it was possible to be anything at age three, let alone the thing that might define me for my entire life.

I have been taught that each person has a vocation—a calling that he or she must use to spread God's love to others. Yet, I've also assumed that one must go on some sort of journey to figure out what this vocation is. If I found my vocation at the age of three, have I skipped this journey? And if I've skipped the journey, does that mean that the vocation isn't real? Or am I just really lucky for having found my vocation so early? Was I really born a writer? Was I born to do one thing and will I do that one thing for my entire life? Can anything be that consistent? That simple? And if I am living out some divine vocation, is that any comfort at all? If I am channeling some divine being in my writing, and everything I write comes from some outside source, where does that leave me? Am I nothing even if I am a writer?

This questioning has not led me to any comforting conclusions. I still wonder if my writer identity has been thrust upon me, and what it means to have someone else determine who I am. If I am a writer, then I am someone who passionately seeks originality—someone who gets pleasure from inventing entire fictional worlds. Yet, if someone—either a teacher or a divine being—is channeling an identity into me, then I am no more original than the characters that I create in my fiction. If my identity is not original, then this identity is not real, and if I am not real . . . I can't even finish this sentence.

I don't know if I really wrote thirty books in kindergarten. It might have been twenty—or fifteen—or ten—or five. I might have made up that part about the special writing desk in Mrs. Meadows' old classroom. I don't know if God predestined me to write masterpieces or if a teacher just casually mentioned that I wrote well and I completely overreacted to the compliment. Questioning my identity as "the writer" has led me to new levels of fear and uncertainty, but this questioning is not going to stop. Even if I one day sit, withered and gray, with a

Nobel Prize for Literature proudly displayed on my desk as I try to crank out one last novel at the age of ninety-two, my thoughts will probably drift back to Mrs. Meadows and those books I wrote in kindergarten. In my old age, I still might not understand my writer identity, but maybe by that point, I will have written a novel about a character with an identity crisis—and maybe the character will have come through all right.

## Reading to Write

1. In this reflection on her writing life and identity, Emily Vallowe considers what it means to be a writer. What do you think it means to be a writer? How would you define the term "writer"?

2. In her penultimate paragraph, Vallowe observes that if "a teacher or a divine being . . . is channeling an identity" into her, then she is "no more original than the characters" that she creates in her fiction. According to Vallowe, what is the relationship between "truth" and "fiction," "self" and "character," and how do these concepts relate to identity formation?

3. Vallowe questions her identity as a writer as she reflects on how she came to identify writing as her vocation. Write a 5- to 7-page reflective essay on some aspect of your identity and how that part of you came to be.

# The Voice from the Window

## *Madeline Kelly*

*As a student at the University of Mary Washington in Virginia, Madeline Kelly wrote "The Voice from the Window" in Sarah Allen's course on the Writing Process. Allen nominated this essay, a reflection on the concept of voice in writing, for the way Kelly "complicates, challenges, and celebrates . . . voice . . . in more than the usual kinds of ways." One challenge for Kelly in writing this piece was knowing that she would "have to take oral criticism in a workshop"—and that she "had to care enough to defend [her] piece or change it."*

Miles down under the sea, in the eternal darkness, there are half-blind fish resisting the pressure of thousands of tons of water on every side. They're not squashed flat as a pancake for the simple reason that their internal pressure is equal to the external pressure. But if one of these fish is pulled from the depths up to the surface, it will explode like a bomb.

We are the same kind of fish. For seventy years we have lived under the pressure of tons of terror, which has permeated everything around us so thoroughly that we have ceased to notice it. It has become an integral part of ourselves, and now that they have tried to drag us up to the surface in a few short years, up to freedom and the sun, we feel terror advancing on us out of the future. But there is no terror in the future—what we are feeling now comes from inside us. We are being torn apart by terror that used to be balanced by the inhuman pressure applied to our souls. They keep on pulling us up higher and higher, and we've already swollen perceptibly, but if only we don't burst in the next few meters, at long last we shall finally glimpse the sun.

—Victor Pelevin, "The View from the Window"

F reedom is scary. Changing habits is scary. Peter Elbow's groundbreaking text *Writing Without Teachers* is scary. It's scary precisely because Elbow, a composition scholar with a radical outlook on the writing process, is asking us to discard traditional writing conventions, in effect, to come up to the surface after years of living under the pressure of teachers. Our writing—and our souls—have learned to live within a thousand and one constraints: We can write an outline. We can write a topic sentence. We can, in short, jump through all the hoops. Releasing the pressure of all those conventions now feels like it could be disastrous. We mistake robotic term papers for good writing, and if we read something with real voice, it makes us nervous. Still, Elbow is relentless, dragging us out of the depths that we know into the sunlight that scares us. *We'll explode*, we whimper. *Never fear*, he says, and cuts the anchor.

Okay, so let's say for a minute we've taken Elbow's leap—or rather, ascent—of faith, and wriggled our way to the surface. What do we have to look forward to? Without conventions and standards, what becomes our writing goal? The new standard becomes *know thyself*; what Elbow wants is for each of us to find our 'natural' way of writing. Be you formal, informal, slangy, or erudite, you'll write best as yourself, so make that the best it can be. Don't prop yourself up with someone else's idea of structure or style. Don't smother yourself under someone else's sea. What's crushing us is conformity; the sunlight we need to reach is voice.

So what exactly is voice? It's a tricky concept to isolate. First, we have to understand that voice denies certainty. Create your own list of "the elements of voice" and inevitably someone will point out something you've missed or scratch out things you've listed. The best we can hope for is what Elbow might call the *dirty truth*—a jumble of associated concepts: "truth mixed with error" (177). So here's the dirty truth: voice is about diversity. It's mixing and matching styles and structures; it's about channeling your energy. Voice is the textual manifestation of your own personal style, and its richness comes from being dynamic, not from obeying set guidelines. The same can be said about defining voice: the very act of codifying something takes away its vitality.

Another key aspect of voice is communication—it takes at least two to make a message. After all, voice is what connects us to our readers. A lot of voice comes, paradoxically, from them. I, for example, will never hear my spoken voice as you hear it; nor will I read my own work as you read it. For Elbow, the act of communicating is a set of instructions for building meaning (152). I write out a set of words in an attempt to guide your thoughts; you use those words as a blueprint for rearranging ideas and concepts you are already equipped with. The former is my part of voice; the latter is yours. Depending on how much I provide, you may have an easier or tougher time building what I envisioned, but we both leave something inscribed on the final product. The reader fills gaps the writer can't anticipate—together, the two can make meaning complete. The bottom line is that voice is about being heard—and the most effective environments for being heard are those that allow for the "team effort" creation of voice. Think of the deep-sea fish. How well do you think he can communicate, limited by all that pressure, all that darkness? Same viewpoints, same ideas—every fish has the same narrow world to work with. But remove the pressure, and suddenly each fish is different, able to fill in gaps and make interpretations that his fellow fish can't. From this collaboration comes voice.

Because they play such a key role in the creation of voice, readers need to be open. They have to be willing to hear your message, just like you have to accept that your work will always be filtered through their understanding. Voice is about understanding, and believing. If we limit our range of possibilities—here's the notion of difference again—then we limit our understanding and believing powers. Our tendency is to strive for agreement, for conclusion. But as readers, maybe it's not our place to put a fixed definition on other authors' words—it's not fair to the author, and it's not fair to other readers who are trying to interpret those words for themselves. Remember, every individual has a personal meaning-building equation: the writer provides instructions, the reader follows them—without being told how. And as shaky as voice is

5

to define, it's a thousand times more ambiguous—more variable—in practice.

For example, if you look at some of the most heated debates of our world, the instinct to impose agreement—to arrive at one voice—is a source of enormous conflict. Scholars, analysts, politicians, all scramble to pin down the meaning of our most sacred texts, but in scrutinizing the words, it's easy to overlook the truths. I wasn't raised in a religious household, so I can only speak from a literary standpoint, but consider the Bible, one of the most influential texts of all time. It's at the core of multiple religions, interpreted in different ways by scores of spiritual leaders and millions of individuals; it stands to reason that there are many strategies for reading meaning and voice in the text. And yet, haven't some of history's bloodiest moments hinged on the need to make others accept a specific reading—a "one voice" version—of the Bible?

We might benefit from asking ourselves what comes from setting the Bible (or the U.S. Constitution, if you'd prefer a secular example) in stone. Does the one-voice model enrich the individual spiritually, or—and hear me out here—does it limit us? Like any text, the Bible should have life, and life-giving powers. It should inspire and uplift, just like the Constitution should uphold ideals. Instead, we fight each other over which voices are there, which voices are imagined. Maybe they're all there; maybe none are. If I were to tell you how to interpret those texts, I'd be doing a rotten job as a fellow reader. We all have a different way of fashioning voice: you, me, the people—human beings, with feelings and opinions—who wrote these texts. Who were they, and what were they trying to say? What's their contribution to voice? As biblical archaeologist Hanan Eschel says, "When you try to get into their minds . . . you get a better sense of the text" (qtd. in Feiler 133). The Bible and the Constitution are extreme examples, but hopefully you're starting to see the differences between the readers' perceptions of voice and the writer's intended voice, how they interact, and that ultimately there's no reason why we should have to settle on just one interpretation. Voice is fluid in a way that totally defies a fixed reading. Elbow is asking us to accept fluidity in our own minds; why not in others' as well? The communicative process is too rich and too subtle; we need to learn to tolerate ambiguity.

After all that discussion and our ultimate non-definition of, well, anything, Elbow's theories for finding voice may sound like a lot to handle. He's asking us to throw most of our writing (and reading) habits out the window; he's asking us, again, to abandon something oppressively safe for a frightening liberty. But a closer exploration of my own writing process has shown me that it's not as hard as all that, particularly if you address more than the literal process and start to consider truths. Elbow's process is about listening to instinct, by writing impulsively first and editing later. In essence it's nothing more than a series of brainstorming sessions for revising and honing ideas. If you compare my process side-by-side with Elbow's, it becomes clear that both are based in the same principles: I tease out my ideas first and then use them to build my message. Another way to think of my writing process is with Elbow's "external cooking" model: the writer puts fragmented ideas onto paper, cuts them up, and reassembles them physically (rather than mentally, which is Elbow's preferred method) into a coherent structure (65). Take this theory and add in a bit more brainstorming, and there you have it. I put down my ideas over the course of several hours—even days or weeks—and seek structure from there. Like Elbow, I discard a lot of my original work and transform most of what's left. Like Elbow, I evaluate as I go.

Within this framework of brainstorming, organizing, and editing, I allow myself a lot of flexibility to make up for my otherwise fickle nature. I have yet to settle on "the perfect writing environment." Sometimes it's only the red pens that work; sometimes lined paper sends my brain into lock-down. I can type, handwrite, or jot. I can scrawl out whole paragraphs or write in individual phrases. Whatever works. Sometimes I'll even try to channel other writers during the creative process. I know I'm not going to become Hunter Thompson or Herman Melville, but it's a good way to perk up my brain. At worst, each method will work only once before losing novelty—but if I'm lucky, I'll discover techniques that aren't just borrowings, they're mine, too.

10      Which leads into the hardest part about Elbow's process: separating what is someone else's from what is yours. After all, we've been so long under water—all squished into the same stifling shape—that our true shape at the surface is hard to guess. Can this blob really be me, or am I just imitating the first form I find? It's a tough call, one that involves your own intuition and a little faith. Ironically, for all Elbow's theory, it takes a bit of readjustment to find yourself again. He's forcing us to make such a change that the first instinct is to cower in his shadow. His ideas are nice—but in practice, it's hard to tell. Which of my ideas are ones he would consider "good"? Where exactly does my voice come from? Am I too attached to my words to edit them? In insecure moments, these sorts of questions plague me. But on the whole, I keep in mind that Elbow is one man, and that not everything he suggests is going to work for me. I need to be willing to try his practices, but without letting his ideas bully mine. As Elbow himself says, the writer is "always right and always wrong" (106).

What it comes down to in the end—once you've sifted through all the theories and all the practices—is that there's no set formula for developing your voice, just like there's no set formula for how others will perceive it. The best instructions we can hope for are simply to find the best way you can to reach other people. Personally, I'm the kind of person who perks up when people start to reveal something of themselves. I like to know what sets people apart. Yes, you went to Paris, but—Eiffel Tower be damned—I'd rather hear about the gypsies you broke bread with in the train station at Souvigny. My favorite authors, professors, mentors, friends, are those with *personality*. Even the teacher who intimidates me to tears earns my affection by having an opinion; even the obnoxious reality TV star wins my vote by having—pardon the language—*balls*.

These have all been extreme examples—from exploding fish to Biblical interpretations to the latest reruns of *Survivor*—but my point is this: Voice is a risk, yet if you're bold enough to have it, it also comes with the implicit promise of respect. And support. Because what all these other voices—writers like Pelevin, scholars like Elbow—are telling us is to take a leap of faith. The depressurization is scary, coming up to sunlight is scary, but in this case, we have to believe we're *not* the fish. We're the writer; we control the metaphor, not the other way around. All our lives we've followed rules because we assume they're the only thing holding us together—they're the pressure that keeps our guts from flying everywhere. But unlike the fish, we don't have a physical force to contend with, all we've got are our doubts and a fleet of high school English teachers. So take the risk, even if all you have to go on is faith, even if you don't know anything beyond traditional writing conventions. Voice is rich and flexible and utterly forgiving. Just make it to the surface. I promise, you won't explode.

## WORKS CITED

Elbow, Peter. *Writing without Teachers*. 25th anniv. ed. New York: Oxford UP, 1998. Print.

Feiler, Bruce. *Abraham: A Journey to the Heart of Three Faiths*. New York: Harper Perennial, 2005. Print.

---

## Reading to Write

1. In her opening paragraph, Madeline Kelly uses two forms of repetition: anaphora, repeating the words at the beginning of successive clauses; and epistrophe, repeating the words at the end of successive clauses. What effect does this use of repetition have on her own writing voice?

2. Kelly uses a controlling metaphor in this essay. She begins with an epigraph about fish under water, pressure, and terror, and throughout the essay, comes back to that metaphor and imagery. Trace Kelly's use of the metaphor throughout the essay. In what ways does her use of metaphor help her create an argument about voice?

3. Write a 6- to 8-page essay in which you both reflect on the concept of voice in writing and use the conventions that best help you develop and display a particular writing voice or tone.

# The Shadow That the Apple Casts
*Thoughts on Exposure*

## Tess Bird

*As a student at the University of Connecticut at Storrs, Tess Bird
wrote this essay for Lynn Z. Bloom's class in Advanced Creative Non-
fiction. Bird wrote this essay in response to an assignment to write
about a "watershed moment," an experience that changed the way
she looked at some significant aspect of her life. Bloom provided this
guidance to her students: "Don't analyze overtly, don't preach; the
meaning should emerge through the narrative or other configuration
of details." She nominated Bird's essay for its "sophisticated and un-
derstated treatment of the subject." In writing this piece, Bird learned
to look at the form of the personal essay in a new way, as "something
in parts, without concrete lines, that comes together in the end through
images and themes."*

**Is to speak of the secrets of the self an exploitation of one's own
stories?**

I wake from a dream in which a woman I don't speak to anymore is trying to get me to talk to her. I am dressed as Death for
Halloween, hidden under a big black cape with slits for eyes and a
mouth. As she follows me down the corridors of what must be a school,
I hiss at her until finally I am forced to scream "Go Away!" at the top of
my lungs, over and over until she finally gives up and leaves.

This same young woman, two years prior, refused to delete two
pictures of me. Out of thousands they were the two I requested she
remove from her library. One of the pictures, an image of me lying
face down on a bed after a party, wearing only ripped fishnets, was

accidentally placed on a CD a few days later and passed on to several male friends. I turned my fury inward, allowing these little crossings of boundaries to build until the final moment, six months later, when she crossed too far by secretly pursuing and eventually kissing the guy I was in a relationship with. Fury, it seems, never evaporates but finds the deepest crevices of your shadow and takes root.

I was bombarded with a different type of anger one Saturday night at Sauna, a monthly gathering of my mother's friends to sit and talk in the steam of a home-built sauna. A few weeks prior, I had published an article entitled "Conversations Between Generations" in the University Women's Center Newsletter and forwarded the link to the women of Sauna. In the article I used an incident where one member of the Sauna group challenged my beliefs as an example to show the tensions involved with feminism. Perhaps I was naive—and unaware that this would cause further tension with this woman—but I was shocked when she told me in the dark of the Sauna, in front of my mother and a friend, all of us naked, that everything she said was to be off the record from now on. For what seemed like a long minute she talked about how she felt bad for a month after the incident happened and then had to go through it all again with the article. And nope, she didn't see how I twisted it around into a positive thing, and she did not want any further explanations. In the dark of the Sauna, the one safe place I know, I felt silenced. I had exposed her, and she in turn had exposed me, and here I was exposing her again via the one thing I cannot decide whether to avoid or embrace: retrospection.

I first began to think about exposure in relation to love affairs nearly two years ago. Keenly aware of feeling exposed numerous times in the bright lights of a locked room while a party raged outside, I understood exposure to be a power struggle among the fumbling of hands and half-clothed bodies. Who could expose whom? Months after the chaos of that year faded, I scribbled recollections into my notebook, contemplating layers of writing about sexuality. As I described the scene, pinpointed by one of those beer cap tables college boys have in their apartments, I realized what I was doing once again: exposing a boy because I had been exposed and then exposing myself in the process. I made the mistake of retrospection once again.

5 Writing cannot dodge exposure. We expose ourselves, the secrets of our families, the words of friends, our relationships with lovers, perhaps because we have also felt exposed. We expose for revenge, representation, or brutal self-honesty. I expose as a way of creating and acknowledging the emotional trials of not just learning how to write, but learning how to live as a writer. In three essays this semester I exposed two key people in my life as well as the sacred room of Sauna. In these exposures I dwell almost at once in my own vulnerability, although perhaps this is not obvious to those whose secrets I allow an audience to see. I have three stories to tell that might help clarify my own self-exposure.

■   ▓   ■

This is a story about truth.

It is in the dark brown room of Sauna, lit only by a lamp lain sideways against a tiny window above the door, that the truth sits. I've witnessed truth in my mother's friends, who flow in and out of safety and challenge, mirror themselves in others, and seek a sense of belonging under the dim light of that wooden room. They sit naked, vulnerable but comfortable, and talk about sex, youth, marriage, children, and the dream of the Sauna float for the Memorial Day Parade. I talk about college and struggles with love and travel, certain things revealed only under the premise that what I say will be held in all that is sacred about Sauna. *I give the same back to you, but you must fear that with my little notebook, alert ears, and often silent tongue, I am collecting, searching your own stories for ones that I can call my own. I take only what is given to me or what is forced upon me, never what is sacred.*

I write about these women as a group because this is something that they have become to me: a fluid body of women moving through the diagonals of my life despite their wildly individual personalities. In my writing they become very close to one, *where what one woman says you all say, and what one woman knows you all know.* This is a literary liberty, and although no one beyond the bounds of the sauna room knows different, it is a lie.

Beth illustrates the fluidity. As something close to a second mom to me, it is her truth that often becomes mine, as when she compares my troubled relationship with my boyfriend to one she had in her twenties. Things become clearer when women who are not your mother but who are your mother's age tell them to you. I explain that all I am asking of him is to take a mirror and look inward. *You all say this is what drives young men away, in the end: the fear of being forced to reflect on-self.* But this is all I really want: for men to live up to self and be present, for men to stop waiting for women to maintain men's peace and guard men's solitude. *You all nod.* Beth talks to me alone for an hour in the dinner tent. Her recognition of my situation makes me cry. Her movements are like vines curving in and out of her body and when she talks to me her eyes see things I'm not sure I said.

*This is what happens with you Sauna women: you know things about youth that I haven't figured out yet. When I come with a satchel of party clothes: jeans, heels, a nice tank top, and a choice of scarves, I emerge with mascara and lipstick and ask your opinions. Tina, you laughed once, recalled partying after a Sauna when you were in your twenties, and you all nod: there is nothing like the feeling of beauty women have after they emerge from a place of nudity, cleansing, and women-love. Nevertheless, I get to the party and feel like it is the last place I want to be. I think you knew this, despite the nostalgia for your own youth and the attraction of a younger generation. I think I am jealous.* 10

My mother holds a more concrete truth. Tina says telling a secret to my mother is like putting it in a locked vault. Sauna is also like this: a locked vault, where things said are not meant to escape the wooden walls. Through her I know the secrets of a group of women, like how insecurities and jealousies blossom under safely formed questions, or how she was left unsettled by a certain woman's comments, or how certain individuals no longer visit alone. From her I witness the cycles of friends and how underneath their truths lie other layers, places of continued learning or unknown knowledge, often of things I have already figured out. I know as we sit in the dinner tent after Sauna that I have knowledge.

*But women, listen, this is my vulnerability: I still sit unsure of my place on the bench in the sauna room.* I never quite know when to leave, when it is natural to slip out to the fire, or when I should get dressed. Slowly, after years, I learn the ways. I am able to navigate with less difficulty. And this is my other vulnerability: my writing. Revealing my words is like sitting naked on the bench in Sauna, under silent exposure. The water drips off our face cloths and someone is heard pouring a cup of cool water over her head. *It is in this room that the truth sits. It forms around you like molds, sculpting your words forever into my own body and memory. What I know becomes my own, what I take is my own, what I write is my own.*

⬛      ⬛      ⬛

And then there is my mother. I steal her stories like I harvest the wisdom of those who have lived before. Her truth, although it emanates from her like the steam that rises after we leave the sauna and enter the cold night air, is that of a mother and I know her struggles. *You've gotten used to it, haven't you? Reading things you didn't know I'd picked up on. I believe that in exposing your stories I am dealing with issues that affect my own growth.*

*I have a story to tell you about representation.*

15      From the time I was very young, a longing for England was instilled in me as it had been instilled in my mother. The women of our family all saw England as a place of representation, freedom, and a matrilineal connection to our own past, immortalized and idealized through stories told by my English grandmother. This past May, at an artists' retreat in a castle in Scotland, I was struck by a sudden urge to be at my grandmother's house. As I was eating breakfast and staring out into the gardens, memories that have dictated my life and writing filtered into me. I imagined the house, a cape built before the American Revolution, attached to a carriage house with a huge barn across the street. I realized what was really instilled in me: a longing for my mother's

home, deep in Connecticut, a site for both childhood happiness and great family pain.

Upon my return, armed with my laptop, a recording program recommended by my musician neighbor, and a miniature speaker, my mother and I trekked to Granny's house on a hot summer day. My mother got her talking as I switched on the speakers, just barely getting her recollections of her earliest memories before she moved on to her childhood. Determined to give her a chance to represent her own voice, I listened intently while my mother talked, knowing the questions to ask and the stories to branch out from. As I look back over the recording of Granny's first memory—sitting in her crib and watching black flies swarm outside the window—I recall my own first memory: breakfast, seven months old and eating melon while watching the sun rise. *I ask you about your own first memory and you relay a distinct feeling of excitement as you were pushed in a stroller through a grove of pine trees.* On my grandmother's twentieth birthday she received flowers from the man she loved, away in World War II, just a day before his sister arrived with the news that he was missing, believed killed. On my twentieth birthday I had mono and went to the party my friends threw for me wearing a see-through shirt over a bikini in a sort of fuck-you-all mentality thinking this was the beginning of the long death called life. *You, with some sense of sadness, resentment, or pain, tell me you do not remember your twentieth birthday, but I know you had been married to your first husband for a year.*

*In order to tell you a story of representation, I have to represent you. In order to tell you a story about how your mother's house fills a place in me that otherwise remains unsatisfied, I must tell your secrets. Like your first marriage, the motorcycle accident, a possible divorce. I know that these are your secrets and to speak of them seems to me a betrayal. Is exposure a betrayal?*

*But the scar on your leg haunts my childhood and will forever affect how I see.* A generation removed, I still feel a corresponding longing and unease for that house. I still desire to walk up those stone steps layered with thyme, climb the awkward stairs past the poppies and birdfeeders, and enter my grandmother's kitchen, only to see her sitting by the fire with her cats, smiling at me with a happiness I have only witnessed in grandmothers. The recording of her interview details her life years before she came to Connecticut. It is not told with sadness, or even happiness really, but with a detached, British matter-of-factness that is impossible to align myself with. It tells of her life in England with little anecdotes that make my mother and me laugh and cry, unable to fully comprehend what it was like to lose a loved one in the war or to grow up during a depression.

What England represents for the women of our family is a mythology. Yes, we drink tea at least three times a day, love making scones, and never felt more at home than we did on a three-week trip to England with my father's mother. But what England represents is not tangible. *And what England represents is deeply wrapped up in what your home means to you.*

■    ■    ■

20    In another world is my father and a long drive in upstate New York while eating apples. This is one that deals with a new type of representation and truth, and that results in an exposure of myself. In this case exposure is initially a period of mystery jokingly referred to in our family as the Missing Years, but eventually the exposure is of our own solitude and shadow-sides. From age sixteen to thirty-three, when he met my mother, my father's life has remained a mystery. The years before are filled in by my grandmother and the years after by my mother. The details he gives me are few, and they are the kind of details I would not want him to read. Every bit of information I get about this period of seventeen years is mapped in my head because I know that it pertains to my own life now. There are mysteries about my father that even haunt the first seven or eight years of my youth—like the time he was smoking in the basement with his friends and I told Mom, not understanding that it was his drinking that made her upset. For most of what I remember of my childhood my father did not drink.

I've given up trying to pull these stories out of him. When we are alone on car rides he sometimes gives me a few tales and I file them onto my mental map, but otherwise he is not one to give up his secrets. On one particular car ride we stop to get apples at his friend's orchard in the Litchfield Hills on the way to look at an MFA program in upstate New York. We buy a bag of Fujis and a half-gallon of cider. It's our breakfast—and as I pull out two apples from the paper bag and hand one to my father, we each take a simultaneous bite, waiting for a moment before mumbling to ourselves about the taste. He tells me he likes to try a different type of apple every time. It's mid-October and I have been looking forward to the time alone with my dad—when you get him alone he dispenses the kind of wisdom you'd expect to get from the ancients, following a long tradition of observation, solitude, and personal expansion.

I ask him if he thinks my brother, who's eighteen, will ever want to spend time with me like I want to spend time with him. I hear again about how my dad lived with his sister, this time in more detail, for several years. "It wasn't like we hung out," he says, "but we saw each other all the time, and we talked." He tells me about how much his ex-girlfriend, his sister, and their friend from high school (a woman I know even now) were impossible to be with due to their feminist views. "They just nailed me about being a man. Oh! It was awful! But I loved it at the same time. I learned a lot from them."

"So, yeah," he says, "it'll take some time but Sam will want to be around you more as he gets older. You'll realize the older you get that the only person who will really know you from the time you were a child is your sibling. Friends don't last. You'll meet a lot of people in your life that you will be forced to leave behind, but not your brother."

What he says hits me. There it is, like a pile of apples falling from a tree in an Isaac Newton cartoon. I tell him about how I've been feeling lately—this sense that my ambitions get the better of me and that I trample people in my path: anyone holding me back.

"It's not like that," he says, assuredly. "You'll learn with time that 25 friends bring you down. There's no growth in them, and if you're going to be the type of person that grows you are going to have to do it alone."

No one really gets the kind of knowledge and learning that pass between my father and me. He's the only one I know who really gets my solitude, and the only man I know who is content being with his wife and children and the few friends he has. The Missing Years haunt me because I know that mistakes untold are the kind of mistakes your children might unknowingly repeat. I try to tell him this but he smiles and says, "when you're thirty-three." I suppose I appreciate that he wants me to figure things out for myself, but the feelings that his golden apples of thought bring to me are impossible to match.

■    ■    ■

I can return now to the dream I started with, the woman who made me see the consequences of exposure. In a lot of ways I feel like my life goes through these cycles, leaving friends or boyfriends behind in the silence of cafés or college parties. The first was a close friend who was beginning to navigate through negative spaces, and I did not want to go along with her. The second was a boyfriend who was playing symphonies alone in his bedroom, unable to enter the world and finish school or be attentive to developing self. The third was the best friend who worked behind my back to seduce my love interest. Not long after, I had a falling out with the circle of young men we were friends with and attribute most of this to my feminism and the fact that I was now dating their friend, the aforementioned love interest. On cold nights, after I wake up from naps and have dreams of being followed down corridors, I often wonder why I constantly find myself in situations of solitude, and I wonder now how linked they are to exposure.

I suppose I should clarify that I dedicated my all to the two girl-friends I no longer speak to. My own silence surrounding what actually happened is painful, and I am often forced to retreat in fear at the thoughts of others: maybe I am the one with a problem. Solitary individuals don't come and go with the laundry, aren't grown like apples every autumn, and when you come across one, they hardly know what to do with their love for you. I am one of those solitary individuals.

I have written letters to this friend trying to resolve the final crossing of boundaries that made me feel like an invaded country. Nothing noteworthy has come of our exchange, and our consequent silence is noticeable to all those around us. I could write another letter to her, but I do not think this will lead to any type of resolution.

Instead I will write to my shadow. To all that symbolizes the darkness of solitude, writing, and exposure.                                                      30

Dear Shadow.

&#9632;    &#9632;    &#9632;

When things go wrong people say, "At least it is something to write about," as if my own pain can be formed into something worth reading. When I agree, it gives me relief. When I disagree, it is because I am wrapped up in the politics of exposure and how much is too much. Would I rather be haunted by dreams of friends who follow me down corridors or not have such images to write about, to live in a world free from exposure and betrayal? The greatest betrayal, of course, is not to expose those around you or expose your self, but to betray your self by ignoring your darker parts.

There's a picture of me as a toddler in a red-and-cream-striped jumper suit standing in front of a box of apples. My grandmother's legs are in the background, and I am leaning over just slightly to grab some apples. I was a wisp of a thing, often depicted alone and searching. There's another picture of me wandering through a field of wildflowers, a color photo, and I was shocked to find a black-and-white snapshot of my father at the same age, wandering through a similar field of wildflowers.

These photographs expose our solitude, but they do not threaten our selves. I think I can learn from that.

1. Tess Bird uses both past and present tense in this essay. Why do you think she puts some sections in past tense and some in present tense? Does she reflect on exposure differently in the different tenses? How so?

2. In this essay, Bird's use of italics signals direct address—sometimes to the women in the sauna as a group, other times to a particular person. What is the effect of Bird's use of italics in this essay?

3. Write an 8- to 10-page essay in which, through narrative and reflection, you consider a topic related to writing that interests you.

# 2 〜

## REMEMBERING PEOPLE AND PLACES
## Memoirs and Autobiographical Narratives

W hat do you remember, and why? What people and places have most shaped the person you are today? How might you more fully understand the significance of these memories? Memoirs and other autobiographical narratives allow you not only to tell important stories but also to reveal the significance of those stories—for your own life and the lives of others.

Memoirs and other autobiographical narratives should be rich in sensory detail; demonstrate attention to tone, pacing, dialogue, character development, and setting; and provide a sense of the relationship between past and present. Many of them make some use of symbols. Each of the selections in this chapter includes nearly all of these elements. Mike Boulter's poem makes strong use of sensory details, from the sound of a horn that "rages" to the stench of dead fish, the taste of salt, the sight of "lonesome scaffolding," and the feeling of a spinning dizziness. Becky Andert mixes a humorous tone and attention to character to show the kindness and care of strangers. Molly Lehman divides her memoir into sections and scenes to pace a story that takes place over many years, and she poignantly employs metaphor to reveal the impact of loss. Susan Collinet's observation of a metal pot, an ordinary but significant object from her childhood, elevates that object to make it symbolic, and she includes a photograph to enhance her narrative. Matthew Treacy creates tension by showing both the strength and the tenderness of his mother—how she shoots a groundhog, crunches rabbits "under the blunt end of a hatchet," and hangs Christmas stockings—by focusing on her actions and the lesson she's taught him about the importance of using one's hands.

As you read the selections in this chapter, consider the people and places that have helped you become who you are today. What objects, scents, sights, tastes, and textures stand out in your memory? What tone would best help you relate your experience to readers? As you write about your own memories, allow the significance to unfold—for both you and your readers.

# 2-2-4 Pelham

## *Mike Boulter*

*Mike Boulter wrote "2-2-4 Pelham" in a poetry workshop at the University of Colorado at Denver. His teacher, Catherine Wiley, asked students to close their eyes and listen to a poem she read. After hearing the poem, Boulter began this piece about Lunenburg, Nova Scotia, where his father and stepmother live, a place he visits often.*

The lighthouse horn rages
only a short gap
between blasts, fog wages
war with visibility.
Scallops and dead fish, the stench.                                                5
Almost overwhelming.
Sea salt rests gently on my lips
as I wander past the docks
and the ships,
sunlight streaming through sails                                                  10
in individual layers
of evening red.

I spend nights and Loonies
at a used book store
down the street from where I sleep,                                               15
but I don't know its name.
Its hours are tired. Opening
when it wants to wake and closing
when it wants to—take it easy.
Thousands of books sleep                                                         20

on its sandy shelves and
in worn boxes like little houses,
sometimes disturbed by strangers
wondering who Mark Twain is.
25    This upsets me, I'm troubled already.
Don't disturb my family,
Literature is the only
one who understands me.

A little further, up a hill,
30    an antique house rests
on the corner of Pelham and Prince
hosting a lonesome scaffolding
where workers will meet
around eight to redo
35    the analogous color scheme
of sky blue and plum.
The old house needs a new coat.
It's chipped and cold.
I'll take any coat
40    because I'm cold and chipped
and ready for a drink.

Destination Knot, the pub.
Not like England,
at least it's not the States.
45    The town drink is whiskey
but everyone drinks rum
and Coke. I'll have a whiskey.
Filtered with charcoal
captured from mines
50    sewing up eyes while drinking
blindness.

Lunenburg is full of
ups and downs, hills
became streets unplowed.
Stray cats painting                                                          55
the night, eyes
glowing hopeful that they
will once know the affection
of a spoiled single child
like myself, and I hope they do.                                            60

I walk past the red wood
museum cramped with fish,
the myths of their masters.
Those who were, not lost
but found by the sea,                                                       65
now reduced to names
carved in glass black pillars
shaped like a compass
so that they might know
where home is, and return.                                                  70
Someday.

I stare out south to where
I was born, past the harbor
and food-filled water,
not wanting to go back there                                                75
and also not knowing that I
am actually looking northwest.
I'm left a little turned around.
Twenty-two spinning
years old, dizzy                                                            80
I long to stay but home
is yet to be found.

## Reading to Write

1. Autobiographical narratives about place include sensory images. Which images stand out to you in this poem? What do those images tell you about Lunenburg?

2. One theme of this poem is looking for home. Who or what is looking for home in this poem? How do you know?

3. The writer identifies with inanimate objects in this poem (counting books as family and feeling "cold and chipped" as the old house that needs a new coat of paint). Think about a place that is important to you. What objects or images are significant to that place? In what ways do you identify with those objects? Write a poem or 3- to 4-page autobiographical narrative in which you consider the significance these objects have for you.

# She

## *Matthew Brooks Treacy*

*Matthew Brooks Treacy wrote this essay in his Rhetoric 101 class at Hampden-Sydney College, a liberal arts college for men in Virginia. His teacher, Lowell Frye, asked students to write about a person, to "create for your reader a sense not only of what or who the person is or was but also why the person should be of interest to your reader." Treacy writes of his mother, focusing on how she "always shingled lessons" into his mind, "leaving each one slightly raised for prying up later on." One lesson she taught him is the importance of using his hands each day. Treacy's essay, judged the best essay written in Rhetoric 101, was awarded a prize that academic year.*

~~~

Mom says, "If you go a day without using your hands, you die." It's a principle that influences the way I do things. Nothing is ever futile. The most horrible chores ever devised by the devil in the days of man do not even leave me with a gutted feeling anymore, though God knows they used to. Repainting a chicken shed or lying prostrate to the sun on a steel roof is never as bad as it sounds; you've used your hands, and at least *that's* worthwhile. My mother has always shingled lessons into my mind, leaving each one slightly raised for prying up later on. There was never a day when we didn't do some meaningless household task just to pass the time. She always used her hands. On top of an adamant refusal to learn the first thing about technology, manual labor just fits her. She used her hands when She shot the groundhog who had one of her zucchinis in its mouth. She used her hands when crunching rabbits under the blunt end of a hatchet for some of the best stew in the Western hemisphere. She used her hands to hang the stockings, even when my sister and I knew better than to believe in a fat guy in a red suit. In the past I have questioned her claim of devotion to me, but there were always ethics to be spaded out of the dirt she was normally covered in, sandy values scraping the back of my neck during a rough hug before bed. Loving me is something She has always done, but with a sharp manner that hides the tenderness I sometimes cry for.

My Mother is not a woman so much as she is a field of energy. Mom is a force, a kind of aura that only takes human form to be that much more intimidating. An order to cut the grass is not a request but an international doctrine, and She sits at the helm of an aircraft carrier just waiting for a rebellious child to give her reason for an atomic strike. Making us cut the grass is her method of control. There lies, somewhere beneath the tile of our kitchen, a proverbial bag of chores just waiting to be opened, like Pandora's Box. I am in constant fear that, one day, a refusal to mow will burst that bag wide open and spill hell into my life, so I do whatever I'm told. These responsibilities have become more of a tradition than a job, so I can't mind them; God forbid I break that custom. The sun bakes me like a scone on early August days, but smiles down on the Mother weeding eggplant, and the neighbors selling lemonade under an oak. She works like a madwoman in the garden, and still keeps an eye on whichever unlucky child has a job outside. When all is said and done, the yard has grown to the heavens, leaving me to give it the haircut of a lifetime under the omniscient eye from amongst the bean rows. It is a task that takes a light-year, but after three hours in the field I'll gladly accept the neighbor's lemonade, no matter what's floating in it. The common image is me standing at attention and She a drill sergeant inspecting my work, looking for any surviving dandelion to give me away. I imagine She would love to find a single uncut weed to justify beating the shag out of me with the garden hose. But then, smiling a smile that would have wilted the grass anyway, She goes to get a beer and watch me finish off the front yard.

There are some unexplainable phenomena between the two of us. These things I've grown accustomed to but have never understood. It's all to do with her. No one else can really grasp just how weird our relationship is, because no one else has ever gone through another like it. The first clue that our mother-son bond was stronger than most was the day I came home to a chaotic scene and She immediately informed me, "Way to go baby, you let the emu out." That night I did homework in electrified silence, forcing down home-grown garden squash and awaiting her return. Finally the door screamed and I prepared for a verbal thrashing only to be greeted with a hug. Everything was forgotten. The homework lay strewn on the table and the snow fell as She unfolded a story that would eventually go down in family lore. It was not a story like the boring epics that college professors pride themselves on, but a *story*. It was like something told by five different people at Thanksgiving with sporadic interjections thrown in through mouthfuls of mashed potatoes and venison. There was a plot line, rising action, a climax, blood, and plenty of cursing. By the time she finished and I had chewed my lip raw, the escaped emu had been recaptured somehow by a turkey call and something resembling a German infantry tactic. I sat there in awe, swallowing repeatedly to wet my vocal cords back into coherence. "That's the most incredible thing I've ever heard," I managed to gasp, unable to get the image of my mom pulling a tackle on a bird from the Cretaceous period out of my mind. The amount of respect She lost for me that night was more than made up by my amazement and overwhelming love for this woman who brought down ostriches. Even being sentenced to double grass-cutting duty and cooking for a week didn't really sting that much. After all, I'd be using my hands.

So many times She would ruin my chances for fun. So many times I was caught when it seemed I could not be, and so many times I would be forced to dry dishes instead of climbing hay bales in the fields. Of course there will always be hay, and there will always be home. She will always be there weeping me away to college and willing me back with that same aura of power that surrounds her. Each time I will argue, but apparently dishes will never just dry themselves. And each time that I think I'm too tired to get up and turn off the dorm room TV,

I will think of my mother and stumble over in the pitch black to use my hands at least one more time that day.

---

## Reading to Write

1. Matthew Brooks Treacy uses repetition to emphasize a lesson he learned from his mother: the importance of using his hands. Consider the three sentences in paragraph 1 that begin, "She used her hands." What do these three sentences tell you about her character? Why do you think Treacy capitalizes "She," even in the middle of sentences? What's the effect of that choice on you as a reader?

2. Metaphors also play an important part in this essay. Treacy describes his mother as "a field of energy," "a force," "an aura," and he uses other comparisons too. Which metaphor do you find most effective? Why?

3. Write an essay about someone who is important to you. Like Treacy does, use metaphor and repetition to give a sense of character—and to show why the person should interest readers.

# The Bucket

## Susan Collinet

*Susan Collinet wrote "The Bucket" for her Advanced Composition class at the University of Arizona. Her teacher, Tammie Kennedy, asked students to use their powers of observation "to gain a new perspective or experience, to know or feel something differently, or to see something familiar in a new way." Collinet says of her own essay: "What began as a story about a kitchen fixture from my childhood evolved into an emotional account of growing up in a family with an alcoholic father and its lingering stigma."*

N ot too long ago, my sister Dorothy phoned me from the East Coast and asked what I wanted from my childhood dwelling place before it went on the market to be sold. Since our father had died some twenty-five years before and Mother had been put in a home for the forgetters, the task of distributing their treasures and inconsolable legacy lay before us, their eleven children.

"Send me the bucket," I said with a quiver in my voice.

"The bucket? Why on earth would you want that beat-up old thing?"

How could she ask why? In our family there survived no heirlooms of Chippendale tables or diamond and pearl cameo brooches or portraits in gilded frames. Our heritage consists of scraps like a notebook of poems written by my father, which my oldest brother now proudly displays in his study; of the rebellious, bright red wicker basket where my mother kept her yarn and mismatched needles, which now sits in the blue and yellow toile French country den of my baby brother's rambling Tudor estate (it was he who painted it so many years ago with a jar of poster paint he stole from his third-grade classroom); and the bucket, which now hangs in my kitchen. The not-so-sacred family relic broods there,

displaying its dents and bruises, guarding its stains from spilled-over memories, and protecting the unfortunate essence of my childhood.

5    The sight of this sad antiquated token of remembrance, dangling by its metal handle from the fancy porcelain knob in my kitchen, evokes images I once needed to forget. Now I gratefully recall them. It memorializes the existence of that old kitchen table etched with kids' initials and eleven lives that were celebrated and regretted, embraced and squandered with a flip of a wrist or a sharp alcoholic tongue.

The old pot's tired, tilted appearance seems out of place in my happy kitchen of stainless steel appliances, shiny marble counter tops, and original paintings of colorful fruit and vegetables created by family members. Nevertheless, it has every right to be there—to remind me of the unbearable stench of diapers boiling at night after supper, or the comforting aroma of the corned beef and cabbage, Mother's famous Irish boiled dinner piled to the brim with potatoes and carrots donated by the church ladies. How I dreaded seeing my mother's face, red with embarrassment when she'd open the front door to the fancy women from Our Lady's Sodality. They smelled of roses and gardenias and wore new coats and shiny patent-leather high-heeled shoes. Arriving in pairs, each would be carrying a small cardboard carton overflowing with celery greens and carrot tops. My mother would rush to the kitchen before them and brush a chair with her apron, making sure it was clean enough for the ladies to sit upon. They'd politely stay for a moment, just long enough to tell Mother what a lovely family she had. After declining an offer for a cup of tea, they'd abruptly rise and head for the front door, leaving behind a trail of fine perfume and an air of condescension that made me feel insignificant, dirty, and poor.

I can see my father sitting at the kitchen table, shrouded in his perpetual angst, cursing about this thing or that, chopping carrots and tossing them in the bucket for his guilt-laden chicken soup. I can hear the ping as each raw slice hits the metal. Earlier in the day, he had probably asked my mother to "phone in sick" for him because he drank too much the night before. She had probably refused. Again. Her refusal probably set him off in a rage; he probably said things he later wished he hadn't. Then he must have sat at the kitchen table, appeasing his guilt by making chicken soup.

My precious heirloom guards the image of my mother standing at the stove stirring fudge, her mind a million miles away, on those rage-infested Sunday afternoons when Dad was hungover—again—and nobody dared speak. Each dent in the bucket harbors my ignorance and intolerance of an insidious disease that came to define a man, a poet gravely misunderstood. In spite of it all, my father was a romantic who wrote poetry and taped it to the refrigerator door, where it was ignored. He inherited the weakness for drink from a long line of Irish alcoholics. Following the accidental drowning of his first-born son at the age of three, he discovered the pint and allowed his life to spiral into despair, anger, and defeat.

A kaleidoscope of flashbacks includes the blob of kids with no identity sitting around the table on freezing mornings before school, staring at the bucket waiting for the Quaker Oats to become oatmeal. One of those mornings, little brother Michael got impatient. With his five-year-old fingers, he reached for the metal ladle sitting in the bubbling breakfast. From the table rose a symphony of screams and murmurs and shrieks from my nine siblings and me. My father came storming out of the bathroom with shaving cream on his face. "Holy Mother of Christ, what the hell is going on here? Michael, get away from there! Where the hell is your mother?"

10       Mother came running from the pantry. "Michael! No! Don't touch! *Mon Dieu!* No!" She swept the child into her arms and ran to the bathroom for a wet washcloth to wrap around his hand. As she returned to the kitchen, the bathroom door slammed behind her with my father's words trailing off: "Goddam miserable son-of-a—." Michael still has the scars from that painful burn, and we all bear a scar from the scathing furor of my father on that frigid January day.

The perfect half moon imprint on its bottom edge where the metal pelted the linoleum floor reflects the memory of my oldest brother, John, carrying the bucket of boiling water into the bathroom for his bath one early summer evening. The weight proved to be too much for his slippery hands and uneven stride. Steaming water splashed to the kitchen floor and scalded his feet and legs. He screamed as he jumped up and down to escape the steaming spill. My father cursed, "Fa chrissakes, what the hell are you trying to do, flood the goddam kitchen?" Sitting at the kitchen table, I lifted my feet from the floor and wept, reacting to John's pain and my father's growl.

Dangling with a smug air of purpose, exhibiting its crude spots of rust and various dimples, the bucket evokes a smile when it nudges my thoughts toward sweltering July afternoons. Filled with ice cold strawberry Kool-Aid, it would bide at the edge of the kitchen table and lure my brothers and sisters and me, and all of our friends, sweaty and dusty from a carefree childhood summer day, to climb the rickety wooden stairs to our second-floor apartment, walk through the opened kitchen door and take turns slurping from the metal ladle filled with the sweet, scarlet drink. Ice cubes would clink against its inside as we'd get in line to wait our turn. My mother would sit by the stove puffing on her Pall Mall and smile at the sight of us.

On those special days when we'd get to lie on the living room sofa, sick with a flu or a sore throat or some unknown or invented ailment, the bucket would be obliged to sit on the floor within projectile range, just in case. I felt an odd comfort, lying there staring down into the empty receptacle.

Today, the bucket is an ongoing source of mockery and derision in my family.

"Is it in the backyard with flowers in it?" one of my brothers jokes.    15

"Do you keep it in your bathroom filled with water in case your toilet gets plugged?" another joshes.

The premature death of our oldest brother defined our childhood and created the dynamics of a defective family. Time has a way of fermenting pain and distilling it into forgiveness. Decades melt the devastation of a tarnished childhood into compassion for parents with limited skills to deal with the worst possible nightmare, the loss of a child. The eleven remaining children suffered while the family tiptoed around the brutal silence of that child's death. That silence is our legacy. The bucket serves as the beloved tabernacle of that warped nobility. That is why each time a family member visits my kitchen and catches a glimpse of it, they recognize that, indeed, I possess the greatest gem of all. Not without reverence they say, "Oh my God, there it is. There's the bucket," and we open the door to our schlep down memory lane and carefully unfold the weathered heirlooms of our tattered psyches.

---

## Reading to Write

1. Susan Collinet uses contrasting details (of objects from her childhood and the places where those objects reside now, of her childhood home and those who visited it) in this essay. What do those details tell you about her childhood and about her life now?

2. Collinet includes a photograph with her essay. What details from the photograph do you recognize in the essay? In what ways do the visual image and the images created by words work together to create a particular meaning or effect?

3. Recall an object from your childhood. In a 4- to 5-page essay, examine the object and the memories it evokes. If possible, include a photograph of the object.

# Arbitrary Encounters of a Traveling Sales Girl

## *Becky Andert*

> *Becky Andert wrote this essay in her Creative Nonfiction class, taught by Don Scheese, at Gustavus Adolphus College in Minnesota. Andert says her purpose was to explore "the situations that follow from crossing physical state borders, personal limits of fitness, and boundaries of expectation." She presented this essay in 2008 at the National Sigma Tau Delta conference in Kentucky, sponsored by the International English Honor Society.*

I dropped my bag beside the door, knocked three times, took two steps back, turned to the side, and looked at my notebook. After fifty-seven seconds when there was still no answer, I jumped forward and knocked again. While I waited for Mrs. Jones to answer her door, I reviewed the names of her neighbors and the sales talk I would use once she opened the door. I looked at my watch; it was almost lunchtime and I still needed to show my books to two more families before devouring my peanut butter sandwich. When there was no answer, I snatched my bag up and ran down the driveway.

Jogging to the next house, I dropped my bag beside the door, knocked three times, jumped back two steps, and looked at my notebook. Waiting for someone to answer the door, I looked down the street. Seven homes were adorned with maroon Sooners flags, three had orange BEAT TEXAS yard signs, and one had a small covered wagon in the front yard with OU painted on the side. The front door crept open, and my rehearsed smile was greeted by a toddler with spaghetti sauce smeared across his pajamas. From a room deep in the house I heard a familiar phrase: "Brandon! Shut the door! You know better than to open it when I'm not there!" A typical three year old, he waved to me and giggled as he glanced over his shoulder and ignored his mom.

Two weeks and 479 families later, I had met seven other Brandons, eighteen Johns, twelve Julies, twenty-one Sarahs, and over 200 other ankle-biters sprinkled throughout Oklahoma City on whom I could count to play with me at the door until a mom or dad arrived to scoop the child onto a hip. As a summer job, I was working with the South-western Company selling educational books door-to-door. Everyone that sold books for the national company followed the same guidelines and schedule. In the months leading up to the summer, we learned a scripted sales pitch and responses to objections the company guaranteed we would encounter. (We saw the books last year. We own encyclopedias. Our kids are Internet-savvy. We already have enough books the kids don't read. Our kids are honor students.) Until I knocked at my first house, I was convinced that there was no way the company could accurately predict the exact dialogue I would have with any given family. Yet, when family after family objected with the same words the company promised they would, and when family after family bought the books after I used the response written by the company, my attitude changed. When I finished talking with any particular parent, I would return my books to their original place in my bag, jog down their driveway, bike down the street, bike up the next driveway, retrieve my books from their place in my bag, and talk with the next family. It may sound repetitive, but our schedule kept us focused on the goal ahead of us.

We had relocated to a state on the other side of the country, and we were living with a host family for the twelve weeks that we sold books. Monday through Saturday we each woke up at 6:00 am, took an ice cold shower long enough to shout a few positive phrases (OKLAHOMA DOESN'T KNOW HOW LUCKY THEY ARE TO HAVE ME! I'VE GOT THE BEST JOB IN THE WORLD! THERE IS NOTHING I WOULD RATHER DO THAN SELL BOOKS!), devoured a carb-filled breakfast, performed an energizing sales dance (imagine an occult conglomeration of a college rouser, the chicken dance, and rowdy music video dance moves), knocked on doors and sold books to families from 7:30 am until

10:30 pm, returned to our host home to turn in our stats, made lunch and dinner for the next day, and went to sleep by 11:00 pm.

5    This schedule made the summer pass quickly, but not without pain. Within four weeks of biking into the back of a truck and shattering the taillight with my knee, I was working across town on the edge of a construction site. Cat calls and whistles followed me as I biked past the building crew, and looking to the other side of the street, I saw seventeen identical beige houses that the new homes would mirror. Nearing the edge of the work site, I felt my bike jolt from something in the road, and looking uselessly for a tree to stop under, I rode to the side of the street and instead stopped in the shadelessness. Spinning my front tire, I saw the head of a metal stud.

To my surprise, the stud kept the air in the tire for the next seven hours. After the seventh hour passed, though, the drone of escaping air was suddenly apparent. Riding the bike on a flat tire, I struggled nine blocks to a gas station. Steering was not viable, balance was difficult, and turning into the gas station I crashed to the ground. My knee erupted in a bloody mess, and my books spilled across the road. I limped into the gas station and opened the phone book. The first three bike shops I called told me they did not offer "house calls" (but I'm at a gas station, not my house), the next phone line was busy, I got an answering machine at the next shop, and finally another human voice. "So you don't have *any* way to get the bike here, and you need your bike to keep working?" That's correct. "Which gas station did you say you were at?" The Holiday Station on the corner of Seventh Avenue and Third Street. "Ooooh . . . Yeah . . . My shop is on Ninety-Fourth Avenue; that's the other side of town. And you haven't had luck with any of the other shops closer?" No. He gave me the name and number of one more shop to try. "Tell them John from Bike Pro told you to call, and call me back if that doesn't work out."

I didn't have to call John back. Leaving my bike at the gas station, I walked the nine blocks back to the neighborhood I had been working in. The owner of the last shop was willing to fix my tire after his store closed, and the manager at the gas station let me leave my bike there until then. I tried my best to wipe off the blood from my knee, but it quickly reappeared and mingled with the embedded gravel. When I knocked at the next house, I didn't even make it through my name before the mom looked down at my leg. "Oh honey!" she gushed, "What happened to your knee?" A relatively new mom (her son was barely sixteen months), she pulled me inside, sat me down on the sofa, ran to her medicine closet, rubbed antibacterial cream on my knee, put gauze over that, an oversized Band-Aid on top, and medical tape to seal it shut. She also gave me a tall glass of sweet tea and a brownie for the road. "Chocolate makes everyone feel better, right? Besides, you've been working hard." You bet, and I never say no to chocolate.

By four o'clock, the bandage had fallen off and another mom noticed my mess of a kneecap. "Darling, I'd love to look at your books, but only if you come inside and put something on your knee. What happened? Have you put anything on that? You know, that will heal better if you dab some hydrogen peroxide on it." Before I could respond to any of her questions, she hurried up the stairs. As a seasoned mother of three, she gave me the hydrogen peroxide and Band-Aids from the upstairs cabinet before sitting down to look at the books. After she signed her order form, I was putting my books back in the bag when her motherly habits surfaced again. "Have you had dinner already? Do you even get a dinner break? Do you eat enough fruits and vegetables while you're working? You know, fruit helps keep you hydrated in this hot weather." Three minutes later I began the nine-block walk back to the gas station munching on a bag of fresh okra.

Arriving at the gas station, it was only a few minutes before a truck pulled up with "The Bike Shop" stenciled on the side. A broad-shouldered man in his thirties got out of the truck and smiled at me. "You must be the one I've been hearing so much about. Having bike problems?" Already exhausted, I did a poor job of covering my confusion. It was true that I was having bike problems, but I didn't know who he would have heard it from besides me. "How many bike shops did you call before I agreed to come?" How many bike shops are there in Oklahoma City? "Well, you should know that people are looking out for you.

Just before you called, I got a call from John at Bike Pro. He told me everything that you did, but also told me to call him back if I couldn't come help you with your bike. He was going to come clear across town—that's over an hour's drive. And after I talked with you, I got two other calls from bike shops telling me the same thing. Someone is looking out for you." Holy buckets! "Holy buckets? You're not from around here are you? My wife says that, and she's from up north in Minnesooooooduhh." He fixed my flat tire and the brake that hadn't worked since the bike was given to me my second week in Oklahoma by a firefighter who was concerned that I would get heat stroke if I walked all day.

10     The next week I managed to stay on my bike, and thankfully the week that followed as well. Oklahoma City was experiencing a record-breaking heat wave, and every day of those two weeks was over 110 degrees. Nearly every house furnished me with water, PowerAde, or sweet tea, and others were willing to let me use their bathroom. I interrupted a birthday party at one house, so instead of water I was given a piece of birthday cake and scheduled an appointment to come back later. A few blocks over, a retired schoolteacher didn't have any kids or grandkids; instead, he gave me $500 cash and asked me to give the books to a family that couldn't afford them. When I inquired about which of his neighbors had kids, he pointed down the street. Using height as an indication of age, he tried to guess their age with the same motions as would be used to exaggerate the size of a recently caught fish: this big; no . . . probably closer to this size; actually . . . they're probably even larger than that.

I had a fifty year old tell me that age was just a number and he'd love to take me out to dinner, and a fifteen year old's voice cracked as he asked if I wanted to go to the movies. Another older man laughed as he told me it was too bad he was three times my age and already unhappily married. "I would tell you I'm the handsomest, richest, smartest man around, and we could elope and be happy. But that old hag won't let me. I would also buy some of your books for my wife, but she still hasn't used what I got her last Christmas." What's that? "A plot of land at the cemetery!"

Several streets later, as I bent down to pick up my bag, I noticed my toned calf in the reflection of the tinted door. Surprised, I practiced flexing my muscles and posing in various muscle man stances. My beach ball is *this* big, and I think the gym is *that* way. After 270 seconds, I once more bent down to pick up my book bag when the front door swung open. Judging by his timing, I was sure this college guy had seen my entire display. His response confirmed my suspicion. "You've got some pretty impressive pipes there, little lady."

"Yeah," I smiled back, and salesman that I was, "I'm selling tickets to the gun show. How many do you want?" I had already fallen off my bike twice, been bitten by a dog, forgotten my entire sales talk when a mom opened the door, left my bag of books inside a house, and seen a small kid run past an open door naked with her mom chasing after in the same lack of clothing. I had spent ten weeks selling books door-to-door, and there wasn't much that intimidated me anymore. I talked with him briefly before walking down the driveway and on to the next house. I dropped my bag beside the door, knocked three times, took two steps back, turned to the side, and looked at my notebook. The company prepared me for all the conversations and objections I would receive when talking about the books, but no one could have predicted any of the other interactions I had.

## Reading to Write

1. Becky Andert creates a sense of character through dialogue and action in this essay. What do the words people say and how people treat Andert tell you about them?

2. Andert creates a sense of place through detail. What details stand out to you? What do those details tell you about Oklahoma City?

3. Write a 5- to 6-page essay about either a job you have had or a place you have visited. Use dialogue, detail, and action to create a sense of character and place.

# On the Riverbank

## Molly Lehman

> Molly Lehman wrote this essay in her Autobiographic Writing class taught by Karl Woelz at the College of Wooster in Ohio. Of this essay, her first memoir, Lehman writes, "I used the assignment—the creative exploration of a significant event or period in my life—to write and think about the death of my grandmother, who passed away from Alzheimer's disease when I was thirteen. As I wrote, I discovered two narratives embedded in the story I was trying to tell: that of my grandmother, whose history and memory were vanishing, and that of myself, entering adulthood and using my own conception of history and memory to understand who and where I was."

### I.

The bridge one mile from my house was over eighty years old and spanned the narrow, muddy Tuscarawas River. It was lined with concrete spires, row after row of smoothly rounded columns supporting its broad sides.

I was finishing third grade when plans were announced to raze the old bridge. It had deteriorated slowly, said the newspaper, and while it had some historical significance, it was no longer sound. Destruction of the old bridge was set for the first of May.

Towards the end of April, the road was closed off. Yellow bulldozers and wrecking balls were parked across the street from the bridge, like guards with folded arms. I imagined the bridge feeling like a prisoner on death row, counting days on the calendar and cowering before the pitiless eyes of its executioners. In a way, it was a relief when the first wrecking ball swung forward and the demolition began.

When it did, my father was at the site nearly every day with a video camera. He was furious with the project and determined to document every second of it. "Look at this," he would say later, pointing at the screen as chunks of eighty-year-old concrete fell into the river or the foundation sank into the mud of the embankment. "That's incredible. Just think of how much history is in every piece of this bridge."

My father is like that, though; he confronts the things that make    5
him angry or frightened or sad. He records them and watches them over and over again, steeling himself, it seems, until he is no longer angry or frightened or sad. I wish I were the same. All summer and into the fall, as the bridge came down, I refused to come near it. When we drove past the closed road I looked away. When my father brought home his video camera I went upstairs to my room and closed the door. My brother and sister would sometimes go on walks with my father down to the site, climbing over the deep gouges in the riverbank and examining the lumps of broken stone, but I could never bring myself to go.

Was it merely to avoid being sad that I stayed inside with a book in my lap while the bridge came down? The sadness was there, the clinging gray kind that hung around for hours and sometimes days. When my father reported that the spine of the bridge had been broken and the last of the dying trestles had fallen, it even bordered on grief.

But I don't think it was the sadness that kept me away.

Watching the bridge come down would mean facing the fact that good things could fail. It would mean that things I had always depended on could disintegrate.

Finally the destruction was finished.

How stupid, to feel abandoned by the destruction of a bridge; yet I    10
felt that way, standing on the riverbank looking across through the empty air where something solid had been. Anger and a new kind of fear pushed at my throat.

Eventually, a smooth new bridge was built over the empty space. I went down often to the site then, watching the young concrete rise in a white expanse across the river. There were no brittle pillars in this bridge; no dangerous weakening in the core, and it was not beautiful. Its efficient blankness was nothing like the delicate grace of its predecessor. I approved.

The old bridge had failed, and that was like a betrayal. It had been destroyed. I didn't want to remember it.

## II.

My grandmother was tall, with a square jaw and wide feet. She was solid. Her hands were gnarled. Behind plastic pink-framed glasses, her eyes were large and dark and surprisingly beautiful. For as far back as I could remember, her hair was white.

She was a seamstress; she called pants "slacks" and had silver thimbles in all of her pockets. She made rag rugs, dividing sheets and flannels into long ribbons and weaving them into fat braids.

15      My father says that the only times she ever said "damn" or "shit" were the times she burned a batch of cookies.

My mother loved her so much that she called her "Ma" even before she married my father.

My grandmother smelled like something called Skin So Soft, a clear oily liquid she would rub into her arms and legs after her bath. The scent brought calm into the room, like a ship pushing a wave.

She had a dog, a gray curly-haired mutt she named Peaches. When my father moved out, he took Peaches with him to live in the country.

Peaches liked everything about the country except for the thunderstorms. If lightning flashed and my father wasn't home, she would run the five miles down the road into town, heading for my grandmother, for the smell of Skin So Soft and the feel of a rag rug beneath her paws.

## III.

20      My grandmother's house was green. Not a subdued, fashionable green, nothing that matched the muted conservative tones of the rest of the houses on the street. The house was the color of parrot feathers

and artificial key lime pie. In the half-dusk, it glowed with an eerie phosphorescent quality, as though it were only an x-ray of a real house. Compared to its soft yellow-brown neighbors, it looked like a fluorescent bulb stuck in the middle of a row of beeswax candles.

I adjusted my wig as I watched the sun sink behind the houses. It was long, black and curly, and it itched. My sister ran up to me, trailing a long gauzy scarf. Her cheeks were smeared with sticky pink rouge. "We're going, we're going, we're going," she shrieked, swinging a plastic pumpkin wildly above her head.

Trickles of kids ran up and down the street. I knew that the thrill in the air had nothing to do with my grandmother's electric house, but it seemed like all the energy in the neighborhood was radiating outward from it like the rays of the sun.

My brother scampered up to us. His eyes were shining through the holes in the sheet. "I want Pixie Sticks," he announced, his bulbous white head bobbing.

"Me, too," said my sister, violently jerking her princess train out of the hedge.

I walked ahead, keeping my chin high and even. I didn't run with them; second grade was too grown-up for that.

I was a gypsy that year, and I was regal. The wig had a red bandanna sewn on the crown. My face was punctuated: my eyebrows two heavy parentheses, the beauty mark like a period just above my red lipsticked mouth. Two gold rings big enough for me to fit a fist through dangled from my ears, snagging on the wool of the shawl I kept gathered at the center of my chest.

The best part of my costume, though, was the skirt. It was a crazed patchwork of colors, scraps and snips of shirts and skirts and bedspreads, curtains and tablecloths and even upholstery. My grandmother had made it, stringing everything up on a length of elastic and stitching it shut on her old Singer. "This is something I would have been asked to make twenty-five years ago," she'd said with her mouth full of pins.

25

## IV.

My father sat with his hands flat on the table, fingers splayed outwards like the arms of a starfish.

"Your grandmother's going to start forgetting things," he said. "Little things. Maybe she won't remember how old you are, or where her glasses are. She might forget our phone number."

30  I was eleven, back in public school for the fifth grade. I traced the wood grain of the table with the tip of my finger and wondered how long this would last.

"Alzheimer's doesn't happen quickly," my father continued. "The doctor calls it a slow deterioration. Her brain cells are starting to die, and as more and more of them do her memory will start to die as well." I pictured my grandmother's brain cells dying, popping and fizzing out like sparks.

I didn't want to sit there. I didn't want to hear that. I didn't want to think about things dying, or failing, or fading away. I didn't want to picture my grandmother's mind crumbling away like the old bridge, and I didn't want to sit and watch again when the cranes came along and pushed it into the river.

My father had stopped talking. He looked at each of us: my brother with his chin resting on one knobby fist, my sister with her blue eyes turned toward my mother. My mother, her mouth set hard, her hands folded. Me, staring down at the table, digging my thumbnail into the crack where the leaves met.

"Let's just make sure we appreciate the time we spend with Grandma," my father said at last.

35  I looked up. "Well, she's all right *now*, isn't she?" My voice was sharper than I meant it to be.

My father glanced at my mother. "Yes, right now she's all right. But it's—she's going to get worse. We want you to be prepared."

"Well, she's all right now," I said, getting up from the table. "It's not a big deal." I could feel their eyes on me as I left the room.

## V.

My mother and grandmother sat on the front steps. They both wore light summer pants rolled up over their ankles and their feet were bare on the wooden boards. Between them was a cluster of bowls, bowls gleaned from every kitchen cupboard: the big egg-colored one, the two plastic ones stained yellow, three of the aluminum cereal bowls, and one tiny sky-blue cup. Clumps of green beans poked over the rim of each. The egg bowl held clean beans. The blue bowl held snapped-off ends.

My mother and my grandmother each had handfuls of beans in the dishtowels spread on their laps. One bean at a time, they would break the ends off, strip the string away, and toss the clean beans into the egg bowl.

Fresh beans are taut and juicy. The skin is velvety, like a caterpil- 40
lar's body, but the flesh is crisp. Breaking one will send flecks of foaming juice spattering on your wrists, and there will be a surprisingly loud sound, like bubble gum cracking under your tongue.

The sound punctuated their conversation, otherwise soft and low. The screen door bulged out as I pressed my forehead to it, straining to hear.

"Did you see in the paper that Al Troyer's daughter got divorced?" My grandmother scooped more beans into her towel. "Such a shame, she had such a pretty face."

"I remember," said my mother. "She was two or three grades above me in school."

"She had a sister, didn't she? Now let me think. Her sister married one of the Madzia boys. Nick, I believe his name was."

My mother brought a clean bean to her lips and chewed thought- 45
fully. "Nick sounds right. Weren't they a wild bunch?"

"Oh, yes. It was strange; their cousins were terribly nice. Have you ever met Jenny Vaughn?"

The name game dominated the porch. Births, engagements, marriages, spousal abuse, lost jobs, moves, divorces, deaths; every milestone—particularly unpleasant ones—was reaped and scrutinized along with the beans.

It didn't stop there, either; the game absorbed every grown-up conversation it touched. They could be discussing almost anything in the beginning: insurance premiums or the weather, recipes for pineapple cookies, how to fix carburetors or ease backaches, hysterectomies, the stock market. By the end, it didn't matter. Every conversation was eventually snagged and funneled into the name game.

The game required an astounding accumulation of gossip. My mother and father went through the paper every morning, quizzing each other, it seemed:

50     "Did you see here that Dottie Showalter's father died?" my father might say from behind the sports section.

"Yes," my mother would trill from the sink, "and Jim Mattson was arrested again for drunk driving."

My father would grow quiet and turn the page. "Dan and Marlene Dutton got divorced," he would say finally, casually, and my mother would flinch and accidentally wash a plate twice.

And playing the name game demanded remarkable recall ability. Players needed to know the gossip, but they also had to find ways to connect it. Maiden names, first husbands and wives, old neighbors, high-school sweethearts, career changes, and medical conditions were crucial. I pictured the memories of game-players like the coiled lines inside the reels of fishing poles: compact and hidden, but once they'd gotten a bite, press a button, the hook swings forward and the line unwinds; they could cast far, far away to haul in more.

Out on the porch, my mother brushed a few stray ends from her towel and stood up, balancing the egg bowl filled with clean beans between her palms. "Watch it," she said to me as she passed, "or I'll drop dinner all over the front porch."

55     My grandmother followed, the rest of the now-empty bowls stacked in front of her. She patted my head and closed the door softly behind her.

## VI.

"What grade are you in now?" my grandmother asked.

"I'm in sixth," I said, picking at the threads on her worn couch.

She nodded, her hands folded in her lap. "All grown up."

I shrugged. I didn't feel grown up. I felt awkward and childish. I'd just gotten braces and the tiny wire squares snagged my lips when I moved them, so I didn't talk or smile much. At school I was back on the swings, reading and daydreaming. During gym class dodgeball games I was "out" a lot, sitting slumped against the blue vinyl mats, watching slack-jawed as my classmates hurled the yellow rubber balls across the floor.

"What grade are you in now?" my grandmother asked. 60

I looked up from the arm of the couch. My grandmother's face, wide and kind, watched me. Her lips were curved. Her eyes were soft.

"Sixth, Grandma."

"Oh, yes," she nodded. "I remember. All grown up." I shrugged again.

It wasn't as if I didn't try to be grown up. I told my mother I had lots of friends at school, so she wouldn't be disappointed. I felt guilty about being unpopular, and afraid that my mother would think she had done something wrong in raising me. I made attempts to fit in. I'd sneak thumb-sized vials of glittery makeup in my lunchbox and put it on before I went into the classroom, pushing the sticky sparkling paste underneath my eyes and across the tops of my cheeks the way football players applied black streaks of No-Glare.

"What grade are you in now?" my grandmother asked. 65

I said it louder this time, even though I knew her hearing was fine. "Sixth."

She nodded, just like she had before. "Yes, you're certainly all grown up."

Was I grown up? I didn't shrug this time. Instead, I put on the same face my mother was beginning to use around her, the same plain wide-eyed smile.

"All grown up," my grandmother said again.

If she repeats it enough, I thought, maybe it's true. 70

## VII.

"Get your things off the table," my mother told me. "We'll have dinner when Dad gets home."

I scowled and gathered up my seventh-grade homework slowly. It was getting harder; math didn't come as easily as it had in grade school. On the way to my room I passed by my grandmother sitting in her chair in the living room, and she gave me one of her blank smiles.

"What grade are you in now?" she called after me.

"Grandma, I have to go," I snapped.

75     I left my books in my room and came back downstairs. The casserole dish in the center of the table steamed with ham and scalloped potatoes and green beans, and the air smelled rich and salty.

Sitting at the table, we stabbed the ham with forks and peeled away the skin. The potatoes made curling patterns of cream on the plates and broke delicately under our tongues, but the beans came out of a can and were soft and dull green.

After dinner, my mother made coffee and passed out mugs to the grown-ups as though she was dealing cards. They went to the back porch, my mother and father. My grandmother stayed at the table, her gnarled fingers wrapped around her mug.

I sat at the other end of the table and played mancala with my sister, the board wedged between dirty plates and bread crumbs. The colored glass pebbles that had come with the game had all been lost, so we played with leftover aquarium gravel. Jumping and gathering the gritty little turquoise stones, we could hear bits of the name game floating in from the back porch.

"Joanne?" my mother said sharply, and I heard the clang of a spoon on the side of a mug. "Her husband's the biggest deadbeat, I swear."

80     "His brother's worse," my father said, his voice deep and warm with coffee. "He's awful. Just awful. Remember the time he came to me asking to borrow money? I told him, I said, 'Frank, you haven't had a steady job in six months.'"

"His father was like that, too," my mother said. "That was before my time—he ran around with my aunt years ago—but I remember hearing about him. What was his name?"

My father hesitated. "I don't know," he said at last.

My sister and I looked at each other.

"Ma would have known," my mother said, almost too quietly for us to hear.

At the other end of the table, my grandmother smiled at us. "Are you the little neighbor girl?" she asked me gently. 85

I turned away. My sister dropped gravel into my side of the board. On the back porch, my parents sipped their coffee in silence.

## VIII.

It wasn't just math. Seventh grade was hard in other ways, too. There was no middle school, no bridge between the child and the adult. Seventh grade meant leaving elementary school behind and entering high school, where we had rows of tiny steel lockers in the basement that had locks with combinations we were expected to remember. It meant class schedules printed on yellow paper that told us we had to switch classrooms seven times a day.

It meant meeting other students. Two other elementary schools sent their newly graduated seventh-graders to the high school, too, and our class was suddenly tripled.

The first day I stood alone on the tile of the lobby, the halls surging with binders and elbows and broad, pimply, unfamiliar faces. Someone grabbed my wrist and I turned.

A fat woman in gym shorts stood next to me. "Want to play junior-high volleyball?" she said. "I'm the coach; we can sign you up right now!" 90

Elementary-school dodgeball flashed through my head. "I don't think so," I told her.

"Come on," she said. "Don't be a wimp."

I tucked my thumb into my book and closed it. I glanced at the list she held in one plump hand. No one I knew.

Who was I hiding from?

95 "Well, I'll try it," I said at last.

Our first practice took place in the gym, which smelled like floor wax and sweat like the gym at the elementary school. I dressed alone in a corner of the locker room and went in. The gym felt too open, too wide. The practice volleyballs were yellow.

"Okay, line up and try serving underhand," called the fat coach.

I stood next to a short girl with long yellow hair. My fingers were slick with sweat. I balanced a ball on the palm of my hand and brought the other back to hit it.

Suddenly it was gone. I looked over at the yellow-haired girl next to me and saw it in her hands. She looked straight at me.

100 I turned away and was bending down to get another ball when I heard someone laughing. I looked up.

"Are you joking?" she crowed. She was holding the ball out to me, her shoulders quivering while she laughed. "Here, take it back. I don't want it. Why didn't you *say* something, for God's sake?"

I took it and she shook her head. "Shoulda seen the look on your face," she told me, stooping to pick up another ball.

I faced the opposite side of the gym, held out the ball, and hit it. To my surprise, it curved in a perfect clean arc over the net.

## IX.

"Grandma, come inside," I said, reaching out to her. "Please."

105 My grandmother held a bottle of Windex, her fingers pressed on the yellow nozzle. The liquid inside sloshed forward when she pointed to the ground.

"I'm cooling off the sidewalk," she said. Her eyes were wide and stared straight ahead, almost childlike.

"Grandma, you really don't need to do this. The sidewalk's fine."

She shook her head. "No, it's a hot day," she said firmly.

I looked at my sister, two years younger than I, and scratched my head. It *was* a hot day. It was July, the summer before my eighth-grade year, and the temperature had risen into the nineties. I wanted to be inside, barefoot in front of the fan with one of my brother's comic books. Instead, I was following my grandmother up the driveway as she hosed it down with window cleaner.

"Grandma—"                                                                           110

"I'm cooling off the sidewalk."

I grabbed my sister's arm. "Come on. She's not going to listen to us, and we need to get her out of the sun."

Inside, I found my mother folding clothes. "Mom, come get Grandma," I told her. "She's gone up the lane with a bottle of Windex."

My mother rubbed her hairline. "Oh, Ma," she sighed.

She went out the door and I saw her walk up the drive and take my     115 grandmother by the arm. My grandmother gestured to the ground again and my mother shook her head. I wandered off to find the fan.

Fifteen minutes later, the screen door banged open and my grandmother came in, guided by one of my mother's hands on her back. She looked angry.

My mother looked tired. The two short vertical grooves just above her nose had deepened, and her cheeks were flushed from the heat. "Sit down, Ma," she said.

My sister had come in behind them, following at my mother's elbow. "What happened?" I asked her. She shrugged.

"Grandma got really mad."

"The disease has gotten bad enough that her personality is chang-     120 ing," my mother said to us, handing my grandmother a glass of water. "She's not the same woman she was before." My mother sat down and examined the pile of unfolded laundry she'd left behind. "I think it might be time for a nursing home," she said slowly.

"Stop it," I said. "Don't say that. She isn't even that bad."

My mother looked at me wearily. "I know this is difficult for you. It is for all of us. But please think about it. She's getting worse, and I can't watch her every minute. She'd be better taken care of in a nursing home."

I stormed up the stairs. Behind me, my grandmother knocked over her glass of water and my sister patted my mother on the hand.

## X.

When my father, the youngest in a family of five sons, was eight, my grandmother planned a trip to the zoo.

125 She wouldn't go along. Instead, she would send her five boys off to the zoo with my grandfather. All day just for the men.

"They'll love it," she told my grandfather.

"Fine," he said, and went into the basement to look for part of a crankshaft for a 1958 Chevrolet Bel Air.

"All day at the zoo with your father," she told my father and his brothers, and after that they built pens and cages out of couch cushions. They kept them up for days, each of them taking turns to crouch inside and roar in anticipation.

A few weeks later, my grandmother woke up early and slid out from underneath the covers. She went into the kitchen and lifted the picnic basket from the top of the cupboards. She opened the breadbox. She took salami and cheese and apples from the refrigerator, cookies from the jar, napkins from the drawer. She made lunch for the men.

130 Then she woke the boys. She tugged a shirt over my father's head and handed my uncles their shoes. In the kitchen, the picnic basket sat in the center of the table while the boys ate toast and kicked the rungs of their chairs excitedly. Sunshine spilled over the windowsill.

My grandmother wiped my father's mouth with the tip of her apron and went into her bedroom. My grandfather was a lump on one side of the bed. She laid a soft hand on his side.

"Durant," she said quietly. He didn't move.

"Durant, wake up. The zoo."

The blanket stirred, but there was no sound.

135 "Durant, please. Today's the day you were going to take the boys to the zoo."

My grandfather opened his eyes and looked at her. His eyes were clear and gray.

"I never want you to say that to me again," he said. "I'm not taking them anywhere." My grandmother lifted her hand from his side quickly. He closed his eyes and turned away.

My grandmother left the bedroom, shutting the door gently behind her.

"I'm sorry, boys," she told my father and my uncles, "but there won't be a zoo trip. Your dad is sick."

She unpacked the picnic basket. In the afternoon, after my grand-     140
father had gotten out of bed and gone into the basement to find spark plugs for a 1952 Impala, my father and his brothers replaced the cushions on the couch.

## XI.

"Tie your shoes!"

The old woman scowled at my nine-year-old brother and stretched out her wrinkled lower lip. We caught a flash of pink gums; she didn't have any teeth left. Whitish crust had collected in the corners of her eyes. A bald-headed plastic doll was tucked under one of her chicken-wing arms.

"I said, tie your shoes!" One bony finger jabbed at the floor, where my brother's dirty shoelaces were undone.

My brother looked at me, bewildered, and knelt down, knotting the laces in a tight bow. The old woman watched him for a few minutes and nodded. She tucked the doll higher underneath her arm and tottered out of the visitors' room, down the nursing home corridor.

I was thirteen and I hated it there.     145

I hated the color of that place. It was green, not the lively color of my grandmother's house but a sickly pale shade of green that made me think of mucus and stomach bile. I hated the smell, the meaty stench of old skin, the sourness of urine and the acrid sting of disinfectant.

I hated the people there. The old woman with her doll and her rubbery pink toothless gums would leer at us and screech. There was an old man who screamed at the nurses. "No, goddamn it!" he would bellow, shoving away the Styrofoam tray in front of him and slapping the hand of the nurse who held out a spoonful of liquefied turkey. "No! I'm not fucking eating that shit! NO! I want out of here. I want the hell out of here. Get me the hell out of here!" Those were the mean ones.

My grandmother was not a mean one. She was a sad one. She sat in her green bedroom with two wrinkled hands folded in her lap and looked out the window. On her bed, the sterilized white sheets were pulled tight and smooth. She looked up when we came in.

"Hello, Brian," she said slowly, looking at my father. "I'm glad to see you."

150 "Hi, Ma," said my father, whose name is Ernie.

I wanted to go home. I was tired of being sad.

We brought my grandmother back to the visitors' room, where one of the nurses was carrying an armload of something soft and gray. She laid it on a table in the middle of the room, and all of the old women, the sad ones, the mean ones, stood up and came over. The toothless woman left her doll gently tucked in the corner of her chair. My grandmother let go of my father's arm and went over as well.

"What are they doing?" my father asked.

"Laundry," said the nurse. She clicked open a ballpoint pen and glanced down at her clipboard. "These women have done laundry most of their lives, so giving them old rags to fold offers a sense of stability and normalcy."

155 She looked up. "The rags aren't used for patients, of course," she said quickly, as though she needed to reassure us. "The linens we use are kept sterilized. These rags are kept for this purpose only, and they simply get washed and folded over and over."

I watched the women bring the edges of the rags together, folding them in tidy squares and stacking them carefully. I thought about all of the clothes that had passed through their hands before. My grandmother was folding on one end of the table. She would have folded boys' jeans, socks with mended holes, and flannel shirts. Coveralls stained with grease. Her flowered housecoat.

My grandmother waved my father over. "Harley, come here." She turned to the withered old woman beside her and said, "This is my son. He's in the service." The woman ignored her and continued to fold.

I hated that place. I couldn't stand to look at my grandmother, placidly folding rags and calling her son by the wrong name—more than that, believing that he was someone else. I couldn't stand the endless repetition, the scrounging for familiarity, the rags being folded over and over again. My grandmother was just another crazy old woman hunting for her memory in a pile of laundry.

I went over and planted myself in front of my father. "Dad," I said, widening my eyes, "can we go? Please?"

My father glanced at my grandmother. Her hands were smoothing themselves over another rag. He opened his mouth as though to say something, then changed his mind.

My grandmother watched us leave. When we reached the door, the nurse came over and swept her arm over the table, toppling the neat stacks of rags into a laundry bag to be washed again.

## XII.

My grandmother died in April, almost five years after the bridge first began to come down, two days after her eightieth birthday. My father was with her the night she died, but I hadn't seen her for months. I wasn't sure what she looked like by then, or how much worse she'd gotten.

At the funeral, I thought of Peaches, looking for the refuge of my grandmother's house when a storm threatened. She had been an old dog when she had died years before, hit by a truck one rainy night on her way into town. It seemed like the closest thing to the way I felt.

I had lost the refuge of my grandmother; she had lost the refuge of her own mind. The bridge had tumbled into the river and was swept away. It had failed.

But in a way, I had failed more. I had gone into hiding, and I wished I hadn't. I wished I had been there to see it, to see its beauty make its long clean arc until the very last moment before it fell.

Reading to Write

1. Molly Lehman writes this essay in twelve sections, most of them specific scenes. What is going on in each section? How do the sections work together to create an overall meaning or effect?

2. Lehman uses several similes and metaphors in this memoir. For example, she compares bulldozers and wrecking balls to "guards with folded arms" and the bridge to "a prisoner on death row." Later, she compares her father's fingers to "the arms of a starfish." Which metaphors and similes do you find most effective or significant? Why?

3. Write a 15- to 20-page memoir in sections. Include scenes, dialogue, metaphors, and similes.

# 3

## RESEARCHING AND INFORMING
## Reports

What are your interests? Are there any topics or issues you would like to learn more about and share with others? Writing reports provides an opportunity to research a topic, synthesize and interpret information, and inform readers about what you find out.

One of the most important elements in writing a report is to narrow and focus your topic. For example, in "The Future of Food Production," Sam Forman writes about food production and its relationship to environmental sustainability, researching the issue in a local community and then providing specific examples that illustrate larger trends and issues. In their ethnographic reports, Rose Locatelli and Kelley Fox also research larger topics—the ways physical spaces and individuals define and affect one another—and they do so by examining specific places and people on their university campus. And in "Xenakis, Cage, and the Architecture of Music," Jonathan Payne reports on the broader relationship between architecture and music, and he makes this broad topic manageable by focusing on two composers and a project of his own.

Once you've narrowed your focus, you have multiple options for the kinds of sources, methods of development, and matters of design you use in researching, developing, and presenting your report. In conducting research, you might be used to starting with information in published texts, as Marin, Forman, and Payne do. Consider other sources of information as well. You might, like Forman, interview experts and practitioners or, like Locatelli, Fox, Forman, and Payne, conduct close observation and other forms of field research. Your instructor can offer guidance on the best sources and methods of research for your report.

In terms of development, you might include description to inform readers about an event, as Maegan Marin does in "Pantoum for Tibetans." Or you might use comparison and contrast, as Jonathan Payne does to inform readers on connections between music and architecture, and as Sam Forman does to show different approaches to food production in Grinnell, Iowa. Depending on your topic, you might use other methods of development as well: causal analysis, definition, narration, or, most commonly, some combination of these various methods.

In considering matters of design, think about whether any visual elements—diagrams, section headings, graphs, photos, tables, or other illustrations—would help you to organize and present the information. Such visual elements can also help readers comprehend and remember your report.

As you read the selections in this chapter, be attentive to the ways in which the writers focus their topics, use sources, and develop and present their information. And take note of any strategies you might use in your own writing.

# Pantoum for Tibetans

## *Maegan Marin*

*Maegan Marin wrote "Pantoum for Tibetans" for a poetry workshop at Saint Joseph's University. Her poem was inspired by Shirley Geok-lin Lim's "Pantoun for Chinese Women" and a line from "Your Ex-Lover Is Dead," the song by Stars, which appears as the epigraph. Marin explains that the line that was spoken before the song begins reminded her of "Thupten Ngodup's famous self-immolation in protest of the Chinese occupation of Tibet" in 1998, and that she challenged herself to use the pantoum's repetitive structure in the same manner as Geok-lin Lim.\**

> When there's nothing left to burn,
> you have to set yourself on fire.
> —Torquil Campbell

When there's nothing left to burn you have to set yourself on fire.
Outside a tin-roofed hut, past the azalea and rhododendron forest,
a man in a garden of ruby snapdragons begs independence.
His bed beneath the altar is neatly made.

Outside a tin-roofed hut, past the azalea and rhododendron forest,          5
they pledge hunger strike, they swear their deaths.
Their beds beneath the altar are neatly made;
they vow, *We will follow one by one.*

They pledge hunger strike, they swear their deaths,
these people in torn clothing feel no breath of hesitation.          10

---

\*A *pantoum* uses a specific pattern of repetition: the second and fourth lines of each quatrain become the first and third lines of the quatrain that follows, except in the final stanza, where the pattern differs. It has various spellings, among them pantoum, pantoun, pantoon, and pantun.

They vow, *We will follow one by one.*
He hides gasoline in a bathroom, plans for days.

These people in torn clothing feel no breath of hesitation
as Delhi police come to haul them away; one slips past the dragnet.
15  He hides gasoline in the bathroom, plans for days.
A quick pulse of flame, a lit cigarette.

As the police haul them away, one slips past the dragnet.
*Bod Rangzen,** he prays; they have been oppressed countless days.
A quick pulse of flame, a lit cigarette.
20  Women toss white scarves around his body, ablaze.

*Bod Rangzen,* he prays; they have been oppressed countless days.
A man in a garden of ruby snapdragons begs for independence.
Women toss white scarves around his body, ablaze.
When there's nothing left to burn, you have to set yourself on fire.

---

## Reading to Write

1. A pantoum uses quatrains that include lines repeated from previous stanzas. What is the effect of the repetition in this poem? In what way does the use of repetition affect the way you understand the event on which Maegan Marin reports?

2. Do an Internet search for a newspaper article on Tibetan protestors. Use key words such as "Tibet," "hunger strike," and "fire." Compare the article to Marin's poem. What elements do the two texts have in common? How do they differ?

3. Choose a recent event on which to write a report. Try writing your report in poetic form, being attentive to images or information that you can reinforce through intentional repetition.

---

*Transliteration of the phrase "Independence for Tibet"

# The Tacit Culture of an Individually Defined (Undefined) Room

## Rose Locatelli

*Rose Locatelli wrote this report for a Research-Based Writing class she took in the first term of her freshman year at Chapman University. Her assignment was to write an ethnographic research report—to "select a community, cultural group, or social environment to observe, interview, possibly participate in, and then represent in report form." Her teacher, Jeanne Gunner, praised Locatelli for showing "a marked ability to vary voice, employ images, and end with reflection on what she learned through the project."*

B lessed are they who see beautiful things in humble places where others see nothing," exclaimed Camille Pisarro, describing the beautiful unseen that lurks beneath the obvious. Individual perception defines actions and prescribes a social code to others; in the same way, the west side of Henley Hall's second floor has created a tacit culture, unwritten rules, for their communal area. These rooms work to isolate as well as to unite; to create order as well as to welcome chaos. In a place of constant compromise, the study rooms act as an individually definable area, a room whose identity is shifted through use.

### MY BIAS

I have been a college student for seven weeks, though I have been romanticizing about being a college student for much longer. My daydreams, of course, ignored the difficult realities of coping with the constant interaction that comes with living in such a communal situation: the noise, the compromise, the drama, and within it all the need to be alone, and to be productive. The study rooms have often been my haven, detaching me from the constant community and providing an environment in which I can focus. I have attempted to, without bias, understand and describe the tacit culture of these rooms; however, I am inclined to believe that all the residents on my floor are responsible, respectful individuals like the ones that I observed: individuals who work hard to achieve their goals and want others to do the same.

Additionally, I am currently in one of the rooms composing this paper—I have imposed a set of rules on the room so that the atmosphere is quiet and studious, which is why I have chosen to refer to these rooms as "the study room." Right now, it very closely resembles the quiet, productive environment of a library or a high school study hall. However, last night, listening to my friends play their guitars, I understood how it could be dubbed "the recital room," and glancing in the window last week to see a group of poker-players stone-facedly studying their cards, I considered "the play room" a more appropriate name. So do not allow the name I am giving the area for identification purposes to define it.

## THE STUDY ROOM

The study room as shown in Figure 1 is actually two rooms separated by a wall, connected by a door, both unremarkable rooms defined by white walls and comfortable, utilitarian furniture clad in patterns that hide the dirt. It is located on the second floor of Henley. One of the rooms is accessible only through the larger study room but is observable, due to a large window, by anyone using the stairs, making it no less open to disruptions than the other room. The main room has a door opening to the hall in the west wing. This larger room holds five chairs, two sofas, two side tables, and a larger coffee table (that I have yet to see used to hold coffee); the smaller room has a large conference table and seven chairs. The furniture is free to be moved around, but is never removed from either room. Because of the large air-conditioning unit that is perpetually blasting cold air into the smaller room, Henley residents refer to that room as "the cooler." The conduct in the cooler is identical to the conduct within the main room; it is merely an extension

**Figure 1**

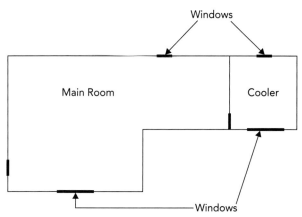

of the culture practiced in the main study room. Though no written rules insist that only studying is done within the room, studying is the main use I observed. Large windows in both rooms offer views both in and out—acting as a distraction (both welcome and unwelcome) but also as a check on conduct: those within the room realize they are being observed, judged, and hence act accordingly (this prevents vandalism, sexual conduct, etc. that might otherwise occur).

## USES OF THE STUDY ROOM

The study room has no written rules, no guidelines for its uses. Its name "the study room" implies a purpose, but I have seen the name changed to "the play room," "the practice room," and so on, as is needed to fit an individual's ideas for its use. Hence, the name does not define the room, does not prevent the room from being redefined; however, each of its rooms is used for only one purpose at a time so as not to interrupt any primary user's activities. In my observations of the room, I found its users to carry similar artifacts: laptops, notes, textbooks,

5

books, pens, pencils and the occasional snack—these are all objects of study. However, often I observed that individuals in the study room would only have a cell phone, seeking somewhere quiet to make a personal call; or guitars and ukuleles, wanting silence for practice or recording purposes. Tasks that required noise from the participants but not others often took place in the study room, the premise of quiet seemingly inviting such noise.

Though the room is an area of relative quiet and rare disruptions, it is understood that others can stop by and say hello. The tacit rule seems to be that it's okay to greet people you know, and to ignore those you don't know or are upset with. In most instances, friends walking by are expected to stop in to greet you or check on your homework progress. However, these disruptions are kept short, acting as momentary relief or inspiration, not wasteful disruptions. One afternoon I observed that as two boys played their guitars, two girls stopped by the room to discuss their music. They requested assorted songs and even danced to them. Though this disrupted the original nature of the boy's practice, neither party found the interaction rude or unusual, perhaps because it did not undermine the boys' original aim, which was to play their guitars together.

The furniture within the room, as shown in Figure 2, is a reflection of its many uses; like the room, the furniture can be, and often was, morphed to what was desired by the user. Very rarely did the furniture stay in the same place from day to day, and often the configurations made no sense to me (though surely they had served some purpose). The two diagrams in Figure 2 depict the furniture on two days and illustrate the drastic rearranging that occurs. Moving the furniture was not only a matter of practicality but also a way to personalize the room, if only temporarily.

## WHO USES THE STUDY ROOM?

The residents of Henley's second floor are the main ones who use the study room. Since every floor in Henley has study rooms, most students

**Figure 2**

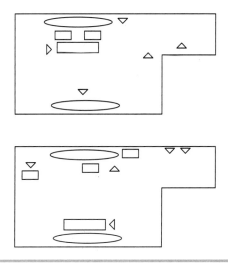

remain on their own floor to work or play. Because the study room is used mainly by a group of individuals who know each other and live close together, the residents feel a sense of proprietorship, creating a sense of respect as well as a sense that they are entitled to change the room's identity (through use, moving furniture, etc.). The residents enjoy using it for its obvious purpose, studying, because it is useful and in many ways necessary; however, they recognize the necessity of adapting that use. It's the only room on the floor large enough to hold a large group of students interested in socializing, and it's the only room where an individual can find silence in order to practice an instrument or talk on the phone. Additionally, the lack of restriction on the room's activities invites change without fear of repercussions. In many ways, the study room is similar to the living room of a house; a living room has a purpose, but it is multifaceted.

No particular clique uses the study room, and so there are no insiders or outsiders; there are simply those who use the room and those who do not. The groups who use it do not have any defining characteristics except that of their room use. Furthermore, those studying within the study room are not considered better students than the individuals who are never seen there. It is an option, not a standard that some choose to utilize and others find unnecessary. Likewise, those observed socializing within the room are not considered more popular or social. This is because the residents recognize that studying and socializing can be done in other environments such as the library or a sorority exchange. In some instances, the study room can create an identity for its users: the boys who routinely practice their guitars together are recognized by other residents as "the boys who play guitar"; other users have other characteristics, such as "night owls" or "procrastinators."

## WHY USE THE STUDY ROOM?

10    Dorm rooms must be versatile, serving as areas for sleeping, eating, and studying; there is no identifiable code of behavior for either residents or guests. Students studying at their computers, wanting silence, are indistinguishable from gamers playing video games on their computers, welcoming company; therefore, visitors and roommates assume company is welcome, creating a difficult environment for studying or other activities that require silence. Rosa, a second-floor resident who was using the cooler to write a paper, explained, "I need to be isolated [when I write]. There are always people coming in and out of my dorm room. People are more considerate in here because they know you're studying, but in my room they just come in." Guests unable to determine what the person in the study room is doing recognize that they must ask and understand, not assume. In this way, an ideal environment for a variety of activities is formed.

Dorm rooms are also shared areas, living spaces comprising constant compromise. One roommate may want to listen to music, while the other wishes to study in silence—and a compromise must be made, creating an arrangement where neither party is completely satisfied. Since a dorm room is very rarely being used for only one task—only when only one person is there—the study rooms become useful, even necessary. The tacit culture of the study room is that the first person there is able to shape its uses, its rules, if only temporarily, while inhabiting the space; the identity of the room is essentially modified, through use, to fulfill a purpose. It takes only a single student to redefine the room's uses and to enforce these uses: A quiet, studious individual averts a talkative crowd, the crowd instinctively recognizing that the temporary rules of the room insist that it is silent and for studying.

## TACIT RULES OF THE STUDY ROOM

The study room, despite its temporary personalization by individuals who shape it to fit their needs, is clearly a shared area, an area to be respected. Personal belongings, remnants of the room's temporary, imposed identity (notes, snacks, etc.), are not left but rather thrown away or taken when the individual leaves, restoring the room to its unidentified purpose, restoring the room into a communal space. However, the furniture, rearranged for various purposes, is not returned to its original arrangement. The study room's users have a blinkered view of how the room is used—they adjust the furniture to make themselves comfortable and feel that this arrangement will suit others just as well; it is not an action of disrespect. Despite knowing the room has other uses, they fail to acknowledge or worry about these other uses.

The tacit culture also dictates any interaction between two users of the room. A person who wishes to use one of the study rooms for a different purpose than someone who was there first would proceed to the other room. If neither one is available, he or she would simply find another area; the use of the rooms is defined on a first-come-first-served basis—no individual's or group's needs hold priority over another's. Even students wishing to use the room for the same purpose tend to move to an unoccupied area, unless they wish to study and no other area is available, or they know the individual already using the room. If two strangers share the room, they tend to sit on opposite couches and use different tables; subsequent strangers attempt to isolate themselves as well, by distance within the shared area, creating their own personal area. A student who was in the cooler reading one afternoon explained to me, "If you just walked in here and sat down [and I didn't know you] and the other room was empty, I would wonder why you didn't choose the empty room. I'd be a little creeped out." However, friends and acquaintances tend to share the same couch or table, allowing the line between their personal possessions to be unclear (papers overlap, etc.). The same is true of individuals talking on the phone: they expect strangers to leave them alone to carry on private conversation. In these rooms, personal space is respected and emphasized especially between strangers.

The unremarkable room at the end of the hall is far more complex than I ever suspected. Its identity changes depending on its use and on who perceives it. The room is definable only on an individual level, and indefinable in so many ways. Yet, the room's rules are universal—the unwritten rules are mutually acknowledged and acted upon. What happens to those who break the rules is left unanswered, but who is to say that the room's rules will remain the same? College students are constantly shifting (much like this room's uses) as they learn, as they grow. Perhaps that is why the room remains versatile, accepting the growth of the students, welcoming their individual development.

## Reading to Write

1. Rose Locatelli explains her own bias in writing this report. In what ways does her use of the room she is writing about affect her representation of that room and her interpretation of its value?

2. In what ways does Locatelli's use of images and section headings contribute to her report?

3. Write an ethnographic report about a room on your campus. As Locatelli does, make your bias clear and use section headings and images to support and illustrate your findings.

# Establishing Identities

## Kelley Fox

*Kelley Fox wrote this ethnographic research report for a Research-Based Writing course at Chapman University. Her teacher, Jeanne Gunner, nominated this report for the way Fox varies her voice and stance, "allowing the reader to experience the environment and its participants and then to follow her critique of both."*

The harvest is always more fruitful in another man's fields.

—Ovid, *Ars Amatoria*

The messy collection of various signs and reminders hastily taped to the door of Room 115 in the Pralle-Sodaro dorm at Chapman University does not even begin to describe the chaos that occurs behind it, the result of three identities being crammed into one extremely small room. Entertaining and certainly very interesting individuals, Griffin, Simon, and Andy are three roommates from three parts of the country with three very different personalities. They each deal with the various social situations thrust upon them in different and unique ways, mirroring their diverse personalities. Upon meeting them, I thought their great differences would keep them apart and inhibit their ability to form friendships. But after watching the dynamics of their room and analyzing their behavior, I have concluded that their actions as well as their interactions with each other establish and perpetuate a specific social order that is central to how they function socially.

Float like a butterfly, sting like a bee.

—Muhammad Ali

On many occasions I have walked into Room 115 only to find Griffin sitting at his computer with a little smile on his face, quietly singing these telling words. It's not a huge surprise, however, as a huge poster of Muhammad Ali, which takes up the majority of the wall next to his bed, is also the screensaver on his computer. Deeply ingrained in this famous phrase lies the encouragement to just "float"; it allows for people to steer clear of involvement, of getting attached to any cause. This idea that not acting is okay puts blinders on its victim, preventing him from becoming deeply involved with any experience. By staying at the surface, one cannot be challenged. By staying at the surface and not probing deeper, one cannot get hurt. But by staying at the surface, one constantly stays at the top of the pecking order, ultimately invincible.

In a sense, Griffin is just that: socially invincible. A varsity basketball athlete, Griffin has no shortage of friends, or of female followers. People seem to simply gravitate toward him, as if being around him makes all their problems trivial. Teammates can often be found in his room, hanging out on his bed, watching ESPN. Girls are certainly not a rarity, and they usually come bearing gifts: pies, CDs, even homework answers. It happens often, and I have a feeling this "social worship" has been going on for a while, although in myriad other forms. Regardless, the constant and excessive positive attention allows Griffin to never have to think about his own happiness; Griffin always seems happy. And it is because of this that, out of the three roommates, it is easiest to be Griffin.

Simon, a freshman only two months into school, has already had several embarrassing nicknames thrust upon him. Tall, skinny, gangly, and freckly, with blatant Jewish features, Simon has been called Steamin' Broccoli, Seamen, and Jerome. Jerome is a name he gave himself, explaining, "It's my black name. I'm a G, a real gangster. That's why I have g-mail." This explanation is usually followed by laughter, causing Simon to turn bright red for probably the tenth time of the day.

The following is a brief conversation between my roommate and      5
Simon that augments my observations:

**TIFFANY:** Simon . . . how come you're always so quiet?

**SIMON:** I don't know. I've always been like this.

**T:** But you seem like you have so much to offer. Do you have your eye on any girls? Griffin and Andy sure seem to.

**S:** No, not really. I don't know. It's kind of a long story.

**T:** Oh c'mon Simon, you can tell us. Who are we going to tell?

**S:** Okay, fine. But you have to swear not to tell anyone, especially Griffin or Andy.

**T:** We promise.

**S:** I don't know. (*Deep in thought, not looking up.*) I guess when I was starting high school this one guy decided to make my life miserable. Everything I did he made fun of. He kind of ruined my social life. I've never really been confident, especially around girls.

Simon is the boy whom everyone beats up on in an attempt to hoist themselves up the social ladder. He falls victim to the classic idea that in order to move up in society, one must put someone else down. Thus, he is and has been stuck at the bottom of the social ladder, both in life in general and in his dorm room. Unlike Griffin, Simon does not have any surplus positives in his life and most likely examines his happiness often.

However, as difficult as Simon's social life is (and although he may not see it this way), he has a specific place on the social ladder. He may not like this spot at the bottom of the heap, but he has a defined social spot he can call his own, a place he easily maintains and a place he feels somewhat comfortable in, being that he's been in this spot for so long.

Andy, the third roommate, ties the three boys' complex but socially remarkable relationship together. A varsity water polo player, Andy is not a typical jock. Obsessed with the video game Halo III, riding his bike around town, and walking around trying to convince people of ludicrous ideas, Andy is usually caught up in his own world (but not quietly). In a way, Andy borrows from the stereotypical roles of both Griffin and Simon: he is an athlete but he is considered "dorky" by many. He is buff and attractive but has to work to reel in girls. While he dresses somewhat fashionably, he loves childish videogames. He is popular among his peers but also classified as a stereotypical nerd. Unlike both Simon and Griffin, Andy has to work diligently to establish an identity. In our college's society, Andy's role is vague and he is constantly forced to challenge his surroundings in order to establish the role in society he wants. He often goes to great lengths to attract attention, a mechanism to separate himself from his peers and establish his social identity. Here's what Simon and Kelley said about him:

**KELLEY:** I didn't used to like Andy. But he's grown on me.
**SIMON:** I don't know. I still don't really like Andy.
**K:** Why?
**S:** He always needs to be the center of attention. It's annoying.

There is less tolerance for the undefined; it is because of this that Andy can never settle down and be his own true self, as he himself may not even know who that is.

There are certain codes maintained in Room 115. While the residents contend they promote the idea that each of them should pick up after himself, messiness seems to be highly encouraged. I had difficulty walking from one side of the room to the other due to all the clean laundry, food wrappers, and plastic, disposable contact containers littering the floor. Society deems messy boys as not only acceptable but even as part of living in a small, crowded dorm room. Cleaning or being too neat would almost guarantee a homosexual insult. Being a messy boy is not only acceptable in college society but also encouraged in order to be considered "normal," which is the reason Griffin, Simon, and Andy live in a pigsty. They may or may not be naturally messy, but being untidy definitely helps them fit in and not be socially unacceptable.

The following is a diagram of Room 115:

---

**Figure 3**
ROOM 115

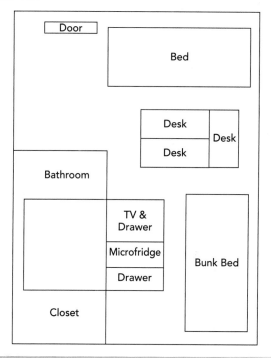

---

The layout of the room and the way the three roommates use this    10
space is telling. When they have down time, if not sitting at their desks
looking at the computer screen or watching television (or playing
Halo, in Andy's case), all three boys can be found relaxing on their
beds. Rarely do they physically interact; the greatest physical interaction I've witnessed among the three is a high-five. They don't like to
have their space threatened, nor do they invade each others' space.

Their behavior follows the heterosexual male stereotype that has been around for centuries. This is the same male stereotype that deemed Arnold Schwarzenegger fit to be a governor. It is the same stereotype that predicts these boys will mature into men with beautiful wives and large, healthy families; will mow the lawn on occasion; will have important, well-paying jobs; and will drive a sports car on the weekend. This male stereotype thrives off of testosterone and is everything these boys aspire to be. The lack of interaction between these three male roommates is typical in a college society that encourages such a stereotype, and suggests that, once again, the motivation behind their actions is centered largely around fitting in.

Room 115 can be seen as a smaller version of a larger social community. The three boys are subject to a social system that dictates how they should behave. They are purposely messy, belch loudly, never physically interact with each other, and watch an unhealthy amount of television instead of doing homework, all requirements for being socially acceptable young college boys who will one day be strong, capable, and successful men. Everything they do fits into the equation that will one day allow them to fulfill the role of the stereotypical male. These are just three roommates in one dorm at a small, private university, yet one could find myriad boys following the same codes at any university or high school across the nation.

Griffin's, Simon's, and Andy's actions are not unintentional or purposeless; their behaviors allow them not only to fit in but also to move up the social ladder. Their roles in society are stereotypical and can be compared to the characters in the 1985 movie *The Breakfast Club*. Griffin is like Andrew Clarke, a varsity athlete, and Simon fits the part of Brian Johnson, the typical high-school nerd. Andy is harder to match to a character and can most closely be compared to a female, Molly Ringwald. Still, all three boys' actions and interactions with each other shadow those of the characters in this stereotypical all-American teenage movie.

These three boys' behavior is especially interesting to track because they are at a socially critical point in their lives. They are young adults and their futures lie in their hands. The decisions they make now, whether about their education, their social life, or their careers, will greatly affect who they will become. It is easy for young people to change certain aspects of their lives now. However, once they're forty and have settled down to raise a family, this is not the case. Thus, the way they want their lives to be in the future in certain ways determines the way they act now. If they follow a certain stereotype, they are pretty much guaranteed a certain result. More specifically, if these boys are dirty and lift weights like the masculine stereotype dictates, they are somewhat likely to end up living the conventional masculine man's life: nice house, great family, secure job, lots of beer with buddies, an overall comfortable life. What boy at this age would not want that? This is why the boys act the way they do, and why boys have been following this stereotype for years.

While this conventional male stereotype might account for the boys' behavior, it is discouraging that they seem to feel obligated to perpetuate this stereotype. They do not use logic to justify their actions; in fact, if I were to ask them why they act the way they do, I would bet my own stereotypical feminine future role they do not realize their actions are all a part of a greater scheme to achieve happiness and self-fulfillment. There is immense pressure placed on young people to act according to the tacit laws of society in order to attain the "perfect" life. This can be a negative factor, as it imposes stereotypes on young people who might otherwise act differently. It forces a faulty thought system upon its victims and does not allow for individualism, something that is harmful to young, developing minds.

Despite these harsh constrictions, the three boys of Room 115 continue to thrive, each in his own way. Griffin and Simon both have defined places on the social ladder and seem to find security in these well-defined spots. While Andy's place in society is a lot less defined, he, too, has much motivation to preserve his space on the social ladder as he has more power than others who are lower on the ladder, namely Simon. While these boys are victim to many stereotypes, they continue to perpetuate these binding roles, something that occurs on college

15

Reports

campuses nationwide. The specific social order of Room 115 is central not only to how the boys in this dorm room function, but also to how they keep their spots on the ever-important college social ladder.

## WORKS CONSULTED

"Breakfast Club." *Wikipedia*. Wikimedia Foundation, 14 Oct. 2007. Web. 16 Oct. 2008.
Peters, John F. "Gender Socialization of Adolescents in the Home: Research and Discussion." *Adolescence* 29.116 (1994): 913–36. Print.
"The Grass Is Always Greener on the Other Side." *Wikipedia*. Wikimedia Foundation, 13 Oct. 2007. Web. 16 Oct. 2008.

## Reading to Write

1. Kelley Fox and Rose Locatelli responded to the same assignment and both studied the relationship between people and a particular place. In what ways are their reports and approaches similar? How do they differ? Which do you find more effective, and why?

2. Fox makes an argument about gender roles and stereotypes among college-aged men. What evidence does she use to support this argument? Do you find her evidence sufficient?

3. Write an ethnographic report about a group of people on your college campus or in your hometown. Like Fox does, provide transcripts of conversations to support and illustrate your points.

# The Future of Food Production

## *Sam Forman*

> *Sam Forman wrote this report for his freshman tutorial at Grinnell College in Iowa. The name of the class was "Our Town: The World at Our Doorstep," and the assignment for this paper was to assess the impact of food production on the environment. In reflecting on his work, Forman describes this report as a landmark in his "development as a writer because of the complexity of the subject matter and the detail that was required to adequately address the issues." He explains, "In addition to the length and detail, synthesizing a coherent argument from several different types of sources was a new challenge to me."*

<br>

The process that food consumed in America goes through to make its way to our mouths is like a Rube Goldberg contraption. The seemingly straightforward process of growing, raising, harvesting, and slaughtering goes on every day, completely hidden from consumers. Very few Americans are aware of the highly complicated, mechanized, and convoluted journey that any given bite of food takes from its origins in nature (or some manipulated approximation of it) to its destination on our plates. Although some people criticize the state of our food system, it is clear that it grew to be the international machine that it is because of demand. More than 300 million Americans want lots of food, meat especially, and they want it cheap. So like every other production process in this country, our food system has been industrialized to produce maximum food calories for the American people at minimum cost. This industrialization of our food system has allowed for population increase and higher standards of living.

But there are significant problems with the industrial food system. Caught up in a drive to maximize production and profit, the industrial food system has grown to a size that is not sustainable. As food production has become increasingly industrialized, concern for the environment and the animals we eat has taken a backseat to expansion. Specialization, rather than integration, has become the hallmark of America's farms. Rather than having chickens, hogs, corn, and hay all on one farm, all these things now reside on separate, much larger farms. There is, however, another, very separate food system that supplements the industrial food system: the local food system. Local food systems cater to people who, for varying reasons, believe that it is better to "buy local" or from a smaller, usually family-owned farm rather than from a supermarket with less-expensive mass-produced food. There are few places where the two food systems are as visible and distinguishable as in Grinnell, Iowa. Poweshiek County has a range of farms in terms of size, as illustrated by Figure 1, taken from the 2002 Census of Agriculture County Profile of Poweshiek, Iowa. As a resident of Grinnell, I have become very familiar with the faces of the two food systems. Wal-Mart, Hyvee, Monsanto Seed, and Fremont Farms are the incarnations of our industrial food system, while Café Phoenix, the farmer's market, and the various family farmers who participate in Community Supported Agriculture programs represent our local food system here in Grinnell. I have become familiar with the producers of food in Grinnell by conducting research, primarily through personal interviews. The interview was a valuable method of research for me because I was able to get a good sense of the interviewees' perspectives, understand their arguments, and sometimes even offer counterpoints in order to force even deeper discussion of the issues I plan to address in this paper.

During my time at Grinnell, I have acquired a very basic understanding of our food systems. Through both reading and personal interactions I have come across all kinds of opinions and arguments from proponents of both small-scale and large-scale agriculture. One theme that everyone agrees on is that our world is changing. Serious

**Figure 1**
FARMS BY SIZE

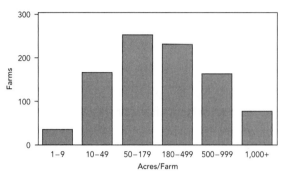

economic and environmental challenges are on the horizon. The current state of our food system in the United States is key to how well the industry will adapt when change comes. The American food system needs significant modification in order to guarantee that we can both eat healthfully and protect the natural workings of the planet we depend on. The most important change that could be made is a return to methods of food production that resemble nature's traditional processes, rather than methods that manipulate nature in an effort to make it work like a factory.

Grinnell is a great place to begin to examine some of the changes that have been taking place in our food system. In Grinnell, as has been the case across the country, there has been a strong trend in agriculture toward larger farms, fewer farms, and fewer farmers on each farm. According to the most recent county census of agriculture (taken in 2002), the number of farms in Poweshiek County has fallen 8 percent since 1997 and the average size of farms has grown 8 percent during the same time period. While growing bigger and industrializing, farms have also changed the nature of their operations to maximize efficiency and profit at all costs. Examples of this trend would be maximizing cropland by demolishing buildings on the farm that used to house livestock or by planting on hilly ground that is prone to erosion. In effect, too much farmland is used to grow crops, and not enough of it is left for livestock to graze on, throwing off the natural ecosystem. This is supported by the 2002 Census of Agriculture of Poweshiek County, which shows that 85 percent of all farmland in Poweshiek County is used to grow crops while only 5.5 percent is open pasture. This great discrepancy begs the question, if so little land is used for pasture and so much is used to grow crops on, where and what do the livestock of Poweshiek county eat?

5    For the most part, livestock, especially those commonly consumed like hogs, beef, and poultry, have been taken off the farm and now reside in an invention of the industrial food system: the Concentrated Animal Feeding Operation, or CAFO for short. In a CAFO hundreds of thousands of animals live together, eating the grain (corn for the most part) that is grown on the land where they grazed green grass long ago. These CAFOs are a prototypical example of how the industrial food system has re-arranged nature to provide the ultimate value-added service: turning cheap, government-subsidized corn into protein and calories, in this case meat. During a phone interview, Professor Mark Honeyman of Iowa State University pointed out to me that by definition agriculture is the manipulation of nature to turn solar energy into caloric energy for our consumption. This logical assertion forced me to stop and ask myself why, if agriculture was by nature manipulating plants and animals, is there anything wrong with the way food is mass-produced in our country today? I quickly reminded myself that there are different degrees of manipulation. The environmental impact of Barney Bahrenfuse, the owner of a 500-acre farm in Grinnell, keeping goats on his farm because they like to eat weeds is minimal because he is not changing anything about the goats' natural habits. Goats like to eat weeds. Greater degrees of manipulation often thwart the animals' natural instincts, reducing their existence to little more

than converting grain into meat. It should be added that small farms are not all good and big farms are not all bad. CAFOs recycle their animals' waste, just as Bahrenfuse does on his farm. The only difference is that while Bahrenfuse hauls his animals' poop across his smallish farm, CAFOs do not usually have farmland of their own and sometimes (because they do not depend on the soil in any way) are not even located anywhere near farmland, and thus have to truck the manure to a buyer, using precious fossil fuels in the process. In a paper entitled "Sustainability Issues of U.S. Swine Production," Professor Honeyman points out that to optimize sustainability, "The relationship of swine population to arable land is important. Large swine production units [CAFOs] built on small acreages or not part of farms that also produce feed grains can have manure utilization problems" (1415). This is certainly not a problem in Iowa, where fecund soil is, well, everywhere. The CEO of Fremont Farms, Steve George, whose farm in Malcolm, Iowa, holds about 9 million hens that lay eggs for liquid egg products, does not have to look far to find a farmer in need of the waste his hens create. Animal waste is usually well dealt with by CAFOs; after all, it is not only environmentally conscious but also profitable to sell your animals' waste as fertilizer.

There are, however, ways in which CAFOs are clearly less earth-friendly than traditional farming. The first way is that they are generally farther from farmland that needs fertilizer, and so the animal manure needs to be transported, a considerable waste of fossil fuel. This also contributes to pollution and global warming, problems we all pay for. Another problem with CAFOs is the health of the animals they produce. Separating the animals from their natural habitat and constantly feeding them subtherapeutic levels of antibiotics weaken the animals' natural robustness. In addition, these practices create antibiotic-resistant bacteria, a threat to the health of humans as well as to the animals that host the resulting super-bacteria. There is much debate about what is the healthiest and safest environment for an animal. Steve George told me in a phone interview that he wouldn't want his chickens roaming around outside, because of all the dangerous pathogens that lurk outdoors. By keeping his hens indoors, he is able to protect them from disease and keep them big and productive by giving them feed with growth-promoting antibiotics in it. In the other camp are Barney Bahrenfuse and Suzanne Costello, who run B&B Farms in Grinnell. According to Bahrenfuse, they raise 600 chickens each year. They let their chickens peck around outside in addition to giving them feed that Barney grows and produces himself. As Costello put it, "One way of looking at it is there's this horrible world out there that we're all at war with," and then there's the way Bahrenfuse and Costello handle their chickens: "If [the chickens] are getting fresh air, and they're getting greens . . . they're healthier beings and they're less susceptible. So the way we view it is, you beef up their health and you don't have to worry about it." Based on direct observation I would have to say they are right. It just so happened that on a drive-by tour of Fremont Farms I observed a truck full of dead hens being covered for highway transport. Apparently about 10 percent of laying hens in CAFOs simply can't endure their situation and die, a fact that is built into the cost of

Fremont Farms

production (Pollan 318). In the close confinement that CAFO-bound laying hens exist in, "Every natural instinct [is] thwarted, leading to a range of behavioral vices that can include cannibalizing her cage mates and rubbing her breast against the wire mesh until it is completely bald and bleeding" (Pollan 317). Bahrenfuse mentions no such problems among his chickens (then again, neither did Steve George). Obviously there are many hundred thousand more chickens living at Fremont than at B&B, but that truckload (which may very well have been full of chickens who had already lived a full life) stands in stark contrast to the three chickens at B&B that "crapped out," as Bahrenfuse put it.

There is also evidence that CAFOs are as bad for the people who live around them as for the animals who live in them. According to Honeyman:

> More than 20 years of studies have consistently shown the negative influences of large-scale specialized farming on rural communities (Allen, 1993). Lobao (1990) found that "an agricultural structure that was increasingly corporate and non-family-owned tended to lead to population decline, lower incomes, fewer community services, less participation in democratic processes, less retail trade, environmental pollution, more unemployment, and an emerging rigid class structure." (1413)

In addition to these findings, large CAFOs, especially hog or beef operations, create public nuisances in other ways. Because there can be hundreds of thousands if not millions of animals living in a densely populated environment, their waste becomes a problem. CAFOs pool the animals' feces in vast open cesspools that can cause huge environmental issues, in addition to attracting clouds of flies that plague anyone living nearby. It is clear that there are major drawbacks to the current industrial method of raising animals. But the question is what choices do we have? There are more than 300 million people living in the United States who need to eat, and eat on a budget.

Not-so-concentrated accommodations at B&B Farms

Proponents of large-scale agriculture argue that it is cheaper and more efficient to produce food following an industrial model. Judging by price tags, they may be right. Often vegetables at a farmer's market fetch a higher price than those sitting in the supermarket do. But the supermarket is not the only place we pay for our industrially produced goods. Mark Honeyman pointed out to me, citing work by J. E. Ikerd, a professor emeritus of agricultural economics at the University of Missouri, Columbia, that many of the costs of mass-produced agriculture are hidden. For instance we all pay taxes to the government, which in turn spends billions of tax dollars a year subsidizing the industrial food system. Between 2003 and 2005 the government spent an average of $11.5 billion per year on crop subsidies, 47 percent of which went to the top 5 percent of beneficiaries ("Crop Subsidy"). This means we are subsidizing a lot, and mostly the biggest agri-businesses. Family farmers, for the most part, receive no government subsidies. So when I told Bahlenfuse and Suzanne that I repeatedly heard from people involved in large-scale agriculture that family farming is nice, but ultimately not very profitable if even viable at all, Suzanne was quick to respond: "You take away [the industrial farms'] government subsidies—they don't work. We don't take any government subsidies, so who's viable?" In fact, Steve George of Fremont Farms pointed out to me that they receive no government subsidies. I looked it up and he was right. According to the Environmental Working Group's website, which gets its statistics from the United States Department of Agriculture, except for a paltry $5,361 in corn subsidies between 1999 and 2000, Fremont Farms gets no government subsidies at all. No direct subsidies, that is. It is important to remember, however, that their operation is indirectly subsidized by the artificially low price of corn in their chickens' feed. By subsidizing the largest producers, the government encourages large-scale agriculture to organize itself along the lines of a machine, operated with chemical inputs and minimal human management, and measured by output.

It is much harder to offer a solution to our increasingly problematic food system than it is to point out its flaws. Some experts, like Bill McKibben, point to local food systems as a more earth-friendly and sustainable solution. Others, like Mark Honeyman, propose many "modest-sized" diversified family farms. Both are plausible solutions, but critics claim that an industrial food system is the only way to feed a country with the size and appetite of the United States. Yet smaller farms do not necessarily mean less food. The solution is integration. Instead of having two separate farms, one a huge corn farm and the other a huge pig farm, we should have several smaller integrated farms. Same number of hogs and acres of corn, just split up. Instead of agriculture existing in enormous monocultures, farms would resemble independent ecosystems. This would simplify and reinforce the nutrient cycle and the health of the farms as a whole. Some might say that this would just be backtracking several decades in agricultural history. But really any change made to improve sustainability would, without a doubt, be a progressive change.

The key to implementing a more sustainable future for our food system is a multilateral effort by both government and consumers. To reshape our food system there needs to be a concerted effort by the 10 government to refocus subsidies along with greater awareness on the part of consumers, because ultimately the consumers have the greatest effect on what the food system produces while the government influences how they do it. Many of the individuals I interviewed noted a growing movement toward local, fresh, chemical-free foods. Tom Lacina, of Pulmuone Wildwood, noted the continual increase in sales of organic foods in the United States. Mark Honeyman observed the proliferation of niche pork markets such as antibiotic-free and grass-fed pork. Locavore, a noun that means "one who seeks out locally produced food," was the 2007 Word of the Year in the *New Oxford American Dictionary*. The local food movement is clearly alive at Grinnell. Many professors and students are conscious of what they eat, and during the growing season local foods are plentiful. From May until October there is a fledgling farmer's market in town. Some local restaurants, most notably Café Phoenix, make a point of buying local whenever possible. But there are also strong signs of the entrenched industrial food system. Wal-Mart and Hy-Vee supply cheap, mass-produced food, mostly to the townspeople of Grinnell, who generally do not have the economic means that people at the college do. This trend is not unique to Grinnell. As Tom Lacina put it, "The top half of the society is willing to pay for local, pure, organic. They have the time to shop; they have the education to shop." But fresh, chemical-free food should not be limited to those with the money and awareness needed to shop locally. Government subsidies to encourage more smaller farms to produce goods for smaller regions could effectively strengthen local food systems and perhaps even result in the kind of affordable prices that supermarket shoppers enjoy today.

There is a clear set of goals for our food industry that we, collectively, as Americans, have to work to achieve. Our food has to be produced in an environmentally friendly way. Our food system must achieve sustainability, meaning it should be able to operate indefinitely in its current state. Our food must be produced in a manner that respects the plants and animals that we consume, and the system must reward the farmers as well. The key is to re-create a system of farming that mimics nature rather than a factory. With that said, there are still daunting obstacles in the way of progress. Most Americans enjoy the quantity of cheap food available in supermarkets across the country. To ensure change, Americans have to cast off the myopia that allows us to enjoy the state of our food system without worry for the future. As a country we must plan ahead for a time when cheap fossil fuel, antibiotics, and government subsidies will not keep a grossly unnatural food system running smoothly.

## ACKNOWLEDGMENTS

*I would like to formally thank everyone who spent his or her valuable time talking to me for this paper. Steve, Tom, Barney, Suzanne, and Mark, your knowledge and perspectives were all invaluable and greatly influenced me as well as my paper. Thank you so much.*

## WORKS CITED

"2002 Census of Agriculture, Country Profile: Poweshiek, Iowa." *United States Department of Agriculture, National Agricultural Statistics Service*. United States Department of Agriculture, 2008. Web. 5 Jan. 2008.

Bahrenfuse, Robert ("Barney"), and Suzanne Costello. Personal interview. 14 Dec. 2007.

"Crop Subsidy Program Benefits." *Environmental Working Group Policy Analysis Database*. Environmental Working Group, 2008. Web. 5 Jan. 2008.

George, Steve. Personal interview. 27 Nov. 2007.

Honeyman, Mark. Personal interview. 18 Dec. 2007.

———. "Sustainability Issues of U.S. Swine Production." *Journal of Animal Science* 74 (1996): 1410–17. Print.

Lacina, Tom. Personal interview. 7 Dec. 2007.

**Reports**

"Locavore." *The New Oxford American Dictionary*. 2nd ed. 2005. Print.

Pollan, Michael. *The Omnivore's Dilemma*. New York: Penguin, 2006. Print.

## Reading to Write

1. As he reports on both large- and small-scale agriculture in Grinnell, Iowa, Sam Forman makes his own position on the importance of environmental sustainability in relation to food systems clear. In what ways does his research inform and complicate his position?

2. Forman uses interviews, observation, and published research in his report. Which of these sources do you find most effective? In what ways do the different sources reinforce each other?

3. Make a list of issues that concern you—or of things about which you would like to learn more. Narrow that list to concerns or interests you can study within your own college or home community. Choose one item on your list that you can research through interviews, observations, and published research. Write a 2-page proposal for a research project on that topic. Your proposal should include your research topic, a review of sources in which your research question has been addressed, and the methods you plan to use.

# Xenakis, Cage, and the Architecture of Music

## Jonathan Payne

*Jonathan Payne wrote this report for his Music and Language class at Columbia University. His teacher, Aaron Fox, asked students to examine music as language and language about music. Payne describes his purpose in bringing together the language of music and architecture, how he wanted "to explore how sound can be abstracted and described visually and verbally . . . but also the way in which it can be constructed spatially." This report, written for an upper-level course in music, assumes some familiarity with the disciplinary fields of both music and architecture. Payne uses Chicago citation, the style generally used in music.*

A recent drawing of mine was a kind of musical score, but not in the traditional manner in which staves, clefs, time signatures, and so on comprise a certain set of symbols for the musically trained to interpret; nor was it scored for oboe, viola, piano, or any other traditional instruments. It was in fact documentation of the architecture of a New York Public Library, a musical score intended for architects and thus requiring no musical training; the instrumentation included staplers, children at play, elevator doors, and hole punchers, and so my definition of "music" was admittedly generous. But it was, broadly speaking, a musical score in that it made legible an arrangement of sounds over time.

The purpose of the drawing shown on the next page was to analyze a local branch of the library with respect to its organization, demographics, and any quality of its design or occupation that was particularly interesting, with the expectation that it would improve the design of my own hypothetical branch library. With my classmate and partner

# Reports

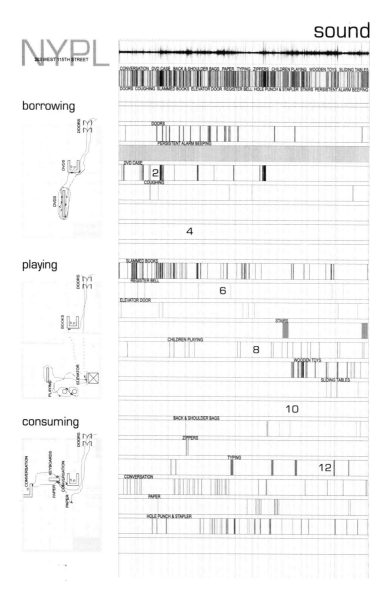

for this project, Sayli Korgaonkar, I found an especially noisy library at 115th Street and 7th Avenue and chose it as our subject for a study in sound. Assuming that the imprecise squiggles and vague colored overlays normally employed by our classmates to indicate sound were not going to work, we were aware of the challenge of drawing sound but knew well the long tradition of symphonic scores, from which we could borrow an approach. In order to make the score legible to the musically untrained, we used a series of horizontal strips—like staves without pitch—and used seconds and minutes as our bar lines rather than a time signature and tempo. We chose fifteen minutes of sound recording from our visit, and by listening selectively to each type of sound, mapped it onto our graph. When a sound occurred, we drew a vertical line in the strip assigned to that sound, the width of the line determined by the sound's duration. The darkness of the line indicated its intensity, as a substitution for dynamic markings. The result was a stack of barcodes, a new kind of musical score that could represent our aural experience of the library.

I was unaware at the time how much this particular drawing would have to do with my research into the work of the composer-architect Iannis Xenakis and the composer John Cage, but I realized afterwards that, in the spirit of Cage, it excluded no sound or silence from its definition of music, and in the spirit of Xenakis, it notated that music both precisely and through a universal system of lines that anyone could understand. With the library design that developed afterwards, which sought to create a musical architecture—an architecture that functioned as a building but played like an instrument—it was a spark to my interest in nonstandard musical notation and the relationship between drawing and music, or architecture and music.

The connection between music and other disciplines is what Xenakis found to be missing from his music education, as he explains in a 1987 interview in *Perspectives of New Music*, "Xenakis on Xenakis," saying that in school, "things were scattered. Each subject was a domain. I wasn't trying to make any connection." He felt that without connections to other disciplines, he had not sufficiently been taught music; "if my professors had really taught me, in the true sense of the word," he writes, "they would have made the connection: they would have shown me music combinatorics which would have opened up for me a more abstract vision of harmony, of contrapuntal polyphony, of form. They didn't do it. They were speaking as musicians."[1] Throughout his career, Xenakis therefore devoted himself to making those connections by developing a musical language and compositional tool accessible to the musically untrained and by making compositions that combine music, architecture, science, history, and many other fields.

5     The compositional tool that Xenakis created was drawing, an especially natural step for an architect-turned-composer to take. Drawing first by hand and later using a computer-based system that interprets lines as sound, he used the method to make his own compositions and to experiment with new sounds, and he had broader visions for the computerized method eventually to become a widespread compositional device used as a pedagogical tool and even as a game for children. "A *posteriori*, I think that drawing came easy to me," he explains. "I was drawing, and my drawings represented musical symbols. I knew traditional *solfège*. But freedom of thought, for me, could not come from there. I was convinced that one could invent another way of writing music. I set myself to imagining sound phenomena, using drawings to help me: a spiral, intersecting planes. . . ."[2] The disadvantage of Xenakis's hand-drawn graphics, however, was that the music could not be heard until he had written it traditionally so that musicians could perform it. Thus, in 1954, following his—presumably laborious—translation of *Metastasis* from graph paper to stave paper, "Xenakis set out to find a more complete, more general way of translating graphically designed music into music notation. His goal was to establish—beyond traditional notation—a more universal way of expressing musical thought, readily interpretable by anyone."[3] The computerized method that he began to develop would gradually offer both translation capabilities as well as real-time feedback and the possibility of distribution for more widespread use.

With the help of an electronic music organization, CEMAMu, which he founded in Paris, he developed the UPIC device: "This is a graphic table, a drawing table, like an architect's. Equipped with a special pen, the musician traces lines on the table. The computer interprets these signs and reconstructs them in the form of isolated sounds or of music."[4] The machine reads time from left to right, and pitch on the vertical axis, making minute variations in frequency possible; while someone unable to read standard music notation could certainly draw a melody by ear in this manner, the aims of the machine were to facilitate invention and experimentation. "With this system, [the composer] writes and the result is immediate," explained Xenakis. "Moreover, he can go hunting for timbres and instruments by drawing—no need for symbols, nor for *solfège*. Nothing but lines having a certain relationship—which one learns very quickly—with the sound."[5] Xenakis had not exactly established a new way of notating, but had rather developed a machine to translate what was already a natural impulse: drawing. "Everybody can understand a line, whereas you have to do specific studies in order to understand what the symbols of traditional writing in music mean," he writes, but simplicity does not come at the expense of function, he is quick to note, because the ease of use and its precision in minute pitch and rhythm variations make possible more of the "complicated things that cannot be discussed or studied with that kind of symbolic and graphic notation; as you know, traditional notation is actually a combination of those two."[6]

More than simply a development in the realm of computer science, the device has certain cultural implications. By drawing music on the computer, Xenakis writes, "with the development of computer networks and of individualized computer science—the computer in the home—an individual will be able to create alone at home, with an electromagnetic table connected to peripherals. I think that in a certain way, the social foundation of art could be resolved by computer science. Finally, the man on the street will be able to *think* in terms of music."[7] Could he be any clearer? Music becomes a language.

Just as Xenakis used drawing and the mathematical techniques from his architecture training to experiment with and generate musical ideas, he likewise invented architectural forms that were influenced by and directly derived from his musical compositions. These forms were what he used for his Polytopes, which were musical-architectural expressions inside and out: the curvaceous shells as well as the audio-visual spectacles contained within were celebrations of what the arts and sciences could accomplish together. "The form of the plastic shell of *Diatope* is a materialization of a project which I have had in mind for more than twenty years," he writes of the Polytope he designed for the opening of the Georges Pompidou Center for the Arts in Paris. "It is a response to the perennial, never-resolved question: What architectural form is to be given to musical or visual performances?" Even without considering acoustics and optimal proportions for seeing or hearing, writes Xenakis, "the effect of architectural forms has a quasi-tactile influence on the quality of the music or show that is performed there."[8] The language of the architecture housing a performance thus alters the music's perception, and so Xenakis used the music to guide the form of the architecture so that their message would be unified.

Tangible architectural forms are thus shaped by intangible musical ones, but Xenakis additionally employs techniques within the Polytopes that enable him to create nearly tangible architecture using music and light as his materials. "If, for instance, the same sonority was performed in succession and with a slight overlap from several loudspeakers, it would create a triangular sound pattern. If many short impulses were heard, they could—depending on their placement in time and space—create a sonic surface."[9] Xenakis mathematically coordinated thousands of lights and loudspeakers in the Polytopes in order to create tectonic connections and surfaces out of sounds and lights, to create an architecture as light and ephemeral as a spider's web. "The spectator, suspended in space like a spider at the end of its filament," he writes, "should no longer have the feeling of living on one plane, but rather in all three dimensions."[10] Xenakis thus attempted to make the physical architecture as musical as possible, and at the same time used the music and lights within to provide the architectural fragility he sought, an ambition that could be realized only because of the intangibility of music as material.

The most direct verbal acknowledgement of the connection be-   10
tween musical and architectural forms is in Xenakis's description of his 1955 *Metastasis* composition in relation to the Philips Pavilion at the 1958 World Exposition in Brussels, a Polytope that was home to a visual and aural exhibit designed by architect Le Corbusier and composer Edgar Varèse. The works in this exhibit were conceived from his interest in ruled surfaces, which are formed by the movement of a straight line in space. In their musical realizations, the straight lines become glissandi, which travel through space by offset beginnings and differing rates of ascent and descent. The architectural realizations of ruled surfaces are the surfaces themselves, of which the Philips Pavilion is entirely composed. "If Glissandi are long and sufficiently interlaced, we obtain sonic spaces of continuous evolution. It is possible to produce ruled surfaces by drawing the glissandi as straight lines. I performed this experiment with *Metastasis*," writes Xenakis. "Several years later, when the architect Le Corbusier, whose collaborator I was, asked me to suggest a design for the architecture of the Philips Pavilion in Brussels," he continues, "my inspiration was pin-pointed by the experiment with *Metastasis*. Thus I believe that on this occasion music and architecture found an intimate connection."[11] Both works were his first experiments with ruled surfaces in music and architecture, a technique that became his signature style; they are the works that launched his career-spanning interest in connecting music and architecture.

Xenakis's career is the ideal example of the relationship between music and architecture, from the two-dimensional drawing through to manifestations in three and four dimensions. On a smaller scale, my own architecture project follows in his footsteps, not in such external features as aesthetics but in the ambitions of the project to link these two disciplines. My initial music score of an existing library grew into a new, musical library using water as material and musical instrument, much in the way that Xenakis used sound and light to describe more ephemeral tectonic structures. Subdivisions in space were fleetingly defined by drips, which in relation to one another formed a web erected out of water, like the filaments that Xenakis envisioned for his Polytopes. The necessary but not always exalted plumbing system thus started to occupy new territory both structural and musical. But my project differed from the Polytope in both subtlety and duration, in that the music benefited not from a multitude of loudspeakers but rather from closer attention, and is intended to be not a temporary exhibition but a lasting structure. In these qualities I found that my project began to have much in common with the philosophy of John Cage: new music already exists but involves a new kind of listening to the activity of sounds in an environment, and that eventually music will be understood not as an isolated experience but as a continuity. In 1961, Cage wrote in "Rhythm Etc." that "eventually we will have a music the relationship of which to what takes place before and after ('no' music) is exact, so that one will have the experience that no experience was had."[12] Nothing is silent, and therefore music is related to all existence.

Curiously, Cage likewise used drawings to compose, appreciating their ability to vary a performance by chance. *Music for Carillon I*, for example, also known as *Graph*, composed in 1952 and revised in 1961, used time and pitch as axes, an approach shared with Xenakis's UPIC, and the one that seems most common for non-standard notational systems. Onto this graph paper, Cage added an array of points, the locations of which were determined by chance—Cage frequently tossed dice and flipped coins as compositional devices. The vertical axis represented a loose arrangement of high, middle, and low pitches. Other scores such as *Variations I* and *II* he composed using transparencies. On these he drew a single line each, and upon tossing them, he allowed the varying arrangement in the overlay to determine the structure of the music to follow. Cage shared with Xenakis the idea that all that is needed for composition is the line, something understood by anyone; what was different was their attraction to the drawing, which for Xenakis meant precision and for Cage meant chance.

Like Xenakis, however, Cage demonstrated in his drawn compositions the architecture he thought most appropriate to music, a connection which may have been subconscious but that he nevertheless articulated. In "Composition as Process II," Cage argues that for the successful performance of experimental music, "The conventional architecture is often not suitable."[13] Cage in this respect shares Xenakis' feeling that the architecture of a performance space changes the ability of the music to communicate. What Cage proposes as more suitable is an architecture like Mies van der Rohe's School of Architecture at the Illinois Institute of Technology—that is, all glass.[14] The belief that the architecture should be transparent to the environment stemmed from Cage's conviction that new music encompasses all the sounds of an environment and never begins or ends. "For in this new music nothing takes place but sounds: those that are notated and those that are not. Those that are not notated appear in the written music as silences, opening the doors of the music to the sounds that happen to be in the environment," writes Cage in "Experimental Music." He continues to relate music, then, to sculpture and architecture: "The glass houses of Mies van der Rohe reflect their environment, presenting to the eye images of clouds, trees, or grass. . . . And while looking at the constructions in wire of the sculptor Richard Lippold, it is inevitable that one will see other things . . . through the network of wires. There is no such thing as an empty space or an empty time."[15] Cage thus related music to architecture, as well as sculpture, and thought, like Xenakis, that they should communicate the same message or speak the same language.

From Xenakis's and Cage's arguments that music and architecture should communicate together comes an interesting proposition, developed by Bulat Galeyev on a machine very similar to Xenakis' UPIC, that the graphic designs of an era necessarily reflect their music compositions. Using a computer that interprets drawings as sound, with time and pitch as axes, Galeyev created limitations on pitch that would allow the machine to conform to the preferred scales of certain eras in musical development, a restriction that Xenakis, who used the device for new creations, would not have been interested in. "We plan to use the computer to test an old hypothesis of mine," writes Galeyev, "regarding possible correlations between the melodic and ornamental structures of the arts of a given culture, in addition to continuing to develop the current software's potential as a means for creating and performing music by drawing."[16] The restrictions placed on the computer system could allow Galeyev to use the device to test the relationship between drawing and music in past cultures as well.

15   A large part of Xenakis's argument in constructing his Polytopes was that music should be linked with other disciplines, particularly sciences, and the argument that he shared with Cage was that the architecture of a performance space should echo the music being played. Therefore it seems that the relationship between architecture and music is somewhat different from that between drawing and music, which, in light of Galeyev's research, could be more closely linked. Architecture's distinction as the practical art may have allowed it to benefit from integration with science earlier than music and drawing, and so an integration of music with architecture and other sciences in the Polytopes could be seen as an architect-turned-musician's gesture towards bringing his later profession forward in the way that he knew it could, as perhaps an architect knows best by experience, by practice. At any rate, for those who speak the languages of music and architecture, a simple adjustment to Cage's most elemental argument is appropriate. "Eventually we will have a music the relationship of which to what takes place before and after ('no' music) is exact, so that one will have the experience that no experience was had," was his argument.[17] Rather, eventually we will have an architecture whose relationship to music is exact, so that one will have the experience that no experience was had. Perhaps this entails more than Cage envisioned as a reinterpretation of the present. Architecture can become a musical instrument, and not just incidentally, but by design.

## NOTES

1. Iannis Xenakis, Roberta Brown, and John Rahn, "Xenakis on Xenakis," *Perspectives of New Music* 25, no. 1/2 (1987): 18.

2. Ibid.

3. Henning Lohner, "The UPIC System: A User's Report," *Computer Music Journal* 10, no. 4 (1986): 43.

4. Xenakis, "Xenakis," 22.

5. Ibid.

6. Henning Lohner and Iannis Xenakis, "Interview with Iannis Xenakis," *Computer Music Journal* 10, no. 4 (1986): 51.

7. Xenakis, "Xenakis," 28.

8. Ibid., 34.

9. Maria Anna Harley, "Music of Sound and Light: Xenakis's Polytopes," *Leonardo* 31, no. 1 (1998): 56.

10. Xenakis, "Xenakis," 40.

11. Iannis Xenakis, *Formalized Music: Thought and Mathematics in Composition* (Bloomington, IN: Indiana University Press, 1971), 10.

12. John Cage, "Rhythm Etc.," in *Module, Proportion, Symmetry, Rhythm*, ed. Gyorgy Kepes (New York: George Braziller, 1966), 200.

13. Branden W. Joseph, "John Cage and the Architecture of Silence," *October* 81 (1997): 102.

14. Ibid.

15. Cage, *Silence*, 7–8.

16. Bulat M. Galeyev, "Melody-Drawing Transformation," *Leonardo Music Journal* 6 (1996): 62.

17. Cage, "Rhythm Etc." 200.

## BIBLIOGRAPHY

Cage, John. "Rhythm Etc." In *Module, Proportion, Symmetry, Rhythm*, edited by Gyorgy Kepes, 194–203. New York: George Braziller, 1966.
———. Silence: *Lectures and Writings*. Middletown, CT: Wesleyan University Press, 1961.

**Reports**

Galeyev, Bulat M. "Melody-Drawing Transformation." *Leonardo Music Journal* 6 (1996): 61–62.

Harley, Maria Anna. "Music of Sound and Light: Xenakis' s Polytopes." *Leonardo* 31, no. 1 (1998): 55–65.

Joseph, Branden W. "John Cage and the Architecture of Silence." *October* 81 (1997): 80–104.

Lohner, Henning. "The UPIC System: A User's Report." *Computer Music Journal* 10, no. 4 (1986): 42–49.

Lohner, Henning and Iannis Xenakis. "Interview with Iannis Xenakis." *Computer Music Journal* 10, no. 4 (1986): 50–55.

Xenakis, Iannis. *Formalized Music: Thought and Mathematics in Composition.* Bloomington, IN: Indiana University Press, 1971.

Xenakis, Iannis, Roberta Brown, and John Rahn. "Xenakis on Xenakis." *Perspectives of New Music* 25, no. 1/2 (1987): 16–63.

## Reading to Write

1. How does Jonathan Payne's representation of his field research into musical architecture compare to his analysis of Xenakis and Cage? Does his example of his own work help inform your understanding of Xenakis and Cage? Why or why not?

2. Payne opens this report with a description of one of his own projects, moves to a discussion of Xenakis's work, and then discusses John Cage's work. Throughout, he makes reference to his own project, and compares and contrasts his work with that of Xenakis and Cage. In what ways does this organization and use of comparison and contrast help to connect architecture and music?

3. Consider two fields of knowledge that many people see as unrelated. Research and write a report that reveals significant connections. Like Payne does, use specific examples and quotations from sources to make the connections clear.

# 4

## STATING A POSITION
### Arguments

**W**hat issues affect you or someone close to you? What controversies or curiosities do you wish to think about in depth? Do you have, or wish to develop, a position on an important issue? How might you best persuade others to take your positions seriously? Whether you start with personal experience and then use research to develop a broader argument (as Virginia Rieck does in "Lessons of My Father: The Double-Edged Symbols of Cowboy Authenticity") or ground your research in peer-reviewed, scientific publications (as Kari Walsh does in "Obesity's Weighty Model"), such arguments allow you to state and support a position, and to persuade others to accept your position as plausible.

The most significant element of an argument is a position you can support. You may make a claim about a larger issue (as Amy Cornell does when she makes an argument about what should constitute "independent" status for loans and tax purposes), but it's important to offer support for your argument (Cornell uses her own experiences along with statistics about financial aid to support her position). Recognize, too, that the complexity of issues worth arguing about means that you'll need to acknowledge and take seriously alternate points of view.

As you develop support for your argument, you can draw from a range of sources in addition to your own experience: governmental and organizational publications (as Cornell does); newspaper and magazine articles (Andrews, Cornell, Hill, Rieck); academic journals and books (Andrews, Rieck, Walsh); and personal interviews (Rieck).

The structure of an argument can also reinforce the main points, as it does in Lindsay Stuart Hill's "One Life," which is structured by purposeful repetition, and in Rieck's "Lessons of My Father," which includes a separate section for each main point of her argument.

The arguments in this chapter also reflect a range of tones. Notice, for example, the difference in tone between Michael Andrews's "Dude . . . Do I Look Fat?" and Walsh's "Obesity's Weighty Model." Although both writers make serious arguments related to health, Andrews reaches a general audience with a casual tone in his argument about muscle dysmorphia in men, claiming that G.I. Joe "would destroy Ken" and referring to Barbie as Mattel's "synthetic sweetheart." In contrast, Walsh, writing for a scientific audience, uses a more formal tone as she considers the genetic and environmental components of obesity in dogs and humans. In deciding on a tone, consider your audience and how you wish to be perceived by them.

As you read the selections in this chapter, pay attention to the ways the writers articulate their positions, the kinds of sources they use, the ways they structure their arguments, and the tones they choose. As you work on your own argument, consider the following questions: Why is the issue or idea important to you? How can you make it interesting and show its importance to others? What sources will best support your position? How might you incorporate alternate views? What structure and organization will best reinforce your main points?

# One Life

## *Lindsay Stuart Hill*

*Lindsay Stuart Hill wrote this poem in the Advanced Seminar in Creative Writing taught by Elizabeth Spires at Goucher College in Maryland. Her assignment was to write a poem about a current event in the news. She begins with an epigraph from the Japanese education minister and uses five words from the epigraph in each line, a form Hill created to give structure to her poem. Explaining that writing this poem helped her "realize the importance of form in poetry," Hill says that "our most effective creative works often arise within the boundaries that are given to us, or those we impose on ourselves."*

~

**You have only one life, and that life is not yours alone.**
               —Bunmei Ibuki, *the Japanese education minister, in*
                    *a plea to a child who claimed he was being bullied*
                    *at school and who sent letters threatening suicide*

Your life: one lost in the sea, not yours, alone.
But that fire of a lie, you have *one*,
one star only: you and your life,
one. Alone, but it's a tree-life, not only
yours alone. Everywhere: you, and the leaves of your life          5
falling in one rain, the life of you, only now ours to have,
we who know you. A life-wind from you to yours in a breath alone.

Only one life? The sun rises before you: another then another life.
But each one is a one, an only, that moon. Life
alone is yours. For, butterfly, what else have you?          10

## Reading to Write

1. Lindsay Stuart Hill chooses to repeat related words such as "one," "alone," and "only" in order to make an argument. Trace her use of these words throughout the poem. In what ways does she use these words to make an argument in this poem? What is the argument she's making?

2. Hill also uses metaphor—comparing the child's life to a star and a tree, for example. What other metaphors does she use? How do these contribute to the argument?

3. Write a poem or a 3- to 5-page prose piece in which you use an article about a recent news story to make an argument. Use the news article as one of your sources.

# Fiscal Independence and the College Experience

## Amy Cornell

*Amy Cornell wrote this argument in her Persuasive Writing class at the University of New Hampshire. Her teacher, Meagan Rodgers, asked students to take a position on an issue relevant to them and the college campus, to keep the argument and any proposed solution manageable, and to use research and evidence as support. In reflecting on her own writing process, Cornell cites two key elements that strengthened her essay: "opening with a personal appeal, and supporting main ideas with multiple types of evidence (quotations, statistics, and more)." In addition, she says that "multiple revisions based on constructive criticism from my classmates and my professor were critical in allowing me to fully develop the main argument of this essay." This argument first appeared in the 2007–08 issue of* Transitions, *published by the University of New Hampshire Composition Program.*

I grew up in an isolated town-city in southwestern New Hampshire. My mother, an elementary school teacher who put herself through college, instilled within my two older sisters and myself a deep and abiding respect for the value of education. We were encouraged to reach for our dreams and not to limit ourselves to the ordinary. However, the one aspect she failed to prepare us for was the price tag that accompanies a college education. With three children entering the collegiate system within five years of each other, there was no possibility that my mom, an elementary school teacher, and my dad, an electrician struggling to run a one-man operation, could possibly afford to support us through college. The burden was to fall solely upon our shoulders.

## Arguments

How many hours of work does it take to earn $68,000, the current cost of an in-state undergraduate education at the University of New Hampshire? At the pay rate of $8.00 an hour, the rate at which I was being paid upon entering college, it would have taken me approximately 8,500 hours of constant table busing (without subtracting living expenses) to be able to afford my tuition. Desperate for financial aid of some sort, I investigated scholarships and governmental options for assistance.

Since I was paying for every aspect of my existence by myself, with the exception of health care, I assumed that it made the most sense for me to be classified as an "independent" on my tax forms for the federal government (and as such be eligible for more financial assistance). However, according to the federal government, for a citizen to be recognized as an independent they must either "be older than 24 years old, be an orphan, be a veteran, be a graduate student, be married, have children, or have extenuating circumstances" (Purgh). According to this definition, even individuals who have graduated from college and are working full-time are still not considered independents until they reach the age of twenty-four. Students who are paying for all living expenses and educational expenses independently should be considered by the government as "independents" regardless of their age or marital status, because they are facing the same kind of financial pressures that every other citizen classified as "independent" under the current taxation system does and should be eligible for the same kind of financial aid.

Overall, students identified as "independents" under federal guidelines are eligible for greater financial assistance than students who are recognized as "dependents" in the form of loans, grants, and need-based scholarships. Low-interest federal loans, which include Stafford and Perkins loans, currently provide students who are independent with greater borrowing opportunities than students who are dependent. For example, a Stafford Loan limits the maximum amount of funds allocated to dependant students at $2,650 per year for freshmen, $3,500 per year for sophomores, and $5,500 per year for juniors and

seniors. In contrast, independents meeting all of the same other quali-
fications are allowed to borrow a maximum of $6,625 per year for fresh-
men, $7,500 per year for sophomores, and $10,500 per year for juniors
and seniors (Federal). These discrepancies in aid allocation result in
thousands more dollars in federal aid being available for independent
students than for dependant students.

Declaring as an "independent" did not always require the stringent       5
measures that it does currently. The federal taxation system used to
specify that in order to receive independent status "parents could stop
claiming [students] as a dependent on tax returns, give them less than
$700 or so per year, no longer house them during the summer, and
schools would then no longer count the parents' income and assets
when determining the student's financial need" ("Nontraditional").
However, during the 1990s the federal government introduced more
stringent regulations regarding who is qualified to receive aid as an
independent in order to prevent abuses of the system.

Since this change in the taxation system was implemented, the
cost of in-state UNH tuition has inflated from $9,715 a year in 1997 to
$17,985 a year in 2007 (almost doubling in a ten-year period) (Taylor).
This fluctuation has not been paralleled by inflation in the minimum
wage in New Hampshire, which remained at $5.15 per hour from 1997
until 2007 ("Minimum"). If minimum wages in New Hampshire are not
being adjusted to compensate for inflation in tuition and living expenses, students working their way through college independently
have no means of applying for the amount of aid necessary to offset
these increases (since they do not qualify as independents according to
the Free Application for Federal Student Aid [FAFSA]).

FAFSA operates under the assumption that "families and students
themselves have the primary responsibility for paying for their educational costs" (Purgh). When issuing loans to students to assist in payment for their college education, it is with the assumption that
matriculated students will be employed by companies and institutions
that will pay them far more than minimum wage, allowing them to,
over time, repay the debt they incurred. However, for undergraduate

students attending the University of New Hampshire to qualify for any federal loan, including Stafford, Perkins, Signature Student, and Tuition Answer Loans, their parents must cosign ("Cosigning"). There is no law that requires parents to perform this service for their children, though, because it financially obligates them to repay the loan if their children fail to do so. If a parent refuses to cosign and the student does not receive enough grant and scholarship aid (which often are "need-based" as well and take assumed parental contributions into account), the dependent student will have enormous difficulty financing his or her higher education.

One of the key concerns FAFSA has in allowing a student to change status from "dependent" to "independent" is that students with families that can afford to contribute to college expenses will take advantage of the system by applying to receive more scholarship, grant, and low-interest loan aid than they need ("Nontraditional"). This is a legitimate concern; it requires millions of dollars to operate all of the services at colleges and universities like the University of New Hampshire and the federal government is not able to pay for the higher education of all of its citizens. The idea of a socialized educational system in which tax revenues pay for the education of independent students is repellant to many U.S. citizens because it would result in an increase in the rates of taxation. However, there is a means of providing all students who are struggling to pay for their college educations and living expenses with aid while still holding them fiscally responsible.

The government would not necessarily need to provide citizens declared as "independent" with a "free ride" through the educational system. In instances when independent students had parents who refused to cosign on loans, the federal government could initiate an "independent loan" with a low interest rate that did not require that parents cosign. In this manner, students without any parental support would still be able to attend a four-year college or university, but would also be responsible for paying for the experience. To verify that students applying for this type of loan were actually independent, FAFSA could determine if the source of student payments came directly from the student's income by requiring the student to submit tax documents. If the student's parents refused to complete FAFSA paperwork, an alternative set of forms should be made available for independent students without parental support. These initiatives would provide all students, even those who are not supported by their parents, with a means of accessing higher education while retaining financial responsibility for the experience.

A significant proportion of students across the country are facing 10 the daunting task of funding their college experience without any financial support from the government or their parents. However, due to policies enacted in the 1990s to limit who can claim themselves as "independent," many of these fiscally independent students have been left with no means of shouldering the heavy financial burden that accompanies higher education (even at in-state schools). They are not eligible for need-based scholarship and grant aid and are not significantly assisted by FAFSA aid when their parents' finances are considered. Students with parents who refuse to cosign loans are left with no way to finance their higher education. By allowing students who are paying for all living expenses and educational expenses to declare as "independents" and making them eligible for low-interest loans without requiring parents to cosign, the federal government could offer such students a way to fund their education without elevating tax rates.

## WORKS CITED

"Cosigning a Loan." *Sallie Mae.* Sallie Mae Inc., 6 May 2007. Web. 10 May 2007.

Dornin, Chris. "House Passes Minimum Wage Increase by a Landslide Vote." *Fosters Daily Democrat.* Geo. J. Foster, 25 Apr. 2007. Web. 25 Apr. 2007.

"Federal Stafford Loan." *Sallie Mae.* Sallie Mae Inc., 6 May 2007. Web. 10 May 2007.

"Minimum Wage Laws in the States." *United States Department of Labor.* U.S. Department of Labor, 1 Jan. 2007. Web. 25 Apr. 2007.

**Arguments**

"Nontraditional Students and Circumstances." *U.S. News and World Report.*
U.S. News and World Report, 22 Feb. 2005. Web. 25 Apr. 2007.

Purgh, Mike. "FAFSA and the Independent Student." *FastWeb.* FastWeb,
2007. Web. 25 Apr. 2007.

Taylor, Toni. "UNH Fact Books." *University of New Hampshire Institutional
Research and Assessment.* University of New Hampshire Office of Institutional Research, Jul. 2006. Web. 6 May 2007.

## Reading to Write

1. Amy Cornell opens this piece with autobiographical details before
   coming to her thesis statement that "[s]tudents who are paying for
   all living expenses and educational expenses independently should
   be considered by the government as 'independents' regardless of
   their age or marital status." These details also provide some of the
   evidence in support of her argument. What other evidence does she
   offer? Which forms of evidence provide the strongest support for her
   argument?

2. One important element of a strong argument is to consider alternate
   positions, as Cornell does when she acknowledges concerns about
   students with families who can afford to contribute to their education
   taking advantage of the system and applying for more aid than they
   need (paragraph 8). In what ways does she address this concern?

3. Write a 4- to 5-page argument in which you take a stand on some
   campus issue that you consider significant. Use several forms of evidence, including personal experience and other sources, especially
   those that provide statistics, expert testimony, and relevant facts.

# Dude . . . Do I Look Fat?

## Michael Andrews

*Michael Andrews wrote this argument when he was a student at the University of New Hampshire. His assignment was to write a persuasive research essay about a topic to which his generation could relate, using both personal anecdotes and research. This piece first appeared in* Transitions 2006–07, *a collection of writings from the University of New Hampshire composition program.*

My brother and I have an addiction. We are gym junkies, supplementing workouts with the latest pills and powders on the vitamin market. Our drugs of choice are Kre-Alkalyn, Muscle Milk, and whey protein. Our dealer is the GNC Corporation. Our dependency is fueled by fitness magazines, portraying what an American man needs to look like. The bombardment of the idyllic body image begins with toys. Action figures with unrealistic muscularity, targeted at young boys, have altered how children perceive their bodies. Just as women cope with eating disorders, American men are plagued by muscle dysmorphia, caused by the "ideal" male body constructed of plastic (Pope par. 4). So, take a seat, Barbie. G.I. Joe has created the unattainable image men have been forced to strive for, reinforcing the mindset behind muscle dysmorphia.

Muscle dysmorphia is a disease commonly seen as the male version of anorexia nervosa (Morgan par. 2). A man with this addiction copes with the need to become more muscular, no matter how big he already is, similar to women with anorexia where too thin is never thin enough. Though the disease can easily be identified as an exercise disorder, the consequences run far deeper. Once immersed in the syndrome, a person exhibits symptoms of depression, consequently weakening both the social and the professional lives of the "bigorexic" (Dickinson par. 3). Nutrition is impaired, from binge eating to crash dieting, from herbal muscle enhancements to anabolic steroid abuse. While the public would expect a muscular man to wear clothing displaying his physique, a muscle dysmorphic, humiliated by his appearance, wears loose-fitting articles, hiding the "puny" stature he identifies with (Muller par. 5).

While some men have mid-life crises, causing a rejuvenated concern for appearance, muscle dysmorphia is not considered a condition affecting forty-somethings. The average age when men begin to exhibit the signs for the disease is 19.4 years old (Maida par. 7). The connection between the earliest childhood toys and muscle dysmorphia is obvious, and the syndrome strikes while men are still teenagers. As men, we have immortalized the "real American hero" through action figures, beginning with G.I. Joe. While our sisters had a Ken doll to enhance their Mattel collections, we had Joe—and frankly, Joe would destroy Ken. This is more than a mere chauvinistic remark; the body proportions say it all. The muscular evolution of G.I. Joe over the past four decades has been startling, especially considering the effects the toy's muscle mass has had on young America.

Introduced in 1964 by the Hasbro Toy Company (Pope par. 11), G.I. Joe was a staple in my brother's and my bedroom before we were in grade school. G.I. Joe not only encompassed my childhood, but even my father's. Yet, in 1964, Joe exuded the realistic look of a man, boasting 12.2-inch biceps when proportioned to a six-foot tall man (Pope par. 12).

5     As the decades passed and social notions of male bodies changed, so did G.I. Joe. By 1975, his mass had increased, biceps measuring 15.2 inches and in 1998 his build exploded, looking like a body builder on a strict diet of steroids and steel. The toy's biceps had grown to a staggering 26.8 inches; if his height were "extrapolated to 70 inches, the G.I. Joe Extreme would sport larger biceps than any body builder in history" (Pope par. 13).

The unfeasible bodies of my boyhood have not crippled the toy trade. Action figures contributed $687 million to the industry in 1994 alone (Pope par. 19). While these playthings are a force to be reckoned with in the corporate world, the implications brought on by the mammoth men of plastic outweigh the earnings. Eating disorders beleaguer more than a million men (Kelly par. 7). Even the youngest males are afflicted with bodily concerns. In an article published in 2000, Amy Dickinson reported that "a recent study showed that 36 percent of third-grade boys tried to lose weight" (par. 3). As a boy grows, he does not appear to become more comfortable with his figure, and boys between the ages of nine and fourteen who want to lose weight are "twice as likely to experiment with tobacco" as a means to do so (Kelly par. 8). All teenagers confront self-esteem issues, but a true "bigorexic" does not grow into confidence. Rather, muscle dysmorphia engulfs his life, hindering relationships, professional growth, and health.

It is human nature to want what we cannot have. Action toys have skewed a man's view since childhood, leaving the "perfect body" all men strive for as the unattainable goal. While every male has some symptoms of muscle dysmorphia, not all men act to achieve the most muscular build possible. Glenn Zorpette of *Scientific American* interviewed thirteen men in New York City, weights ranging from 185 pounds to 290 pounds, and discovered that twelve of the participants believed their size was not big enough. Weighing 258 pounds, one gym dweller considered himself an "average Joe," going on to say "I feel like I weigh 150 pounds. People look at me and say I'm big, and I take it as a compliment. But I see myself like I weigh 150 pounds" (qtd. in Zorpette par. 7–10). The mental effects of muscle dysmorphia cause a downward spiral of self-doubt, leaving a huge man no more sure of himself than a little boy.

There's a misconception that this exercise disorder does little more than add hours to the weight room. But this disease drastically affects all aspects of normal life. Some men turn down professional promotions because of the fear that with new responsibilities would come the need to cut hours lifting and working out. And the notion that this disorder thrives strictly in the gym is wrong. Many men dealing with the disease are too embarrassed by their "puny" size to even leave home, thus leaving the extent of the disorder widely unknown (Muller par. 5).

The number of muscle dysmorphia casualties is undetermined. Partly because of shame, but also because of cultural stigma, this disease goes widely unnoticed (Morgan par. 3). Machismo has always been the way of American men: the providers, the protectors, the strong. Women, on the other hand, have had to fight the connotations of being weaker, feeble, and helpless. As another women's movement occurred in the latter twentieth century, a fight was waged between the marketing executives and American women. Women fervidly confronted the stereotypes of a "dream woman," body issues, and the media's negative influences. School counselors were instructed to look for young girls with image issues and to sympathize with their plight, but not to do the same for young boys (Stout par. 5). The subject is not simply an American problem, but a global one. At the United Kingdom Body Image Summit, the editors of women's magazines were ordered to remove images of women deemed "unhealthy" for the female psyche (Morgan par. 2). However, there was no mention of men (Morgan par. 3).

10     An unwritten norm exists among men: do not discuss emotions, insecurities, or doubts. This "Boy Code of Silence" means a male will not ask for help, whether it is for directions to the highway or assistance overcoming the crippling effects of muscle dysmorphia, according to William Pollack (qtd. in Stout par. 12). It is no surprise that those enterprises encouraging muscle dysmorphia have had their own take on the syndrome. In a *Men's Health* article entitled "It's All in Your Head," Ron Geraci explains, "if you have a really weird habit, you can elicit sympathy instead of criticism by referring to your quirk as a syndrome" (par. 3). After defining muscle dysmorphia, the fitness magazine offers its take on the disease: "Take steroids and only one body part will become puny" (Geraci par. 4). Encouraging words from a magazine based upon health.

I am as self-conscious as any other teenager. I worry about not being as brawny as my other guy friends and that I will not be attractive to girls. My female friends express their image of a perfect man, with rippling muscles and perfect abs. They comment negatively on my arms and praise my "sexy boy cuts" on the bottom of my torso. The pressure to look perfect is very real—I still dream of marrying a Victoria's Secret Angel. As a young man on the verge of the 19.4 age where most dysmorphics are identified, I feel the pressure to emulate the male magazine models and to desire the female models.

In 1998, Mattel gave its synthetic sweetheart a make-over. Barbie was once again changing with the ages, and this time, realistic beauty was flawless. Barbie donned smaller breasts and lips, larger hips and waist, and less make-up than ever before (Morgan par. 1). G.I. Joe, the same year, had muscle measurements impossible even on the world's most renowned body builders. Isn't it time to give our boyhood superman a break, too? Lay off the bench press, Joe; the cobra soldier is the least of your worries. Barbie is still America's picture of perfection even after her transformation. Her male counterpart, Ken, looks fit but realistic. G.I. Joe has more muscle than Ken will ever have, but in the end, we all know who Barbie goes back to the toy chest with.

## WORKS CITED

Dickinson, Amy, and Lisa McLaughLin. "Measuring Up." *Time* 156.21 (2000): 154. *Academic Search Premier*. Web. 19 Nov. 2005.

Geraci, Ron. "It's All in Your Head." *Men's Health* 13.2 (1998): 46. *Academic Search Premier*. Web. 19 Nov. 2005.

Kelly, Marcy. "Body Image and Advertising." *Media Scope*. Media Scope, 2009. Web. 19 Nov. 2005.

Maida, Denise Martelo, and Sharon Lee Armstrong. "The Classification of Muscle Dysmorphia." *The International Journal of Men's Health* 4.1 (2005): 73–91. *Academic Search Premier*. Web. 19 Nov. 2005.

Morgan, John F. "From Charles Atlas to Adonis Complex—Fat Is More Than a Feminist Issue." *Lancet* 356.9239 (2000): 1372–73. Web. 19 Nov. 2005.

Muller, Susan M., Dixie Dennis, Sidney Schneider, and Robert Joyner. "Muscle Dysmorphia Among Selected Male College Athletes: An Examination of the Lantz, Rhea, and Mayhew Model." *International Sports Journal* 8.2. (2004): 119–24. Web. 19 Nov. 2005.

**Arguments**

Pope, Harrison G., and Roberto Olivardia. "Evolving Ideals of Male Body
      Image as Seen Through Action Toys." *International Journal of Eating
      Disorders* 26.1 (1999): 65–72. Web. 19 Nov. 2005.

Stout, Eric J., and Marsha Wiggins Frame. "Body Image Disorder in
      Adolescent Males: Strategies for School Counselors." *Professional
      School Counseling* 8.2 (2004): 176–81. Web. 19 Nov. 2005.

Zorpette, Glenn. "You See Brawny; I See Scrawny." *Scientific American* 278.3
      (1998): 24–25. Web. 19 Nov. 2005.

## Reading to Write

1. Michael Andrews develops his argument through comparison and
   contrast (comparing muscle dysmorphia to anorexia nervosa in
   paragraph 2 and comparing and contrasting toys throughout). In
   what ways does this use of comparison and contrast strengthen his
   argument?

2. Like Amy Cornell, who also wrote her argument for a class at UNH,
   Andrews combines autobiographical details and outside research in
   his argument. How do their uses of evidence differ? How are they
   similar?

3. Andrews opens his argument with an extended metaphor that relates his and his brother's fitness and diet routines to an addiction,
   comparing them to junkies with drugs, dealers, and dependency.
   Write a 4- to 5-page argument about a topic of concern to you. Begin
   with an extended metaphor.

# Obesity's Weighty Model

## *Kari Walsh*

> As a student at the University of California at Davis, Kari Walsh
> wrote this argument in a class on how genetics is being used to under-
> stand obesity. Her assignment was to write a persuasive essay on a
> controversial topic related to obesity. This piece was first published in
> Prized Writing, an annual publication put together by the Writing
> Program at UC Davis. Her teacher, Craig Warden, commended
> Walsh's work for the way she "smoothly integrates information from
> diverse publications into a persuasive argument." Walsh uses the
> APA style of documentation.

A s humans shifted from hunters to consumers, only the dog moved with us: from pointer to companion. Indeed, when our traditional mainstay of fat and protein changed to today's diet of convenient carbohydrates, our dogs' diet of lean meat switched to one of processed kibble. And now the effects of these changes are similarly expressed—obesity and many of its health consequences are problems common to both human and hound. Despite the striking resemblance between us, the dog has been little utilized as a model for human obesity. With the recent sequencing of the dog genome, it is time to examine the potential role of man's best friend as man's best model.

As long as 500,000 years ago, humans and the gray wolf competed in the same environment, and for as long as 100,000 years we have mutualistically shared the same society (Wayne et al., 1999). An excellent example of this reciprocal relationship can be found in the Inuit culture, where the dog was critical to the society's resiliency. Dogs enabled the Inuits to move efficiently by pulling sleds of supplies and, in exchange for this service, the dogs were cared for. When they hunted, the Inuits divided the meat between themselves and their dogs and were careful to provide each with the parts of the kill that were the easiest for them to digest. Humans ate mainly fat, while the dogs primarily ate lean meat (Phinney, 2004). This division of food and labor worked well for their society, as can be seen in its long, successful history in one of the world's harshest climates. Similar relationships existed in many other areas, with man and dog sharing work and the benefits reaped from it (Lindblad-Toh et al., 2005).

When people began domesticating the wolf, they selected dogs that could assist them in their line of work (Lindblad-Toh et al., 2005). Our ancestors' choices are still seen in today's breeds: pointers, herders, and retrievers. The artificial selection used to shape these breeds was often a response to the selection their owners labored under. For instance, a hunter and pointer had to travel for hours without tiring and be observant enough to identify prey. If they couldn't, neither one ate. Herding dogs had to gather and protect vast numbers of prey animals. Like their owners, these dogs had to interpret the other animals' behavior and respond appropriately to it. If either owner or dog failed to react, the herd would scatter and become vulnerable. In the above examples, the dogs had different requirements for temperament and conformation because of their owners' disparate needs. These requirements were often similar to the attributes their owners needed to possess to be successful. This makes the dog a simplistic yet unique reflection of some of the phenotypic variability existing within people today.

Yet the phenotypic differences between dog breeds are more easily categorized than the phenotypic differences seen in people, because the dog is a product of artificial selection. As M. W. Neff describes in an article in *Cell*: "artificial selection leaves an indelible mark on the genetic architecture of the organism—traits selected by man stem from macro-mutations of observable effect" (2006). When dogs were selected in the past, they had to be suitable for the job they were bred to do, but another trait that was often selected for was the ability of the dog to thrive on limited resources. Feed efficiency is readily measurable, which means that it is possibly one of the macromutations Neff describes. For obesity researchers, finding the mutations that enable animals to maximize food resources would be of great interest because they may be a major contributor to today's high rate of obesity.

In human populations, almost 66% of people are overweight, and 5 in dogs, the incidence is as high as 40% (German, 2006). As in people, being obese in dogs is associated with a higher mortality rate (German, 2006). It is generally agreed that obesity is a risk factor for many health problems, such as orthopedic disorders, cardiorespiratory disease, reproductive disorders, neoplasia, and hypertension (German, 2006). However, the differences expressed among obese patients in their presentation of these diseases is still an area of active research.

One of the most significant obesity-related diseases in people is diabetes mellitus, and the incidence of it is increasing (Rand et al., 2004). Although no published research links obesity to increased risk of diabetes in dogs, dogs show equivalent forms of human type 1 and gestational diabetes (Rand et al., 2004). There is growing evidence of a genetic as well as an environmental component to these diseases with the discovery of a haplotype that makes dogs three times as likely to develop type 1 diabetes as dogs without the haplotype (Rand et al., 2004). This haplotype is comparable to a genetic sequence found in humans that may also result in an increased risk of diabetes (Rand et al., 2004). While the similarities between human and dog diabetes make the dog a worthwhile model to study, it may be our differences that are even more revealing. To date, no studies have shown an equivalent form of human type 2 diabetes in dogs, even though dogs develop absolute insulin deficiency (Rand et al., 2004). What prevents the dog from developing the marked signs of type 2 diabetes, while the human must suffer from its complications? The answer is in our genomes.

Another obesity-related disease for both humans and dogs is hypertension. The correlation between weight and blood pressure has been well established in humans and has recently been shown in dogs by Montoya et al, (2006). The human and dog closely model each other in the detrimental consequences high blood pressure has on the eyes, brain, and kidneys. However, the incidence of stroke and heart disease in dogs is low, which is another significant difference between us. This difference can be explained in one of two ways: first, that there is not enough data to accurately represent the incidence of heart disease in dogs, or second, that the molecular variability between us changes the expression of the same disease. Unfortunately, Montoya's paper references studies that induced obesity in dogs, which is different from naturally occurring obesity. Such an experimental design could have confounded the results and demonstrates the need to look at the variation that already exists in dog populations for weight.

Even though people and dogs show a few peculiar differences in the symptoms of obesity-related diseases, the traditionally proposed treatment for obesity in both is the same: diet and exercise. In humans, these treatments have been extensively researched, and no diet or exercise program has shown long-term results for losing weight and then maintaining the loss. Some may say that weight loss is more achievable in dogs because the dog generally does not feed itself. This is true; yet for many owners, when their dog begs or follows a command, they are usually persuaded to feed them an extra treat—even if their dog is obese. They identify so closely with their canine companion that they feel guilty withholding food from it. This can be seen in the steadily increasing rate of obesity amongst companion animals (German, 2006). But with this increase in obesity has come a greater awareness of its consequent health issues. No one wants their dog to suffer unnecessarily, a fact that has led to a new market for diet formula feeds that closely resemble their human counterparts.

But how effective are these diets? A high-protein and low-carbohydrate diet was tested in dogs by Diez et al. because the same diet showed success, however debatable, in people (2002). The principle behind this choice was simple: in humans and dogs, a diet with higher levels of protein conserved lean body mass. Diez's experimental design was basic: eight obese dogs were split into groups based on body weight and sex, and these groups were given either a high-protein or control diet. There was no significant difference in weight loss between the two groups; the dogs with high-protein diets lost about 80% of their excess body weight from fat, while the dogs on the control diet lost about 70% from fat. The p-value is not statistically significant at the 95% level for a difference between the control and high-protein groups for weight loss from fat.

This lack of statistical significance could be from the flaws in the ex-  10
perimental protocol. Only eight dogs were used, a low n value. The dogs were from the same breed and housed in the same colony, but there was no mention of the familial relationship between the animals. As obesity is proving to have a critical genetic component, the pedigrees of the animals is essential information. The high-protein diet had a high vegetable component (ingredients two through six), and both diets used were high in fiber. Human obesity studies have proposed that diets high in fiber have a greater effect on satiety. Diez used that assumption when composing the experimental diet in her study with only the word "tradition" to support her reasoning. If this experiment had used a meat-based, high-protein diet, the results might have shown statistical significance.

This prediction is suggested by Phinney's research, which showed that people who returned to eating a native diet, like the Inuit diet of high fat with moderate protein, showed weight loss with almost 100% coming from fat stores (2004). Dogs would not be able to tolerate the high-fat diet the Inuits ate, as the Inuits well knew, feeding their dogs only the lean parts of the kill. But perhaps researchers studying dogs could also utilize the lessons learned from the Inuit culture and design a study with a lean, high-protein diet. This would be the dog equivalent of a "native" diet, and may prove to be more healthful for them.

As with humans, obesity studies with dogs have not shown a significant correlation between energy requirements and activity level, even within a distinct activity category (Butterwick et al., 1998). Studies investigating the effect of exercise on obesity have similar conflicting results for both humans and dogs (Butterwick et al., 1998). But the majority of researchers are still unwilling to look for alternative treatments and cling to the notion that diet and exercise must cure obesity—there just hasn't been an experiment that is well designed or sensitive enough to prove the correlation (Butterwick et al., 1998). These unremarkable results may have a simple interpretation. Obesity likely has a strong genetic component, and the varied responses to exercise and diet help to show that. It is a condition that will not be successfully treated until genetic mutations are found and treatments are designed for each.

However, obesity is a disease that needs to be controlled right now, and researchers must continue to try to find treatments that work for a majority of people. One of the main problems confronting researchers in human obesity is that it is extremely difficult to replicate the home environment in a laboratory. Even well designed, effective treatments in a metabolic ward may fail when implemented by people on their own. Once again, our genetic makeup drives our varied responses to the current obesity-promoting environment, and the signaling differences that affect our behavior must be elucidated. It is in this respect that the dog's potential as a model for humans is most apparent.

A common joke about dog owners is how closely their dogs resemble them in both physical appearance and disposition. While this joke is only a joke, according to Neff et al. there is a perceptible resemblance between dog and human personalities: "Fear, aggression, loyalty, anxiety, and playfulness are but a few canine temperaments that resonate with us, and their genetic roots are likely to echo in our genome" (2006). As Neff proposes, these temperaments may have a genetic basis. And they are likely the result of the long history we share. In order for us to have lived mutualistically for perhaps thousands of years, we had to understand the needs of the other without the benefit of verbal communication. This ability may now prove to be exceedingly valuable to obesity researchers because behavior is a critical component in the treatment of obesity. And no other animal so closely models basic human personalities as the dog.

15      There are many other reasons to consider the dog model as opposed to the mouse or human model more typically used in obesity research. Rigorous experiments that a person would not agree to could be performed with the dog. For instance, humans will not eat processed pellets for years, but dogs are routinely fed kibble of known nutritional

value. Humans tend to lie about their diet, exercise program, and weight, because these are sensitive and emotional issues. But people tend to be less emotional when speaking about their dog's weight, and so researchers could obtain more precise data using surveys. Dogs' reproductive patterns are also more useful to researchers than humans' patterns: dogs produce multiple litters with large sibships, and dogs from similar lines are bred together. Inbreeding, because of the genetic uniformity it produces, has proven to be a valuable tool to researchers. Obviously, people cannot be forced to inbreed or produce litters of offspring, making these tools unavailable to human geneticists.

Using the mouse model instead of the dog or human model gives a researcher even greater access to inbred lines of offspring and a much shorter generation time between litters. But mice cannot model the natural phenotypic differences between people as accurately as the dog can because they are so highly inbred and have induced mutations. As Neff explains, "Studying adaptive traits in a natural context stands in sharp relief to investigating induced, defective phenotypes in the laboratory" (2006). Mice have very practical, useful applications when studying major gene effects on human obesity. But the dog may have a much more useful genome for studying the effects of multiple genes on naturally occurring obesity, and this is the direction in which obesity research must soon head.

Numerous topics might be explored using the dog model, and each could provide exciting new information on obesity and obesity-related pathologies. Elucidating the mechanisms that contribute to absolute insulin deficiency in dogs could clarify the difference between this and human type 2 diabetes. If dogs are somehow protected from developing overt type two diabetes, the pharmacological ramifications would be enormous. Another study could examine the percentage of obese dogs that develop heart disease, and if the correlation proved to be low, it could lead to a more precise understanding of how adiposity affects the heart. As heart disease and obesity are such prevalent disorders in humans, a more precise understanding of their interactions would be valuable.

## Arguments

Researchers could also perform experiments with dogs to clarify the genetic and environmental components to obesity. One possible design would be to take different families of siblings and separate the sibs into groups for different diets. Changes in adiposity could be measured and the sibs compared to each other and to unrelated families. While the sibs would not have the homogenous genetic background that identical twins or inbred mice have, the limited differences in their backgrounds could prove useful for finding obesity genes, particularly if sibs developed different levels of adiposity in the same environment.

Studying dogs as models for human obesity shows such promise. The artificial selection used with dogs has made genetic differences phenotypically visible. Obesity-related diseases have similar pathologies and our differences may lead to the discovery of better drug therapies. Dogs' personalities are highly discernable and closely reflect basic human temperaments and behaviors. And there are millions of dogs: millions with extensive pedigrees, millions with weight issues, and millions that are suffering from obesity-related diseases. This vast resource has become even easier to utilize with the sequencing of the dog genome, and the dog is merely waiting for the right person to realize just how weighty a model it is.

### REFERENCES

Butterwick, R. F., & Hawthorne, A. J. (1998). Advances in dietary management of obesity in dogs and cats. *Journal of Nutrition, 128*(12), 2771S–2775S.

Diez, M., Nguyen, P., Jeusette, I., Devois, C., Istasse, L., & Biourge, V. (2002). Weight loss in obese dogs: Evaluation of a high-protein, low-carbohydrate diet. *Journal of Nutrition, 132*, 1685S–1687S.

German, A. J. (2006). The growing problem of obesity in dogs and cats. *Journal of Nutrition, 136*, 1940S–1946S.

Lindblad-Toh, K., Wade, C. M., Mikkelsen, T. S., Karlsson, E. K., Jafee, D. B., Kamal, M., . . . Zody, M. C. (2005). Genome sequence, comparative analysis and haplotype structure of the dog. *Nature, 438*, 803–819.

Montoya, J. A., Morris, P. J., Bautista, I., Juste, M. C., Suarez, L., Pena, C., . . . Rawlings, J. (2006). Hypertension: A risk factor associated with weight status in dogs. *Journal of Nutrition, 136*, 2011S–2013S.

Neff, M. W., & Rine, J. (2006). A fetching model organism. *Cell, 124*, 229–231.

Phinney, S. D. (2004). Ketogenic diets and physical performance. *Nutrition & Metabolism*, 1(2).

Rand, J. S., Fleeman, L. M., Farrow, H. A., Appleton, D. J., & Lederer, R. (2004). Canine and feline diabetes mellitus: Nature or nurture? *Journal of Nutrition, 134*, 2072S–80S.

Wayne, R. K, & Ostrander, E. A. (1999). Origin, genetic diversity, and genome structure of the domestic dog. *BioEssays, 21*, 247–57.

## Reading to Write

1. A carefully written argument includes any necessary background information. Kari Walsh provides information on the ways in which canines and humans have shared a relationship for thousands of years. In what ways does Walsh use this background information to help support her argument throughout the essay?

2. One of Walsh's points in support of her argument is that dogs and humans have similar personalities (paragraph 14). What other points does she make in support of her argument? How does she support each?

3. Walsh wrote this argument for a genetics class. Some conventions of writing differ between writing in the humanities and writing in the sciences (for example, there are differences in citation practices and in how you use direct quotation). Consider two courses you are enrolled in this term for which you are writing or reading arguments. Write a 3- to 4-page paper in which you analyze one important difference in disciplinary conventions of argument and support between those two courses.

# Lessons of My Father: The Double-Edged Symbols of Cowboy Authenticity

## Virginia Rieck

> Virginia Rieck, who grew up on a ranch in Texas, wrote this piece at
> Duke University in her first-year seminar on academic writing, one
> centered on the theme of authenticity. When Rieck was a senior in
> high school, her family lost half of their ranching operation and was
> forced to move to another town. Shortly after the move, her father
> began wearing a cowboy hat, which, she says, "led me to a more gen-
> eral interest in cowboy culture and authenticity, which was the topic
> of my essay." Her teacher, Kristin Solli, says of this argument, "Not
> only is Virginia able to produce very thoughtful writing about issues
> that matter deeply to her on a personal level, but she is also able to
> make an interesting contribution to the academic debates surrounding
> questions of authenticity, identity, and subcultures."

My dad is a cowboy. He wears the Wranglers, he wears the
boots, and his calloused hands wear the marks of hard
ranch work, but for as long as I can remember, he never donned the
hat. This year, all that changed. Dad made the purchase in Gibson's
grocery store, and when I asked him why, after all these years, he decided to trade his puzzling square-topped cap for a traditional cowboy
hat, he told me he wanted a broad rim to protect his ears. They were
getting "weathered." Sure, Dad. Looking back, I think I understand:
This year, a ranch my dad leased for twenty-eight years was sold and
divided among four heirs—a beautiful piece of land, chopped up, never
to be whole again. It might as well have been my father's heart. Perhaps my dad bought the hat as a subconscious attempt to hold on to
the ranch and lifestyle he poured his soul into. Of course, he would

never admit to that, and it might not even be true. Nonetheless, these observations make me wonder what being a cowboy means to my father. It is obviously much more than a job description, and contrary to popular belief, there is more to being a cowboy than our mythical understanding entails.

Although researchers have long studied the iconic cowboy's effect on modern America through pop culture, they have overlooked one pertinent question: How have cultural influences affected today's *real* cowboys? Scholars seem to view the cowboy as less than human. He is either a popular mythical icon or a dinosaur—the Marlboro man or an artifact. Ironically, the ubiquitous cowboy concept as it is preserved in literature and the minds of the general population contributes to the contemporary working cowboy's demise: literature disregards him and the myth swallows him. Yet, nothing has impacted the contemporary cowboy's identity more than the threat of urban assimilation. What does this mean or matter? Kembrew McLeod, in "Authenticity within Hip-Hop and Other Cultures Threatened with Assimilation," lends some insight: "By mapping the range of meanings associated with authenticity as the meanings are invoked discursively, we can gain a better understanding of how a culture in danger of assimilation actively seeks to preserve its identity" (134–35). McLeod's main interest is hip-hop culture, but his work provides a useful mechanism for studying any group faced with absorption into the mainstream as well as a foundation for my study of cowboy authenticity claims.

In my research, I sought to understand what meanings today's working cowboy associates with being an authentic cowboy by interviewing my father and drawing on past experiences in my rural hometown. Since this project is personal for me, and my father is only one working cowboy among many, I do not mean for the conclusions I draw to be taken as the last word. My goal is not to find the definitive answer, but to provide a backdrop for and inspire new work. In my investigation, I found urbanization has caused the cowboy to adopt three symbols of authenticity—land and agriculture, origins, and a code of ethics—as a means to preserve his identity in the face of assimilation.

## Arguments

This essay scrutinizes each of these symbols to understand exactly what they entail, how the contemporary working cowboy uses them as preservation mechanisms, and the possible negative implications they may hold for him. Ultimately, these findings will add to our understanding of the nature of authenticity claims in the grander scheme of waning subcultures.

## AUTHENTICITY CLAIMS OF THE CONTEMPORARY COWBOY

### Agriculture and Land as Symbols of Authenticity

Like me, my father grew up on a ranch, but he did not spend his childhood wanting to be a rancher. In fact, my dad earned a degree in accounting and assumed the position of chief financial officer at a hospital for several years before realizing he was not made for deskwork. Thus, when a ranch lease near his hometown became available, he jumped at the chance to escape the city life of Houston, Texas, and act as a steward to land and livestock in the country. The attachment Dad developed to his ranch land underlies his description of what he views a true cowboy to be: "A cowboy is someone who has roots in agriculture. He has a unique appreciation for land and nature." To cowboys, land represents more than a resource or a commodity. Though most people understand how a piece of land holding memories and life lessons can take on sentimental value for a cowboy, less clear is why it might be employed as a symbol of authenticity.

5      Perhaps a cowboy invokes authenticity with his connection to the land because from it he derives part of his identity. Studies referencing the cowboy vocation as much more than a profession exhibit the inextricable nature of the cowboy's life and work. In an essay examining the origins and early use of the term "cowboy," James Wagner concludes that we cannot use "cowboy" as a blanket description for every Anglo who works with cattle (14). This deduction supports the idea that the definition of "cowboy" is more than a job description. Actually, a cowboy's personal and professional life is one in the same. He cannot leave his work at the office because he lives at the office. By using a

connection with land as a criterion for authenticity, today's working cowboy draws a line between himself and those who do not understand the function of land as a life source—figuratively and literally. Highlighting his intimate tie with nature allows the cowboy to preserve his true identity.

Land may provide a useful symbol of authenticity for the cowboy, but it is not foolproof. With changing environments and technological advances making the rural lifestyle obsolete, urban encroachment threatens cowboys. My family and I are not the only ones who have lost a ranch. A joint study by American Farmland Trust and Texas Cooperative Extension reveals that "Texas's rural lands are being splintered into 'ranchettes,' endangering wildlife and the family farmers who make their living off the land" (qtd. in Shackelford). Growing populations spilling into rural areas across America are generating an increase in demand for land, creating economic pressures too high for ranch owners to overcome. Michael Fritz reports that "prices are increasingly driven by urbanites—from sellers of apartment buildings seeking to defer capital gain taxes through 'like-kind exchanges' and people seeking recreational property, to deep-pocket investors turned off by the stock market" (32). Such a situation combined with the cowboy's identification with the land leads to a captain-going-down-with-the-ship effect: Without a ship, a captain may feel utterly lost. In choosing to sink with the vessel that defines him, he avoids the anguish of drifting through life without a purpose. Accordingly, by linking himself to the land, the cowboy ensures that when it goes, he will as well; with the current trend of urban infringement, this may be sooner than he would like.

Regardless of its implications, using a connection to land as a symbol of authenticity implies that while one may frequently encounter wannabes in the cities, finding a working cowboy on the subway would be difficult. Nevertheless, complications can arise: wealthy landowners who purchase land and animals with no emotional investment in their "purchases" obscure the line between authentic cowboys and well-heeled men in cowboy hats. In this situation, knowing a person's background may be helpful in ascertaining their genuineness. After all, a cowboy's connection with land is crucial, but it is a relationship that generally must be cultivated early in life. Hence, I will now address how origins have become a symbol of authenticity in cowboy culture.

## Origin as a Symbol of Authenticity

Dude ranches and how-to books offering the chance to become a cowboy abound. However, such promotions are scoffed at by cowboys because apparently, one does not become a cowboy, he is born that way. Horse-trainer Jason Masterson, when asked in an interview what he had to say about those who want to be cowboys, replied, "It's hard if you weren't raised that way. I mean, going from an apartment high-rise to a farm-house is a big adjustment, and learning the ropes without someone who knows what they're doing is nearly impossible." He puts it politely. My dad, a little more frank, says that the chances of someone *becoming* a cowboy are slim to none if he does not have the background. One's social environment shapes his identity. In other words, those who do not grow up drenching cows (administering medicine to them), docking lambs (cutting off their tails), or waking at five or six every morning to start ranch work, could never truly appreciate what being a cowboy means. Daryl Hunter, writing for the *Upper Valley Free Press*, reports that when "cowboy poet and humorist Baxter Black was asked, What made you decide to become a cowboy? he replied, You either are one, or you aren't. You never have to decide." Such a consensus shows that heritage is important to a cowboy's identity, but it does not explain why.

Just as hip-hop culture does not fully accept those who do not grow up on the street or in the ghetto, cowboy culture does not recognize those who were not raised living the cowboy lifestyle as authentic. However, some, like Kembrew McLeod, might assert a cowboy's roots are significant because—like many other subcultures threatened by assimilation—true cowboy culture uses its origins to highlight its stable position in the rushing stream of society. In his discussion of hip-hop culture, McLeod explains, "[B]y invoking authenticity, one is affirming that, even though hip-hop music was the top-selling music format in

1998, hip-hop culture's core remains pure and relatively untouched by mainstream U.S. culture" (146). To apply McLeod's supposition to the case at hand is tempting: perhaps a cowboy calls on his heritage to underscore his loyalty to the original cowboy essence amid its romanticization by pop culture. Perhaps—but probably not. Cowboys' authenticity claims do not fit neatly into the mold McLeod establishes. Today's working cowboy has changed a lot since the 1800s, so to argue that today's cowboy has not deviated from the cowboy archetype would be difficult. After all, he has gone from a British Loyalist who stole cows to an iconic hero who saves the town and rides off into the sunset (Carlson 5). Most cowboys are not even aware that being called a cowboy was once an insult or that the word "cowboy" had such varied meanings.

Indeed, my dad would be surprised to find that just a few decades ago, as a rancher, he would not have been considered a cowboy. Apparently, according to *The Modern Cowboy,* ranchers or cattlemen often played prominent positions in the community while cowboys did not. Ranchers took breaks whenever they felt the need. Cowboys, on the other hand, did not govern their own schedules. John Erickson indicates the differences that existed between cowboys and ranchers when he writes, "The rancher and the cowboy may dress alike, talk alike, and even think alike, but at six o'clock in the evening, one goes to the . . . barn while the other attends a meeting in town" (5–6). Such distinctions do not seem to matter to the contemporary cowboy. More than just asserting his loyalty to the cowboy prototype, the cowboy's use of origin to claim authenticity serves as an attempt to remind people that real cowboys still exist: they are not the characters dressed up in bars, and they are not the fabricated heroes we read about in books. Sometimes, trees continue to stand even after they die; by clinging to his roots, the cowboy proves he is still alive.

While a cowboy's origins might effectively confirm authenticity, using origin as a criterion for such a large part of the cowboy identity holds major ramifications. If the cowboy's roots are cut, if urbanization eliminates the possibility of growing up on a ranch or living the cowboy lifestyle as a child, the contemporary cowboy may cease to exist.

10

**145**

Granted, like the trees mentioned earlier, he may continue to stand, but only as a memory—a remnant of things past. Notably, the effect of losing this authenticity claim would ripple to my third symbol of analysis: the cowboy ethics code.

## The Cowboy Ethics Code as a Symbol of Authenticity

Even if one was born and raised a cowboy and loves nature, if he does not acquire a certain level of honor and integrity, he cannot—in the eyes of today's working cowboy—legitimately call himself a cowboy. In my interview with my dad, I sensed that one of the things that makes him most proud of his identity are the ethical standards he believes a cowboy represents. According to my father, the cowboy ethics code made famous by many western movies is more than a theatrical fabrication; it is a bona fide convention in a cowboy's lifestyle that sets him apart from the rest of us.

The code of ethics is not complicated. It basically entails following one's conscience. As my dad relates, "When you spend your whole life working with animals and nature, you learn to view the difference between right and wrong clearly. You can learn a lot just from watching the environment around you." One story my father shared with me illustrates perfectly the proud and serious code today's working cowboys share. Dad agreed to a $20,000 lamb sale with no more collateral than a handshake—no contract, no proof of purchase, just two men and their words. When I asked him how he could place so much confidence in a stranger, my dad said, "I don't know. It's corny, but I knew he was a cowboy; I could trust him."

Why is the ethics code such a valuable symbol of authenticity? Its purpose seems similar to that of other authenticity claims within a subculture. Stephen Duncombe observes that members of a subculture invoke authenticity to "distinguish themselves from the mainstream culture that threaten[s] to absorb them" (qtd. in McLeod 146). Another study, by Sarah Thornton, reveals like findings: "The social logic of subcultural capital reveals itself most clearly by what it dislikes and by what it emphatically isn't" (qtd. in McLeod 146–47). In line with these views, the cowboy, by holding himself to higher moral standards than the rest of the population, highlights yet another difference between working cowboys and the materialistic urban world threatening to consume them.

Nonetheless, in assigning such great significance to this ethics code   15
as a symbol of authenticity, the cowboy once again ensures the preservation of his identity for only a short while. As my father pointed out, being a cowboy in the city is difficult because extreme social pressures make abandoning one's values easy and adhering to a cowboy ethics code arduous. Moving to the country may seem overly idealistic, but having lived in a small, rural town, I can confirm that cows, horses, and the people who tend them generally do not worry about issues of money or power. Waking every morning to watch the sun rise over a valley filled with bluebonnets or even gnarled mesquite trees, a cowboy acquires an early appreciation for the many things in life that cannot be purchased. Nevertheless, as the city and its accompanying worldly influences continue to spill into rural America, the ethics code the cowboy uses to confirm his authenticity could gradually be eroded.

## CONCLUSION

Though I derived these authenticity symbols from experiences with my dad, to assume other cowboys might utilize such criteria is not unreasonable. After analyzing what inspired the authenticity claims of cowboys and how they function, I hope I have helped build a greater understanding of the implications they hold for the contemporary working cowboy. Consider for a moment land and agriculture, origins, and the cowboy ethics code in terms of how they work together to serve as the cowboy's life preserver—literally. A connection to the land is the main flotation device, keeping the swimmer afloat. Without this portion of the life jacket, assuming the cowboy cannot swim, he has no chance for survival. Origins, like the straps of the jacket, provide shape and meaning: they substantiate the cowboy's connection to the land. Lacking straps, the jacket would just be a floating piece of material, but with them is almost a structured, functioning implement. Lastly, the cowboy code of ethics acts as the buckle. Though the jacket could almost operate without it, a certifiable, effective life preserver requires this key component. Accordingly, if any of these parts are missing or deteriorating, the life jacket is a futile mechanism and a burden, a heavy piece of substance strangling and weighing the swimmer down.

Symbols used to invoke authenticity do provide a defense against absorption into mainstream culture. Yet, the extent to which a symbol can preserve a subculture seems to depend on one key characteristic: stability. Cowboys, deriving much of their identity from a physical symbol, land, encounter a problem of an impermanent, diminishing resource. America's steady trend toward more urbanization and indus-trialization reduces the efficacy of the contemporary cowboy's founda-tional symbols of authenticity, contributing to his destruction rather than preservation. Eventually, the only places one will find working cowboys are in countries or territories where city streets and buildings do not suffocate the land and the lifestyle it promotes. Paradoxically, the cowboy's authenticity symbols are entwined so inextricably with his identity, he cannot live with them, and he cannot live without them. After all, without the criteria from which he derives his concept of self, the cowboy can no longer exist.

Does this mean all subcultures are inevitably doomed to lose their individuality and become part of the mainstream? No. If this was a viable conclusion, Kembrew McLeod probably would have beaten me to it. In his study, hip-hop's authenticity claims give the subcul-ture staying power because its symbols, such as race and gender, do not disappear. This leads me to believe that while a subculture's claims to authenticity may serve as useful preservation mechanisms, if symbols are concrete like land, or can be negatively affected by time and other changes, they may become counterproductive. My study of cowboy culture reveals that authenticity claims, as such an integral part of identity, cannot be extracted from a subculture. Therefore, ultimately, the degree to which authenticity claims can preserve a social group depends on the enduring nature of the claims themselves.

Perhaps the cowboy cannot be saved, but by understanding the function and implications of land, origins, and the cowboy ethics code as double-edged symbols of authenticity, I have not only gained a greater appreciation of today's working cowboy, I have come to know my father on a whole new level. I cannot give my dad his ranch back, but I must hold on to its memory: more than recompense for a home, symbol, or a piece of land, maybe my dad wears his new Stetson as a tribute to a lost part of himself. In that case, I'll keep my own hat safe—that way, if Dad ever loses his, I can lend him mine.

## ACKNOWLEDGMENTS

*I could not conclude this essay without thanking the cowboy who inspired it: my dad. Without the insight he provided in our interview and long-distance telephone calls, this text would not have been possible. I must also acknowledge Kembrew McLeod, whose work on hip-hop culture laid the foundation for my study of the contemporary cowboy. My mom and the other members of my Writing 20 class—especially Jeff Edelman and Mario Moreno—deserve thanks for lending patient ears and suggestions. I would also like to express gratitude for the advice shared with me by Chris Weburg of the Duke Writing Studio. Without the support of all these people, my essay would have remained a shapeless blob of emotion. Last, I would like to stress that in writing this paper, I have adhered to the Duke Community Standard.*

## WORKS CITED

Carlson, Paul H. "Myth and the Modern Cowboy." *The Cowboy Way: An Exploration of History and Culture.* Ed. Paul Carlson. Lubbock: Texas Tech UP, 2001. 1–10. Print.

Erickson, John R. *The Modern Cowboy.* Lincoln: Nebraska UP, 1981. Print.

Fritz, Michael. "Still on a Tear." *Beef* (Oct. 2006): 32–34. Print.

Hunter, Daryl. "The Cowboy: An Endangered Species." *Greater Yellowstone Resource Guide.* Upper Valley Free Press, 26 Apr. 2006. Web. 26 Oct. 2006.

**Arguments**

Masterson, Jason. "Interview with a Real Cowboy." *Associated Content.*
    Associated Content, 12 Apr. 2006. Web. 26 Oct. 2006.
McLeod, Kembrew. "Authenticity within Hip-Hop and Other Cultures
    Threatened with Assimilation." *Journal of Communication* 49.4 (1999):
    134–48. Print.
Rieck, Robert. Personal interview. 9 Oct. 2006.
Shackelford, Julie. "Study Shows Texas Farm and Ranch Lands Getting
    Carved Up." *AgNews.* Texas A&M University System Agricultural
    Program, 12 May 2003. Web. 31 Oct. 2006.
Wagner, James R. "Cowboy: Origin and Early Use of the Term." *The Cowboy
    Way: An Exploration of History and Culture.* Ed. Paul Carlson. Lubbock:
    Texas Tech UP, 2000. 11–20. Print.

## Reading to Write

1. Virginia Rieck's use of published research is complex; she uses it to
   support, complicate, and deepen her argument, and yet she also
   contradicts the claims of others and uses an analysis of her father
   and his words and experiences as proof. Trace Rieck's use of sources
   in this piece. Which of her points do you find most compelling? How
   does she support that point?

2. Rieck lays out her thesis in paragraph 3, claiming that "urbanization
   has caused the cowboy to adopt three symbols of authenticity: land
   and agriculture, origins, and a code of ethics as a means to preserve
   his identity in the face of assimilation." Note the structural features
   (headings, transitions, and repetition) she uses to reinforce her argument. Which of these features do you find most effective, and why?

3. Research and compose an argument about an issue that is important
   to you. Use interviews, personal experience, and published research
   to support your points. Consider using sections to structure your
   argument.

# 5 〜

## CALLING FOR CHANGE
## Proposals

What would you like to see changed? What plan of action can you suggest to remedy a problem you see? What support can you find for the position you hold? Proposals take many different forms. Whether you're writing a grant proposal, like Donna Johnson's feasibility report, or a feature story like Alissa Steiner's piece on depression, proposals allow you to carefully define a problem and propose a manageable solution.

You can accomplish your initial task in a proposal, clearly defining a problem, by using vivid description, as Daniel Edwards does in his poem "Lunchbreak"; by describing a personal experience and connecting it to a broader problem, as Steiner does in "Depression in College Students"; or by incorporating outside research to set the parameters of the problem to which you will offer a solution, as Andrew Skogrand and Katy Kreitler do in their proposals.

The solution you offer should fit the scope of the problem you define. For complex issues, you might offer more than one solution—as Steiner, Skogrand, and Kreitler do—but if you do so, make sure the solutions you offer are complementary. Otherwise, you'll need to choose between potential solutions, analyzing the problem and potential answers and showing why the solution you offer is the best or most feasible, as Johnson does. In any case, you will need to provide clear support, both your own analysis and outside research, for your proposed solution. Strong proposals also frequently end with a call to action, providing readers reason and motivation to act now.

## Proposals

As you read the selections in this chapter, be attentive to the ways the writers define a specific problem, articulate a manageable and appropriate solution, provide support, and call readers to action. As you write your own proposal, consider these questions: What problems most concern you? What solutions can you offer? What kinds of support can you provide that will help readers see both the significance of the problem and the viability of the answer you provide? How might you best persuade readers to take the action you suggest?

# Lunchbreak

## *Daniel Edwards*

> *Daniel Edwards wrote this poem in a poetry workshop taught by April Lindner at Saint Joseph's University in Pennsylvania. In response to a freewriting exercise, Edwards composed this piece about his experience working in a psychiatric hospital. He says that writing this poem helped him to expand the breadth of his "understanding and empathy for the patients" and to reflect on one of his first experiences with a violent adolescent, which in turn helped him deal with later "volatile situations with similar patients."*

she lies, crucified
wrists and ankles crimped in tan leather cuffs
feet and arms pulled apart across the plastic, sheetless bed
her shirt rides up her rotund belly
covered in a landscape of past pain: bruises, scratches and scrapes          5

she lies, face up,
her eyes peel the paint off the ceiling,
looking for a way out
thick piston legs having just pummeled
the left side of my chest                                                       10
in a valiant attempt to decapitate me
with her feet

she lies in the center of the bare seclusion room, and when she
sees me
her face begins to pinch and squeeze tears from her pores               15
as she apologizes to me through a saline regret
perhaps for donkeykicking me halfway across the room
but maybe it wasn't even meant for me

**Proposals**

these children of the sacrifice become artists of apology
20      counting their wrongdoings like lashes to their backs
when so often
they are the ones owed an apology

---

### Reading to Write

1. Daniel Edwards includes many images of violence in this poem, from "crucified" in the first line to "lashes" in the final stanza. Make a list of the violent images in this poem. Who is doing violence to whom? In what ways do these images help Edwards define the problem he lays out?

2. At the beginning of the first three stanzas, Edwards repeats the words "she lies." What is the effect of this repetition? How does it make you see the subject of the poem (the girl)?

3. Because this is a short poem, the proposal part—that abused children, even those who enact violence themselves, should be apologized to—is shorter and less developed than it would be in a longer proposal. Write a poem or short essay in which you describe, using vivid imagery, a problem that you recognize. Use your last line to propose a response to that problem.

# Feasibility Report for Solar Decathlon Grant Committee

## *Donna Johnson*

> *Donna Johnson wrote this feasibility report for her technical writing class at the University of Louisville. Her teacher, Geoffrey A. Cross, asked students "to present to your audience the significant details of the problem that you investigated, the results of your investigation, and the conclusions and recommendations that you wish to make." He nominated Johnson's piece because of its concision and use of tables, her analysis of criteria, and because she went beyond the requirements of the assignment, saying that "by going the extra mile to examine the Louisville building code and space limitations of the house to decide what and where in Louisville to build, Donna achieved excellence."*

### INTRODUCTION

Thank you for the opportunity to submit my proposal for the grant to build one of the five solar-powered houses from the 2007 DOE's Solar Decathlon. The goal of the Solar Decathlon was to build a solar-efficient house. My goal is to examine these five houses and present to you my proposal to build one of these houses. But, rather than build a solar-powered house, I would much rather build a solar-powered *home*. Of the five houses, Darmstadt, Maryland, Santa Clara, Illinois, and Missouri-Rolla, I felt the "homiest" house was the Santa Clara house. I didn't, however, base my decision solely on that criterion.

### CRITERIA

All of the houses had strong qualities. In order to narrow my choice down to one house, I used seven criteria to select the most appropriate house.

**Proposals**

- Architecture
- Engineering
- Market Viability
- Comfort Zone
- Energy Balance
- Appliances
- Curb Appeal and Aesthetics

Because I am selecting a home, I weighted some of the criteria differently than the DOE's Solar Decathlon. The total points available are 1,000, with the points assigned to the various criteria weighted differently to best select a home, not simply a house.

## METHOD

I gathered my information on each of the houses from the Solar Decathlon website. In addition, I checked the zoning laws in Louisville.

## EVALUATION

### Architecture (100 points)

5   This category was based on the following three areas:

- Firmness—Soundness of the structure and the use of building materials
- Commodity—Ease of use of the house, flow from one room to the next, and space adequacy
- Delight—Stepping outside of the box on materials and their usage

It would have been more useful if the points had been broken down more for architecture in the committee's criteria. Commodity and firmness should have been weighted more than delight, and there was no indication that they were. This is why I felt it was necessary to lower the points from 200 to 100.

| Total points | Darmstadt | Maryland | Santa Clara | Illinois | Missouri-Rolla |
|---|---|---|---|---|---|
| 100 | 96.25 | 94.75 | 61.675 | 77.25 | 53.5 |

## Engineering (150 points)

This category focused on the main engineering design and implementation and how well the house lived up to its annual energy goals and consumption. Since this is the goal of a solar-powered house, the points were kept at 150.

| Total points | Darmstadt | Maryland | Santa Clara | Illinois | Missouri-Rolla |
|---|---|---|---|---|---|
| 150 | 136.395 | 127.35 | 119.145 | 114.75 | 111 |

## Market Viability (150 points)

The judges looked at three main criteria: livability, buildability, and flexibility. The build teams chose for whom they were building these houses. If all the houses were designed for the same size family, the points awarded would have been less subjective. When looking for a home, livability is one of the most important criteria. Buildability is truly the most important, but livability is a close second. If the point values were broken down, we could see the weight given these factors. The point value was again kept at 150 points.

| Total points | Darmstadt | Maryland | Santa Clara | Illinois | Missouri-Rolla |
|---|---|---|---|---|---|
| 150 | 106.41 | 112.5 | 106.23 | 114.345 | 109.5 |

## Comfort Zone (150 points)

This criterion is based solely on performance of the heating and air conditioning of the house. Heating was judged on how well the house remained at a temperature between 72 and 76 degrees, and for cooling, relative humidity was to stay between 40 and 50 percent. Both of these

Proposals

items are important in Louisville due to cold winters and hot and humid summers. Comfort is an important factor in keeping peace in a home, and I changed the point value from 100 to 150.

| Total points | Darmstadt | Maryland | Santa Clara | Illinois | Missouri-Rolla |
|---|---|---|---|---|---|
| 150 | 106.41 | 112.89 | 111.24 | 122.01 | 111.14 |

### Energy Balance (100 points)

10 The point of the competition was to build a solar-powered house. Of course when there is no sun, there must be backup batteries. The points were awarded by the extent to which the energy taken from the batteries equaled the energy supplied to the batteries.

| Total points | Darmstadt | Maryland | Santa Clara | Illinois | Missouri-Rolla |
|---|---|---|---|---|---|
| 100 | 100 | 100 | 100 | 87.24 | 92.67 |

### Appliances (250 points)

This is the one category that can really make a house a home. The only subjective portion was the entertainment. The rest of the category: refrigerator function, freezer function, dishwashing, clothes washing and drying, television hours, computer hours, and water evaporation, are easily measured. These things are all what we have grown to live with; we can make some sacrifices, but giving up these comforts is just too much to ask. I made this portion worth 250 points; we may build houses, but we live in homes.

| Total points | Darmstadt | Maryland | Santa Clara | Illinois | Missouri-Rolla |
|---|---|---|---|---|---|
| 250 | 220.56 | 163.59 | 238.52 | 160.62 | 197.02 |

## Curb Appeal and Aesthetics (100 points)

This part of the evaluation looked at how well a house would fit the zoning laws and rules for the City of Louisville. There, it states that a house should blend into the surrounding houses when looked at from the street. For example, if the location for the house was downtown New York, and it was to be built on the rooftop of a skyscraper, the Darmstadt house would score higher. But this house would never fit in Louisville.

| Total points | Darmstadt | Maryland | Santa Clara | Illinois | Missouri-Rolla |
|---|---|---|---|---|---|
| 100 | 45.65 | 78.54 | 83.63 | 88.95 | 93.45 |

Total points for all seven criteria (1,000 points)

|  | Arch. | Eng. | M. V. | C. Z. | E. B. | App. | C. A. | Total |
|---|---|---|---|---|---|---|---|---|
| Points | 100 | 150 | 150 | 150 | 100 | 250 | 100 | 1000 |
| Darmstadt | 96.25 | 136.395 | 106.41 | 106.41 | 100 | 220.56 | 45.65 | 811.675 |
| Maryland | 94.75 | 127.35 | 112.5 | 112.89 | 100 | 163.59 | 78.54 | 789.62 |
| Santa C | 61.675 | 119.145 | 106.23 | 111.24 | 100 | 238.52 | 83.63 | 820.44 |
| Illinois | 77.25 | 114.75 | 114.345 | 122.01 | 87.24 | 160.62 | 88.95 | 765.165 |
| Missouri | 53.5 | 111 | 109.5 | 111.14 | 92.67 | 197.02 | 93.45 | 768.28 |

## CONCLUSIONS AND RECOMMENDATIONS

The result of the seven criteria has the Santa Clara house finishing in first place, with the Darmstadt house finishing second.

The Darmstadt house lagged in both appliances and curb appeal. Of the five houses, the two that are the most livable are the entries from Missouri-Rolla and Santa Clara. These two houses not only have private bedrooms, but also well-defined living and kitchen areas. The Missouri house does the best with a separate kitchen, and the Darmstadt does the worst with just one large room.

15       One of the five houses does not meet the criteria for what I think of as a home. The Darmstadt house does not have a truly private bedroom. Having this private space is very important. In the Darmstadt house, the beds are under the floor in the main living space. A well-defined kitchen area and dining area are also important. Only one of the houses has its own kitchen, the Missouri-Rolla house. The Santa Clara house does separate the kitchen from the living area with the entryway.

Selecting which house to build is only one part of the equation with the end result being a livable home. Being energy independent is a great goal, but all of these houses are very small. This means little storage for everyday necessities, groceries, toiletries, and cleaning supplies. Because of this, I feel a building site close to shopping and entertainment is a must. This is just one of the reasons I believe the Highlands area in Louisville, Kentucky would be the logical choice.

Lot size is another factor involved in this decision; the Santa Clara house is 650 square feet. It is important that the house does not get lost in a large lot; the house lots in the Highlands are of a smaller size. Under the LDC (Land Development Code) for the City of Louisville, the zoning for the Highlands is *Residential Single Family*. This means that for a house of 650 square feet, the smallest lot size is 1,300 square feet. The ideal lot for a solar house would be on a corner lot with streets on the south and east sides of the lot. With this corner lot, I would not have to worry about neighborhood trees or other houses casting shadows on my solar collectors.

There are some things that all of these houses would need in order to be built in Louisville.

- These houses are all considered factory-built, and because of this, they must have a masonry-type skirting from the ground to the bottom of the exterior walls. This should not affect the design or function of the Santa Clara house; this house is already built slightly elevated for the storage of bicycles and other things.
- The general compatibility standards also state that the front-facing windows must have consistent size and proportion to the

adjacent houses. The Darmstadt and the Maryland houses would have the most trouble in this respect.

- The minimum width of the house's first floor must be at least equal to the average of the two nearest houses. Again this is why the Highlands is an ideal location; there are smaller single-story houses in the Highlands, and the Santa Clara house would blend in with its smaller footprint. In addition, the Santa Clara has a nice wraparound porch that would make it appear much bigger than it is.

Again, let me thank the Grant Committee for your time and consideration. I hope that in the future I can have all of you over for a glass of sun-brewed ice tea in what I hope is the first of many energy-efficient homes. It is time we not only build with the future residents in mind, but with the future of our planet in mind as well.

## Reading to Write

1. Donna Johnson uses several visual features—section headings, tables, and bulleted lists—in this proposal. In what ways does her use of these features help structure and support her proposal?

2. One important element of a proposal is the tone. How would you describe the tone of Johnson's piece? She begins by thanking those who will be reading her proposal for the opportunity to submit it. Where else does she address her audience directly? What is the effect on you as reader of the use of direct address?

3. A proposal can take many different forms. An application for a fellowship, grant, internship, or job is a kind of proposal. Find something for which you would like to submit an application (students.gov provides information about government-sponsored grants, internships, and study abroad opportunities). As you write your application, consider, as Johnson does, both tone and structure.

# Depression in College Students

## Alissa Steiner

*Alissa Steiner wrote this piece in response to a feature article assignment for her journalism class at the University of California at Davis. This piece first appeared in the 2007–08 issue of* Prized Writing, *which is published by the University Writing Program at UC Davis. Her teacher, Cynthia Bates, nominated Steiner's piece because it demonstrates "how compelling a feature article can be when the author identifies a significant topic, develops it with powerful specific support, and writes cleanly and directly."*

Nima Shaterianl was the 2004–05 student body president at Tamalpais High School in Mill Valley, California. He starred in plays, wrote volumes of poetry, and played the piano. I knew Nima—he was a year behind me in school and a friend of my sister. I heard him speak at his graduation, awing the audience with his wisdom and his wit. As I had, Nima went on to study at UC Davis, where he made friends easily and was known for being charismatic, friendly, funny, and bright. Nobody guessed that on January 3, 2006—the day before he planned to return to Davis for winter quarter of his freshman year—he would shoot himself to death. Seven hundred people attended his memorial, all trying to understand why someone so popular, gifted, and warm would want to end his life.

Nima is one of the 11 UC Davis students who committed suicide between 2000 and 2006.

Depression and suicide are major issues not only here in Davis, but also at college campuses nationwide. A striking number of college students are being diagnosed with depression, and that number is consistently rising. A study by the American College Health Association in 2005 showed that 15 percent of college students around the country have been professionally diagnosed with depression, up from 10 percent in 2000 (Stone).

Understanding depression, its symptoms and its consequences, can help us identify and help friends and family members who may be suffering. Also, if counseling services on college campuses were better able to publicize and reach out to students, perhaps more students could get the help they need before it is too late.

## RECOGNIZING DEPRESSION

Depression is an illness that inhibits a person's ability and desire to 5 function normally from day to day. People who suffer from depression typically experience a loss of interest in once-pleasurable things, along with sadness, irritability, fatigue, weight changes (loss or gain), inability to sleep, and feelings of hopelessness and despair. The symptoms of depression can be easy to mistake for moodiness or stress, and students who suffer from these symptoms often fail to get help in time.

Depression is caused by chemical changes in the brain. The brain sends out neurotransmitters between cells to regulate mood. In depression, these chemical messages aren't delivered correctly between brain cells, disrupting communication. When this happens, people lose access to their positive moods, and they feel anxious, stressed, and depressed. In addition, research in genetics has shown that people can inherit a vulnerability to the brain chemistry changes related to depression. When someone has a stressful or traumatic experience, that vulnerability may be triggered and can lead to the onset of a mental illness. The hormonal changes experienced during the teen years can also cause chemical changes in the brain that inhibit neurotransmitters, meaning depression is not merely a passing condition. College students need to recognize both the causes and the symptoms of depression so that they can get help if they need it or seek guidance about how to help a friend who is depressed.

## TRIGGERING FACTORS

College is a time when students often experience a variety of pressures that can initiate depression, leaving college students at a higher risk than other age groups to develop mental illnesses. Diana Hill, a doctoral intern at the UC Davis Center for Counseling and Psychological Services (CAPS), attributes the high number of depressed students to the challenge of balancing multiple life demands. While in college, students often juggle school, work, extracurricular activities, family, relationships, and friends, among other things. "Students have to play all these roles at once and often feel a lack of support in that process," says Hill. She also notes that students may not have fully developed the coping skills needed to deal with the stress of all the transitions they make during their college years.

According to Hill, the stress starts at the very beginning—the shock of leaving the support of family life at home for independence can be enough to traumatize a student. And once college students are in school, more pressures abound. Demands are increasing for students to earn advanced degrees in order to have top careers, and students must achieve high grades so that the top graduate schools will admit them. Such heavy workloads and competition can certainly play on a student's psyche. In addition to academic stress, many students must also finance their own educations. Working to support themselves while trying to keep up academically is difficult and can fuel anxiety and hopelessness. Finally, many students take on new kinds of relationships for the first time during college, and the instability caused by the building and breaking of interpersonal bonds lends itself to feelings of depression and anxiety. All of these stressors can easily trigger depression, especially in students who are genetically predisposed.

Hill identifies another reason for the increase in students experiencing depression and seeking therapy: the recent advance in psychopharmacology. "Over time, we are seeing more cases of people making it to college who have been depressed earlier in life and had good treatment," she says. In effect, students who in the past may not have been capable of attending universities are able to further their educations. When these students are exposed to college-related stressors, they often find themselves re-experiencing depression and anxiety. Some will seek treatment once again, though others may not.

## DEPRESSION AT ITS DARKEST: SUICIDE

Depression in college students can have devastating consequences;   10
over the course of a single year, 1 in 12 college students in the United States will make a suicide plan, and about 15 of every 100,000 college students die each year from suicide. It is the second leading cause of death among college students, second only to accidents. Massachusetts Institute of Technology (MIT) chancellor Phillip Clay stated, "Indeed, the death of a student is one of the most painful losses a college community can suffer" ("Elizabeth Shin"). MIT, which has a reputation of being an academic pressure cooker, recorded 12 suicides between 1990 and 2000 ("Elizabeth Shin").

The most shocking of these suicides was that of Elizabeth Shin, an MIT sophomore who set herself on fire in her dorm room in 2000. On the surface, she was popular and lively, busy and self-motivated. She was an accomplished musician, athlete, and student who had many friends in her dorm. But she dreamt of death, of escaping the pressures she put on herself to feel worthy, productive, and loved. She told her suicidal thoughts to some roommates and friends, who feared for her life. And though she shared with various counselors at the MIT counseling center that she was regularly cutting her wrists, having suicidal fantasies, and not eating, they neglected to tell her parents or admit her to a hospital. On April 9, 2000, Elizabeth confessed to a friend and a counselor that she had seriously contemplated sticking a knife in her chest. Two days later, her dormmates heard Elizabeth crying and smelled smoke coming from her locked room before immediately calling for help. The fire squad found her engulfed in flames, flailing on the floor in the middle of her room. On April 14, Elizabeth died in the hospital of third-degree burns that covered 65 percent her body.

Elizabeth's death brought national attention to the state of students' mental health. In an article in the *New York Times Magazine*, Deborah Sontag wrote that colleges and universities were sharpening "an evolving national conversation about a more demanding, more needy and more troubled student body. Colleges are grappling to minister to what administrators describe as an undergraduate population that requires both more coddling and more actual mental health care than ever before."

## COUNSELING SERVICES AT UC DAVIS

UC Davis faces the same challenges as colleges around the country in providing adequate mental health care for its increasingly distressed students. Davis' Center for Counseling and Psychological Services (CAPS) is designed specifically to aid students with any psychological stress they are experiencing, be it situational or long-term mental illness. CAPS works on multiple levels and aims to be a welcoming and available service to any student who should need psychological support. Students can attend group support sessions, and they can also receive individual therapy support for up to five free meetings before being referred to a psychiatrist. CAPS also offers structured skill-based programs to educate students on health and wellness, relaxation skills, sleep strategies, and other self-care strategies. As Hill sees it, CAPS is an excellent program because "we provide a continuity of care for our patients—we provide many services and work as a team so students don't fall through the cracks." It is their hope, says Hill, that "clients will have a place where they can reconnect with their own coping skills and strengths." Students can walk in any time between 8:00 A.M. and 5:00 P.M. and talk to the counselor on call.

Despite the caring effort behind its programs, CAPS is not as widely utilized as it could be. A survey conducted three years ago showed that only about 70 percent of the student body knows about CAPS, even though the Center does have some outreach programs. According to Hill, one of the biggest challenges CAPS faces is a lack of funding, leading to fewer counselors than are really needed to serve the number of students coming in. "The counselors here are very busy," she laments. "There are just not enough people here." Students who have visited CAPS notice the same problem. Hagar Liebermensch, a student and former resident advisor at UC Davis, says, "In my experience, it has been challenging to schedule appointments there, often making sessions few and far between." Liebermensch believes that a lot can happen between sessions, so a student who needs a great deal of help may not find it at CAPS. With more money, CAPS could also do more with prevention and outreach, rather than just crisis intervention. This way, more students would know about the services CAPS provides. Perhaps students would in turn know more about what depression looks like, and when and how to seek help for themselves or their friends.

## LOOKING OUT FOR EACH OTHER

So what can we do for a friend who is in crisis or appears to be mentally unhealthy? The first step is acknowledging that friend's feelings. Expressing concern for our friend's well-being, while at the same time validating that it might be hard to speak out about feelings, is crucial. As Hill phrases it, "the first piece with friends is listening, offering support, and knowing that if someone doesn't want to seek help, all you can do is try to support him or her." Should a friend appear to be a threat to himself or herself, or to others, the problem should be addressed immediately. Hill recommends in such situations that concerned students either come into CAPS themselves or bring their friend in directly.

15

I will never know for certain why my classmate Nima took his life. Maybe if he and his friends had been more aware of counseling services on campus, he or they would have sought out support. Perhaps he did not realize that what he was feeling was far more common than it seemed.

## Proposals

If students are more informed about what depression is and how to detect it, they may be quicker to seek out someone to talk to, and possibly less likely to consider suicide as a solution. For though the college years may be commonly referred to as the best four years of a person's life, they are packed with turmoil. Hopefully, as universities come to realize the importance of students' mental health in academic functioning, they will make funding their counseling services a priority. Perhaps then fewer college students will suffer needlessly—or take their own lives.

### WORKS CONSULTED

Birch, Kristi. "College-Level Coping." *Arts & Sciences Magazine, Johns Hopkins University* (Fall/Winter 2005). Print.

*Depression.com.* GlaxoSmithKline, 2007. Web. 30 Nov. 2007.

"Elizabeth Shin." *Wikipedia.* Wikimedia Foundation, 2007. Web. 30 Nov. 2007.

Hill, Diana. Personal Interview. 20 Nov. 2007.

*iFred—International Foundation for Research and Education on Depression.* International Foundation for Research and Education on Depression, 2007. Web. 30 Nov. 2007.

Kennedy, Talia. "UC Regents Hear Plan to Prevent Suicide." *The California Aggie* 29 Sept. 2006. Print.

Liebermensch, Hagar. Personal Interview. 3 Dec. 2007.

Polonik, Wolfgang, and Shahar Sunsani. "Counseling and Psychological Services Unit Visit 2006–2007." *Student Services and Fees Administrative Advisory Committee.* University of California Davis, 22 Feb. 2007. Web. 30 Nov. 2007.

Ryan, Joan. "The Darkness behind His Perfect Smile." *San Francisco Chronicle* 15 Jan. 2006: B1. Print.

Sontag, Deborah. "Who Was Responsible for Elizabeth Shin?" *New York Times Magazine.* New York Times, 28 Apr. 2002. Web. 30 Nov. 2007.

Stone, Gigi. "Depression, Suicide Stalk College Students." *World News Tonight.* ABC News, 8 Oct. 2005. Web. 30 Nov. 2007.

"Youth Suicide Fact Sheet." *American Association of Suicidology.* American Association of Suicidology, 2007. Web. 30 Nov. 2007.

## Reading to Write

1. Alissa Steiner effectively uses sectioning in this article. In her first section, she draws readers in with a personal example (paragraph 1), links that example to a larger problem (paragraphs 2 and 3), and proposes a solution to that problem (paragraph 4). Look closely at the other sections Steiner uses. How does she use these different sections to support her definition of and solution for the problem of depression in college students?

2. Steiner uses many kinds of sources in this piece: articles, personal interviews, encyclopedias, and a news report. In what ways do these sources help her define a problem and offer a solution?

3. Identify a problem that affects students on your college campus. Write a proposal in which you use sectioning and different kinds of sources (including personal interviews) to define and offer a solution to that problem.

# Making Waves: Finding Keys to Success in the Failures of the Fish Industry

## Andrew Skogrand

*Asked to investigate a problem in need of a solution, Andrew Skogrand wrote this proposal when he was a student at the University of San Francisco. This piece, nominated by his teacher Darrell g.h. Schramm, first appeared in the 2004–05 edition of* Writing for a Real World, *published by the USF Program in Rhetoric and Composition. Skogrand introduced his proposal by explaining that "Overfishing is a problem with hundreds of solutions, all offered by various interests. I felt compelled to sift through the solutions, filter out the destructive ideas and allow an articulated solution to flow forth."*

W e are the efficient, bargain-bound consumers of America. Our wages are well earned, and our money well spent. After a hard day's work, we can retire to the warm atmosphere of Red Lobster and settle down to the appetizing "Crown of Shrimp" entrée. In keeping with the American way, this meal—fit for a king—comes at the low price of $7.99 (now through January 30th). We receive a dozen delectable bamboo-skewered shrimp, and we deserve it. But the deal doesn't end at the dozen shrimp; no, we are thriftier than we thought! We pay not only for the twelve tantalizing shrimp we are served, but for every pound of shrimp we purchase, we also purchase ten pounds of assorted fish (McGinn 22). Although this fish is thrown back into the ocean, never actually making it to market because it's dead when caught alongside our now tempura-battered shellfish, we maximized our return ten-fold! Our money funds the paving of the ocean floor, turning the painfully complex ecosystem of the marine depths into a convenient underwater parking lot (20). And yet, remarkably, the dollar goes even further. Our kingly cuisine pays for blockades in Gulf ports and waterways by shrimp boats because of fierce conflict between fishermen and Coast Guard personnel (Margavio and Forsyth 33). All this for fewer than ten dollars! Yes, America is amazing, and the dollar can do so much, much more than we knew—it's practically a steal.

Behind this innocuous act of purchasing seafood there lurk countless consequences that remain unknown to and hidden from the average consumer. Most of the world still operates under the mindset of the nineteenth-century professor William Carmichael M'Intosh, who stated that the "fauna of the open sea ... [is] independent of man's influence" (Marx ix). People look to the overwhelmingly large oceans and deduce that the marine resources they contain must be equally vast and impressive. We eat tuna with much concern for the safety of dolphins, but we hardly think twice about the tuna. In other words, we view the dolphin as a rare and endangered animal, but tuna is seen as an infinite, inexhaustible resource.

Despite popular belief, seafood staples such as salmon and tuna are in precarious positions themselves. Currently, "11 of the world's 15 most important fishing areas and 60 percent of the major fish species are in decline, according to the U.N. Food and Agriculture Organization" (McGinn 11). Similarly, the Pew Oceans Commission, a bipartisan group composed of politicians, scientists, and activists, traveled the country in 2000 and found that populations of "New England cod, haddock, and yellowtail flounder [have] reached historic lows. In U.S. waters, Atlantic halibut are commercially extinct—becoming too rare to justify ... commercial fishing" (5). In a letter to the president, Retired Navy Admiral James D. Watkins, chairman of the U.S. Commission on Ocean Policy, warns that "unsustainable exploitation of too many of our fishery resources" has put "our oceans and marine resources in serious trouble" (United States 5). In both the heavy reports filed by scientists and the light catches brought in by fishermen, the truth has surfaced. America's fisheries, along with global fisheries, face eminent collapse.

Proposals

## HISTORIC PILLAGING

History provides the key to a better understanding of modern fishing practices and outlooks, as well as the current crisis. Marine researcher Peter Weber reports that during this century alone "marine catch rose more than 25-fold" (11). This substantial rise can be attributed to a great increase in fishing activities—an increase during the 1950s and 1960s that was so large that the trends of augmented catches exceeded world population growth. This was a crucial time period; from this experience an "entire generation of managers and politicians was led to believe that launching more boats would automatically lead to higher catches" (Pauly 10). These glory days would soon expire. The effects of the enlarged fishing fleet began to manifest themselves, and by "the 1960s, the yields from major marine fisheries . . . were topping out and beginning to shrink" (Weber 11). The plight of the Peruvian anchovy, a species constituting one-fifth of the world's catch in 1970, quickly came to epitomize unstable fisheries when the annual catch fell from thirteen million tons to two million tons between 1970 and 1974 (McGinn 13). This bottoming out of a fishery sent shockwaves through the commercial fishing world, and the need for change became clear.

5     Sadly, the Peruvian harbinger did not result in a change in fishing policies, but rather a change in fishing practices. The crisis only spurred the industry to consolidate and modernize its fleets, thus using technological advances to make up for losses in overexploited and diminishing fish stocks. Apparently, the historic catches of the fifties and sixties may have died out; however, the misinformed midcentury mindset that accompanied it did not. Nonetheless, fishing industries contended that these new tools would be coupled with "models of single-species fish populations . . . [that provided a] maximum sustainable yield" (Pauly 9). The supposed strategy was to use technology to bring in the most fish possible and—with the aid of these models—still leave enough fish for the stocks to rebound. Daniel Pauly, director of the Canadian Fisheries Centre, laments that these models were followed "only in theory" and that, even today, "fishing technologies . . . fail to

account for ecosystem processes" (10–11). In short, to cope with increasing demand, fish equipment simply ate up everything in sight. Even today, fishermen keep what they want and casually discard the rest; unwanted fish and wildlife, or "bycatch," are sent back into the ocean dead or dying. The equipment may be effective at catching; however, it is far from efficient in catching its *target*. Although this may be a small difference in adjectives, the effect is enormous. Fishing equipment not only destroyed fish populations, but it began to ravage the environment in which they lived.

How efficient was fishing equipment? Researcher Anne Platt McGinn with the nonprofit Worldwatch Institute reports that when the orange roughy fish was "pitted against modern vessels, high-tech gear, and seemingly unlimited capital" the "catches of this species plummeted by 70 percent in just six years." Similarly, the 1960 introduction of commercial trawlers in the Gulf of Thailand led to an 80 percent decrease in daily catches within two decades (McGinn 14). The fewer fish there were in the ocean, the more adept the fishermen became at hunting down the remaining stocks, all for the sake of keeping their nets full. This futile effort has been characteristic of fishermen for the past four decades. The fishing industry's response to smaller catches has not been to allow populations to replenish, but rather to tighten its grip on fisheries by increasing productivity and further threatening the species.

## MODERN PLUNDERING

The idea that "more boats equals more fish" proved disastrously untrue for the industry, but with an ocean full of trawlers, fishermen have to keep working and meeting quotas. Fishermen now utilize the ominous technique of descending the food chain in order to maintain their catches. The idea behind this practice, which the industry believes to be "good and unavoidable," stems from a side effect caused by severely limited populations of large fish such as tuna or mackerel (McGinn 10). The various fishes these predators used to eat are in greater abundance. Fishermen do not see this abundance as a cautionary indictor that the ecosystem's scales have been dangerously tipped, but rather they view it as the next natural step in fishing. In short, the moment "top predators are fished out, we turn to their prey, for example shrimp in place of cod." Unsurprisingly, this "good" technique has led to the "unavoidable" and gradual eradication of "large, long-lived fishes from the ecosystems of the world oceans" (10). We fished for the big fish, until they were too few in number. Then we began to fish for the smaller fish, whose fate will be no different. When their numbers dwindle, it stands to reason that we will descend again. We will descend the food chain to catch smaller fish, just as we will descend the ladder of environmental ethics to fill our appetites.

After overfishing such species as tuna and mackerel, crippling their native populations, it hardly seems prudent to then exploit their source of food, once again hindering their chances of survival. Imagine the absurdity if hunters believed they could help endangered lions by turning their crosshairs toward shrinking populations of zebra. While the industry may feel it can relieve pressures on some species by moving down the food chain, temporarily shifting its focus to smaller fish, realistically, we can only descend the food chain so far.

Humanity's tinkering with the marine ecosystem does not stop at the subverting of the food chain. Currently, in order to reach the remaining commercially viable species, the industry utilizes "fish[ing] gear that drags along or digs into the seafloor, destroy[ing] habitat needed by marine wildlife" (Pew 8). Researcher Paul K. Dayton of the Scripps Institution of Oceanography reports that due to trawling, "thousands of square kilometers of benthic habitat and invertebrate species have been obliterated . . . massively [altering] many coastal marine communities" (821). Once again, these communities are offered little chance to rehabilitate. Most areas of the ocean are trawled, at the least, once a year—despite the fact that most of these systems need a minimum of five years to recover (Pew 8). In order to meet demand, fishermen have not only endangered certain species, but they have begun to threaten marine biodiversity and ecosystems that, unlike fish, don't "bounce back." These are foreign, fragile systems that science knows little about, and while reconstructing the systems remains out of the question, other possible solutions to the crisis still exist.

## FUTURE PROTECTIONS

The first and most critical step in restoring our oceans lies in restoring    10
the federal programs that protect them; without a functioning agency,
any policy changes made hereafter would fail to be enforced. Today's
system is plagued by an overabundance of laws and agencies that have
few means of interacting. Currently there are 140 federal laws that
concern the ocean and its coastlines. In turn, these laws are under the
supervision of six departments in the federal government and more
than a dozen federal agencies (Pew 14). The U.S. Commission on Ocean
Policy reported the same bottleneck when noting "eleven of fifteen
cabinet-level departments . . . play important roles in the development
of ocean and coastal policy" (United States xxxvi). There is no central
entity in charge of creating ocean policies, enforcing ocean policies, or,
most importantly, studying the effects of ocean policies. Homer was
right—too many kings do ruin an army.

The system is buckling under the force of its own weight. Policies in
the past for fishermen and coastal industries have simply been indefi-
nite and problematic. One fisherman noted his feelings towards the
current ocean administrations when he complained, "The fishermen
are going fucking crazy with all the rules and regulations. Could you tell
me if it is okay to use fishtraps on tilefish right now or not? How are
these guys supposed to know all that crap" (Helvarg 168). Without a
clear mandate, fishermen will not respond. There remains a desperate
need for a single and definitive authority in the fight for ocean health
and fishing sustainability, and that authority needs to be NOAA.

The National Oceanic and Atmospheric Administration, or NOAA,
could merge with other appropriate ocean agencies to remove federal
clutter. Consolidating the various agencies would ensure "improved
communication and coordination [that] would greatly enhance the ef-
fectiveness of the nation's ocean policy" (United States xxxvi). NOAA

would become an agency that consults "the scientists and resource users who know the fish stocks and appreciate the . . . [ocean's] complex ecosystem" (McGinn 69). It would operate as a natural resource program that would show concern for the economy in light of the environment.

It then falls on the shoulders of Congress to assign NOAA the great tasks it is to undertake. Congress would pass a new ocean policy act that would lay down clear and concise rules on how fisheries must be managed. Although this new policy would entail hundreds of regulations—as any act of Congress does—a select few would act as keystones. These vanguard policies could include regulation of fishing gear, ecosystem-based planning, individual transferable quotas, and bycatch reduction and monitoring.

The regulation of fishing gear will help severely damaged areas, prohibiting the practice of trawling by indiscriminate equipment. In order to protect marine ecosystems, NOAA would allow only approved fishing gear to be used in various zones. Currently, fishermen "are not required to prove that their actions cause [any] damage" and it is up to society "to prove actual or serious impact" has occurred (Dayton 822). Under new administration, the burden of proof will be reversed, and it will be the task of the fishermen, not the society, to prove with "scientific information . . . [that] these activities can be conducted without altering or destroying a significant amount of habitat" (Pew 24). Once this has been accomplished, fishermen would be free to trawl. The time has come to take precautionary measures when dealing with fish stocks; practices are to be considered harmful until proven safe.

15 Just as gear restrictions would ensure the protection of marine habitats, ecosystem-based planning would keep marine reserves viable. Ecosystem planning would change the way fish stocks are assessed, and thus how many fish can be caught. Fish industries would begin to take into account the many factors that determine fish population, such as "age at capture, the availability of nursery or spawning areas, and the availability of critical habitat on migration routes" (Alden 27). Due to the interrelated nature of marine habitats, the industry

must look at the health of the entire ecosystem, not simply the populations of targeted fish. Ecosystem planning may result in small losses
for fishermen initially, but due to science's extensive scope, the health
of fisheries and fishermen will be protected in the long run.

Once fishing limits are calculated environmentally, fishermen will
be given individual transferable quotas, or ITQs. Weber describes an
ITQ system that would give each boat owner "a share in the annual
catch, and quota holders could buy, sell, or lease them like property"
(35). The effect would be twofold; first, fishing would become a closed
system. Closing the market relieves pressure on fisheries and compet-
ing fishermen by limiting the entry of new boats. Second, ITQs would
act as an immediate response system. The system would give fishermen a stake in the fisheries and encourage them to "go to greater
lengths to protect the total stock, and thereby enjoy greater individual
returns" (McGinn 63). In other words, the quota for each fisherman is
based on total fish populations; more fish in the fishery means more
fish for each fisherman. Phenomenal. Financially, it becomes advanta-
geous for the fishermen to fish responsibly. In the past, fishermen
rarely considered the long-term effects of overfishing. The ITQ system,
however, would provide fishermen with immediate feedback through
quota fluctuations.

Many skeptics of the ITQ system complain that quotas encourage
fishermen to discard inexpensive fish, filling their boats only with
high-priced species to maximize profits. The now dead and unwanted
fish is wastefully thrown back into the ocean. Bycatch reduction and
monitoring would be a countermeasure against such unhealthy practices. Under the new system, it would be illegal to "discard and waste
one species because [fishermen] are in a target fishery for another"
(Pew 25). If the true cost remains the lives of millions of fish, then all
caught fish must be brought in. If a fisherman catches it, it's part of
his quota.

Bycatch measures also must be taken in the case where the caught
item isn't marketable, for example, sea turtles. NOAA would create a
mandatory program for the use of TEDs, or turtle exclusion devices.

## Proposals

These devices allow turtles and other unwanted organisms to escape nets via a release device. Not only do TEDs "exclude 97 percent of the turtles," but they also save on "fuel costs through drag reduction—the less bycatch, the less drag" (Margavio and Forsyth 5–6). Adoption of such a program has been slow in the past, but NOAA would provide training and technical assistance to fishermen when needed. The program would emerge gradually. The program's first year would be optional, and fishermen who volunteered to participate during this time would receive the TED device at no charge. Especially in matters of equipment, fishermen must feel that they are actively participating in the ocean's rehabilitation and not unwillingly contributing to their own destruction.

NOAA would not only change the way that fish managers think, but it would also change the mindset of the public. A consumer campaign composed of "publishing cards, lists and brochures on what seafood to eat and what to avoid" would inform consumers as to what fish should be purchased (Skladany and Vandergeest 24). Moreover, NOAA would implement a certification system to mark which fish have come from responsibly managed fisheries so that consumers can easily identify environmentally sound choices. History has shown that a better-informed consumer will purchase the responsible product, as noted in similar successful campaigns such as "sustainable timber, dolphin-friendly tuna, organic food and fair-trade coffee" (24). The sad truth remains that until consumer demand fades, cooks like "Michelle" from New York will continue to purchase endangered fish as long as people want it. In her words, "Until we can't get it . . . I will continue to buy it" ("Still Serving" par. 8). If demand is undercut for forbidden fish, however, the industry will have little reason to evade NOAA regulations. For a solution to become effective, we must not only look at how fishermen exploit natural resources, but also at why they do. The fish industry is simply folding under consumer pressure, and the system can reach equilibrium only by educating the public on the right choices.

## PAYING FOR PROGRESS

The large reorganization of NOAA and the creation of many new ocean    20
initiatives will not be free of cost. Two sources of income would provide ample resources for the new ocean policies and, notably, neither
source would cause increased tax pressure on the public. The U.S.
Commission on Ocean Policy readily identifies the first fiscal source as
the "outer Continental Shelf oil and gas revenues that are not already
committed to" other various marine initiatives. This translates into
approximately four billion dollars in unclaimed revenues annually
(United States liv). Each year, this sum would be wisely placed in an
ocean trust fund.

The second source of money would again be a redirection of already existing assets. The United States takes part in a global trend of
paying out large subsidies to the fishing industry. Internationally, these
figures were estimated to be between 14 and 20 billion dollars in 1995.
Currently, these funds encourage fishermen to continually operate at a
loss and "[participate] in the downfall of their own industry" (McGinn
32). Why continue to pay for fishermen to operate unsuccessfully if
there remains little hope of such subsidies reinvigorating the mori-
bund industry? New subsidies will come under the control of NOAA;
they will not encourage unsuccessful fishermen to stay in the business, but rather they will pay for education and training for fishermen
to find new jobs in other, more open markets. Subsidies, as they were
intended to do, will pay for brighter futures.

## THE POWER OF POSSIBILITY

The time has come to face realities. The fate of the fishermen and the
health of the ocean are inextricably linked. Eventually overexploited
fish stocks will bottom out and, ironically, it will be the fishermen who
will face extinction. Overfishing does not simply concern marine health,
but the health of the fishermen and the health of the economy. Therefore, the ocean must be treated as an investment—one that must be

Proposals

allowed to mature wisely; it is not a honey pot in which we can end-lessly dip our hands. Although current trends are bleak, the future remains full of possibility; restructuring the system may initially upset the fishing industry, yet "300,000 related fishing jobs could be gained from better management and protection of fish stocks" (McGinn 33). Fishermen of the near future stand to increase their catch by 25 percent—or twenty million tons—if they simply allow fisheries to rebuild (Weber 8). The scientists, the economists, and even the politicians have unanimously sounded a clarion call for reformation. Let us not wait until the time has passed to respond. If we fail to heed the warning, if we are slow to act, then our pockets may be full and our stomachs may be satisfied, but our oceans, our hopes, and even our futures will be empty.

## WORKS CITED

Alden, Robin. "A Troubled Transition for Fisheries." *Environment* 41 (1999): 25–28. Print.

Dayton, Paul K. "Reversal of the Burden of Proof in Fisheries Management." *Science* 279 (1998): 821–22. Print.

Helvarg, David. *Blue Frontier: Saving America's Living Seas.* New York: Freeman, 2001. Print.

Margavio, Anthony V., and Craig J. Forsyth. *Caught in the Net.* College Station: Texas A&M UP, 1996. Print.

Marx, Wesly. *The Oceans: Our Last Resource.* San Francisco: Sierra Club, 1981. Print.

McGinn, Anne Platt. *Rocking the Boat: Conserving Fisheries and Protecting Jobs.* Worldwatch Institute Paper 142. Washington, D.C.: Worldwatch, 1998. Print.

Pauly, Daniel. "Empty Nets." *Alternatives Journal* 30 (2004): 8–13. Print.

Pew Oceans Commission. *America's Living Oceans: Charting a Course for Sea Change.* Arlington: Pew Oceans Commission, 2003. Print.

Skladany, Mike, and Peter Vandergeest. "Catch of the Day." *Alternatives Journal* 30 (2004): 24–26. Print.

"Still Serving Chilean Sea Bass." *Day to Day*. By Alex Chadwick. NPR, 20 Aug. 2003. Web. 30 Oct. 2004.

United States Commission on Ocean Policy. "An Ocean Policy for the 21st Century." National Oceanic and Atmospheric Administration, 20 Sept. 2004. Web. 14 Nov. 2004.

Weber, Peter. *Net Loss: Fish, Jobs, and the Marine Environment*. Washington, D.C.: Worldwatch, 1994. Print.

## Reading to Write

1. One element that makes Andrew Skogrand's writing effective is his use of word play. In paragraph 1, for example, he refers to a "Crown of Shrimp" entrée, calling this inexpensive meal "fit for a king," and then later in the paragraph refers to the greater price of this "kingly cuisine." Read through the rest of this proposal, noting Skogrand's use of word play. Where is it most effective, and why?

2. Many strong proposals include a specific call to action. Skogrand includes such a call in the final paragraph. Do you find this call to action motivating? Why? What strategies does he use to encourage readers to act?

3. Research an issue that you believe is important, and then write a proposal that defines the problem and offers a solution. Try to use word play as Skogrand does, and include a specific call to action at the end.

# A Quenched Thirst, A Clear Conscience—The Best Part of Waking Up: The United States and the Global Coffee Crisis

## Katy Kreitler

*Katy Kreitler wrote this proposal for her freshman writing seminar at the University of San Francisco. Her teacher, Darrell g.h. Schramm, asked students to investigate a social issue that went beyond but also included the United States and to propose a detailed solution to the problem. Kreitler says that one of her goals in attending college was to "learn skills to change the world"—and that "At my Jesuit, social justice–focused university, and in the freshman seminar course in which this paper was written, I learned to connect basic logic and language tools to my larger goal, and to see writing for what it can be: a tool with which to enact change." This proposal first appeared in USF's 2004–05 edition of* Writing for a Real World.

### INTRODUCTION

American traders . . . had no concern for what was happening to the landscape of [coffee] supplying countries. American consumers knew virtually nothing of the ecological or social circumstances that supported their daily rituals: a first morning cup at home, a mid-morning coffee break at the work place, and then a final cup with dessert in the evening.

—Richard P. Tucker, *Insatiable Appetite:*
*The United States and the Ecological Degradation*
*of the Tropical World* (qtd. in Brown 248)

C offee is one of the most profitable commodities in the modern world, second only to oil, and no country consumes more of it than the United States (Brown 249). We Americans drink coffee daily to help us wake, to warm our bodies, and to feed our cravings for caffeine. Coffee, our nation's third largest import, is consumed so frequently by U.S. citizens that the quantity purchased by American coffee roasters in one year averages somewhere from 18 to 19 million bags (253). Yet while companies like Starbucks pull in about $3.60 per pound for their quality roasts, coffee-farming families throughout Latin America, Africa, and Asia are paid next to nothing for their labor (252). In fact, coffee bean prices are currently so low that farmers are often paid less for their crop than it costs them to produce it, forcing them to work in constant debt ("Fair Trade Coffee" par. 1). While these farmers labor intensively over their fields, they do not have the means to feed and clothe their families, and poverty and malnutrition are rampant in the developing countries whose economies rely on coffee exportation.

The low wages for coffee growers around the world are the result of a global coffee crisis caused by the collapse of the U.S. International Coffee Agreement, a global oversupply of the coffee crop, a sharp decline in coffee prices, poor bean quality, and an indirect trade system, some of which can be linked to the United States' preference for free trade over fair trade. The coffee that we consume so readily in our country is purchased in an unregulated, busy market characterized by the exploitation of farmers, their families, and an environment that struggles to support our capitalist demands. If we wish to reform the coffee market so that every person involved, from producer to consumer, gets a fair deal, we must adopt a trade system that is fair and direct. The solution to the global coffee crisis must include participation and cooperation on all levels: U.S. citizens must make purchases that coincide with humanitarian values, fair trade organizations must join together and give media attention to their cause, the United States government must return to its commitment to human rights and rejoin

Proposals

the International Coffee Organization, and coffee producers across the globe must join together in farming cooperatives and diversify their crops to ensure economic stability. Only then can the world coffee trade suit the needs of all people working within it.

## ORIGINS OF THE PROBLEM

> For capital, the whole world, nature and humanity alike, lies before it as a field of exploitation.
> —Joel Kovel, "The Struggle for Use Value: Thoughts about the Transition" (qtd. in Gareau 96)

Joaquín Elías Valencia Franco has worked as a coffee farmer in his native country of Colombia for thirty-five years with his five sons and wife of twenty-five years. Now Franco is having his farm repossessed and sold because he cannot sell his beans for a price high enough to pay off his enormous debts to the bank. Franco, unfortunately, is one of 12,000 Colombians facing this situation. Because of the rapid drop of coffee prices, this man, many of his fellow countrymen, and coffee farmers around the world are left in debt without the ability to work it off. Franco laments, "We don't have even the minimum resources for food, schooling, and health" ("Going Bust" par. 1–6).

According to J.D. candidate Grace H. Brown in the *Georgetown International Environmental Law Review*, the situation that farmers find themselves in today reflects a number of problems in the recent history of the coffee industry, problems that have allowed the industry to become the way it is today: unjust and unsustainable. It cannot be said that the United States alone is responsible for these problems, yet because of the massive size of the American coffee industry, our country's actions played a vital part in its breakdown. By backing down from the International Coffee Agreement (ICA), the United States proved its importance in global coffee trade.

5     Each of these agreements, overseen by the International Coffee Organization and signed by a coffee-consuming country, set export

quotas for coffee producing countries in an attempt to stabilize the market. President Kennedy signed an ICA in 1962, and the United States was part of the global fight to keep trade fair. However, as the demand for coffee rose in the United States, it was clear that under the regulations of the ICA, the new consumer coffee demands of the nation could not be met. The National Coffee Organization (a group that represents the larger coffee companies in the United States) declared that "the interests of the U.S. coffee industry are best accommodated by free and unrestricted trade of coffee," and the United States took its name off the ICA. Though the government argued that this move best reflected the beliefs of our nation and a commitment to the free market, it clearly had other direct motivations. The United States was putting the interests of its own economy and demanding consumers above those of the meager wage-earning coffee farmers, and it set this example for other nations (Brown 251). The selfish attitude of the United States is common among major coffee corporations, and it would come to represent the entire industry.

Soon after the United States, the world's largest coffee-consuming country, reneged on its commitment to the International Coffee Organization, all pacts fell out of existence. By 1989, the last ICA was no more. This would have catastrophic effects for the coffee industry. Brown writes that while quotas forced farmers to sell only certain amounts, most were producing more than they could sell; with the ICA regulations gone, these extra bags of lower-quality beans were put on the market. This would mark the beginning of the current global oversupply of coffee (251–52).

In addition to the collapse of the ICA, which prompted the immediate sale of old bags of coffee beans, two things happened that would increase the rates of coffee production, adding to the oversupply. First, Brazilian coffee producers rejoined the market. Brazil had suffered frosts following the ICA's 1989 breakdown, and the country downsized its production immensely; however, in the late 1990s, the weather had cleared, and regular production resumed. Second, Vietnam entered the market. This would be significant, as Vietnamese coffee production was soon the second highest of any country in the world. Adding Brazilian and Vietnamese coffees to an already heavily supplied international market created the global oversupply that now exists in the industry (252–54).

An oversupply of a commodity like coffee has distinct consequences. Like any product, an increase in supply causes prices to drop; however, because this particular product is inelastic, that is to say, its supply does not greatly affect its demand, these low prices do not necessarily lead to a greater rate of purchase. In other words, supply increases at a faster rate than demand. This is devastating to farmers, who must sell their crop at a cheaper price in order to compete with others in the market, yet whose rates of sale remain the same. Profits decrease drastically.

This is where the path of the coffee industry has left farmers like Joaquín Franco, slaving over crops that will not generate enough profit to meet even the most basic of needs. Yet, while we can pinpoint these specific events in history as causes of economic distress, we cannot look at them as solely responsible for the current coffee crisis. There are many other contributing factors to this crisis that are active today, as in the management of the market, in the systems of trade, and in the methods used in the growth, transportation, and sale of coffee. All of these factors together create a problem that goes beyond coffee beans. In this market of excessive gross production there are detrimental consequences for growing third world economies, fragile ecosystems, hungry farmers, and even money-hungry American consumers. The game that we are playing with mother nature and coffee suppliers across the world is a risky one. Without reform, we shall all lose.

## GRAVE SITUATION, GRAVE CONSEQUENCES

> I really don't care at all about coffee. I care about people. In Guatemala, I see their poverty, their suffering, their lack of future.
> —Bishop Alvaro Ramazzini Imeri, Roman Catholic Bishop
> of the Diocese of San Marcos, Guatemala, and
> winner of the Letelier-Moffitt Human Rights
> Award on fair trade (qtd. in Morrow 28)

Every so often, I get a craving for a delicious, freshly blended coffee drink. Whether prompted by an uncontrollable sweet tooth or the sight of a tempting advertisement, the idea will not leave my mind until I am in a brightly colored armchair at Starbucks, smelling the comforting aroma of roasting beans and sipping something warm and sumptuous, preferably with chocolate. Four dollars never tasted so good. As I am writing this paper, I continue these sparse visits, but they come at a cost. As I watch my coffee purchases slowly drain my wallet, I am frustrated that when I shell out four dollars for a drink made with about a half cup of coffee, the producers of this crop will see virtually nothing of my money. My dollars will combine with the money spent by my fellow coffee lovers to become gas money for the Starbucks employees, a down payment on the company head's new yacht, and start-up money for the next two thousand Starbucks cafés.

No matter how much more coffee the American public consumes, no matter how high prices become at coffee places, the farmer will never see the difference. Instead, the extra cash is pocketed by corporation leaders. A farmer in Honduras or Guatemala who harvests his own coffee for exportation has no way of knowing what I pay for my grande caramel macchiato here in the states; facts like these are conveniently kept from third world producers.

The isolation that these coffee growers face is due to a multileveled trade system that severs their connections with the U.S. companies that roast and sell their beans. In this system, independent farmers usually must sell not directly to American companies, but to "exploitative middlemen" commonly referred to as coyotes (James 221). According to Grace Brown, coyotes have access to market information about which most local farmers are clueless, giving the former the ability to demand any price they wish, and naturally to profit immensely (Brown 254). True to the nature of unfair business, these people "generally pay [farmers] less than half of the export price" (James 221). This unnecessary step both lowers the profits of coffee farmers and increases the costs of the final product for coffee drinkers. In the end, "the amount accruing to the farmer from the retail sales price of a cup of coffee in a coffee shop is probably less than two percent," says the ICO ("Coffee Crisis" par. 11). This gap in profits between a family farmer and a company like Starbucks is detrimental for both producer and consumer.

In truth, the only ones receiving tangible benefits from this exchange are those in the middle: the coyotes and the major coffee-selling corporations. Brown writes, "The price of coffee becomes so inflated by each party along the way that consumers ultimately pay the same price" (254). In other words, whether middlemen are fair or not, my drink still costs me the same amount. Price increases are completely up to the companies, and have no reflection on the cost of the coffee beans. American coffee drinkers are kept ignorant of the origins of their morning coffee, and therefore are freed from any responsibility to make a humane purchase.

It would be unfair to place all the blame on corporations, however. A number of coffee-exporting countries, as well as individual farmers, plant and harvest only coffee beans. Relying on one crop to sustain a nation's economy is extremely risky, especially with coffee. The coffee bean is a cash crop; it cannot be eaten or made into clothing. If farmers cannot sell any beans, they are left with nothing; if a country full of farmers cannot sell any beans, an entire nation is left with nothing. This makes it a practical business decision for farmers to switch to more efficient methods of production. Unfortunately, these switches are often damaging to the environment as well as to local wildlife.

15      One such conversion has been the move from shade-grown coffee to sun-grown coffee. The idea of growing coffee in the sun began as a means of protecting the leaves of coffee plants from rusting, but though "fears of such problems never materialized," farmers continue to use this industrial growing method on their land. While the trees used for shade-grown coffee provide natural mulch (Brown 256), and a habitat for migratory birds, insects, and other animals, sun-grown coffee promotes soil degradation and water pollution ("Environmental Benefits" par. 1, Brown 256). In addition, maintaining sun-grown crops requires chemical fertilizers and pesticides that are detrimental to the health of indigenous animals and even to the farmers. Still, "Forty percent of the

coffee bean plants planted in the past fifteen years have been con-
verted to sun-grown coffee" (256). This trend is a threat to the natural
environment of the coffee-exporting countries and could have dire
consequences for the future of the trade.

This is merely one negative aspect of an unregulated market. There
are, in fact, a great deal more. But perhaps we should now focus on the
possible effects of this business if the market is not altered. One is poor
bean quality. In a desperate attempt to make some sort of profit, farmers often sell whatever beans they can, regardless of their condition.
The USDA currently has no criteria for the purity or pesticide application of imported coffee, so farmers have no reason to hold back any
beans (256–57). Also, of the two types of coffee beans (arabica and robusta), arabica, the kind most profitable to farmers and generally the
highest in quality, is becoming increasingly uncommon. Coffee sellers
are purchasing a majority of robusta beans because they are cheaper
and can easily be used as "filler" in premium roasts (Scholer 37). So,
while bean quality decreases, so does bean variety.

Another consequence yet again affects the farmers. When a field
full of coffee crops fails to yield sufficient profits, a farmer must employ desperate measures. In order to keep the crops alive, farmers all
too commonly put their children to work in the fields. If this is unsuccessful, the only remaining options are to switch to elicit crops, such as
coca and opium poppy, or to abandon the fields entirely (Brown 255). In
the words of the International Coffee Organization, "[This] situation
stimulates emigration to cities and to industrialized countries" such as
the United States ("Coffee Crisis" par. 4). People who were once helping
our economy, if so exploited, could soon become a strain on it.

It is these realizations that make my trips to Starbucks less and
less enjoyable. More importantly, they make me frustrated. I should
not have to feel guilty after drinking a cup of coffee, I should not have
to worry that the majority of my drink is made with low-quality beans
that were grown with pesticides and other chemicals, or that farmers
are starving even though they sell their crops easily. In a nation that
stresses human rights and equality, businesses should be compelled to

give every person a fair share. I should be able to assume that the four dollars I pay for my coffee goes to all the right people. Unfortunately, this is not the case.

## TRADING FAIR

> It's trying to open other markets.... It's defending the worker's rights.... It['s] a commitment that is very broad and extensive.
> —Bishop Ramazzini (qtd. in Morrow 31)

President Bush tells us, "America will be prosperous if we embrace free trade. I want to end tariffs and break down barriers everywhere, entirely, so the whole world trades in freedom" ("President" par. 6). As idealistic as his words may sound, this exact ideology is what causes problems in the coffee trade. Starbucks and Folgers are *free* to charge any price for their coffee that the American people will pay. Farmers are *free* to use any harmful pesticides and chemical agents in the growth of their beans. We are *free* to purchase a packaged item that was produced in inhumane conditions. The free trade system that we glorify in America is not as positive as our president would like us to believe, especially when it comes to coffee. With this commodity, a free market system is unhealthy for the environment, the consumer, and the producer alike. It leaves countless farmers without jobs and without hope. And while it may be a symbol of our commitment to free market capitalism, it is a violation of our commitment to basic human rights. It cannot continue.

20  Fortunately, there is an alternative to free trade: fair trade. This system is intended to prevent overproduction and poverty as a result of unregulated trade, serving as an alternative to today's risky, mainstream means of exchange. The fair trade system creates relationships between importing and exporting countries so that both producer and consumer get a fair deal. These coffee beans are purchased from farmers at consistent, fair prices: $1.26 for conventional beans, $1.41 for organic (MacQuarrie par. 5). Fair trade companies ensure that their

products are high quality and environmentally safe, and each one strives for "democratic organization, education, community development, and sustainable agriculture" (Gareau 108). A group of fair trade organizations from the United States and nineteen other countries, called Fairtrade Labeling Organizations International (FLO) ("What is" par. 1), has set five criteria for this type of coffee production:

> (1) a guaranteed fair price for all coffees, higher for organic; (2) democratic cooperatives of small farmers; (3) direct, long-term, stable trade between producers and importers, eliminating "coyotes" or multiple intermediate brokers; (4) a line of pre-harvest credit from importers, and (5) environmental protection. (Morrow 29)

These requirements establish the mission of the fair trade movement, and set basic guidelines for organizations wishing to promote the sale of fair trade coffee.

Fair trade coffee beans, which, according to the International Trade Forum, make up only "about .3 percent of world production" (Scholer 26) are distinguished from other coffee beans by a fair trade label. High quality is guaranteed. Unfortunately, the prices are also high. Fair trade beans average only six cents a cup, yet the difference in price between mass-produced coffee beans and these slightly pricier fair trade beans is enough to scare off the American consumer (Morrow 29). Frugal shoppers throughout the United States fail to recognize the importance of this small label, if they notice it at all.

Regardless of a lack of supporters for a somewhat unknown cause, fair trade organizations in the United States, such as Transfair USA and Global Exchange, are actively working to increase the production and sale of fair trade products, and struggling to convert Americans into socially conscious buyers. Oxfam is currently working with Starbucks, Proctor and Gamble, Kraft, and Sara Lee in an attempt to persuade these influential companies to sell fair trade coffee. So far, Oxfam's Coffee Rescue Plan has been relatively successful. Both Starbucks and

Proposals

Proctor and Gamble now offer fair trade varieties of their coffees ("Coffee Scorecards" par. 1). As a result of pressure from organizations like Oxfam, Starbucks now sells 1 percent of its beans at fair trade prices (MacQuarrie par. 12). Oxfam considers this a success, as even a small percentage of Starbucks' enormous yearly revenue is still a large amount; yet any critic can see that supporting fair trade by converting a single percent of a company's products can hardly be considered a commitment to the cause. The movement has a long way to go.

On the whole, the production of fair trade coffee beans has increased. Transfair certified two million pounds of fair trade coffee in 1999 and ten million pounds in 2002 (MacQuarrie par. 9). Unfortunately, no significant, large-scale changes will be made until major coffee corporations, American consumers, and the United States as a whole make a commitment to ensuring that every coffee bean imported, roasted, and consumed is a result of fair, humane trade.

## A PRACTICAL SOLUTION

> (1) Everyone has the right to work, to free choice of employment, to just and favorable conditions of work and to protection against unemployment. (2) Everyone, without any discrimination, has the right to equal pay for equal work. (3) Everyone who works has the right to just and favorable remuneration ensuring for himself and his family an existence worthy of human dignity.
> —From Article 23 of the Universal Declaration of Human Rights

Fixing a large-scale problem like the global coffee crisis will not be easy or simple. Fortunately, there are some easy, simple things that can be done to make a difference and that should stimulate necessary global changes in the coffee market. Many solutions have been proposed in the past that have been less than successful. Today, still more are proposed. Donald N. Schoenholt, specialties editor of the *Tea and Coffee Trade Journal,* roaster of sustainable coffee and CEO of Gillies Coffee Company in Brooklyn, says that the answer lies in the purchasing power of the people. Internet auctions and a proper certification system can ensure the farmers a fair deal (12–14). Morten Scholer, senior market development advisor for the International Trade Centre, has a similar idea. Like Schoenholt, Scholer proposes that coffee organizations promote consumption and also that farmers diversify production (par. 19–28). Realistically, a feasible, effective solution requires the participation of all people involved in the coffee market. I propose the following:

First, all pertinent nongovernmental organizations (NGOs) must join together to create a unified fair trade campaign. Currently, a number of fair trade organizations are in connection with each other, yet they work on separate funding and have separate advertisements, etc. If these groups were to band together, money could be used more effectively, and a single successful advertising campaign could be created.

Second, media attention must be given to the issue. People must be made aware of the benefits of fair trade coffees before they will consider purchasing them. Whether in the mainstream media or the alternative press, advertising should be the primary goal of all NGOs working to reform the coffee industry. With any luck, the proper campaigns will create more demand for fair trade coffees and other fair trade products as well.

Third, once fair trade is a mainstream issue, or when the demand for fair trade rises, NGO campaigns can reach out to the major coffee-selling corporations. Starbucks, for example, could be pressured into converting its coffees to fair trade with the proper consumer demand. A switch to more fair trade coffee could be appealing to Starbucks if it could elevate its image in the public eye as a socially conscious company. NGOs should base their campaigns on this idea: that a caring corporation is more appealing to the common citizen.

Next, and most importantly, the U.S. government must make a strong, final commitment to human rights and sustainability in the coffee trade. This should be done in two ways. First, the United States must sign a new International Coffee Agreement, and pledge its commitment to the International Coffee Organization. Secondly, the USDA should create a national quality standard for imported coffee beans.

25

This slows the production and trade of our coffee, and ensures quality, fairly priced beans. What stands in the way of these governmental moves is our nation's commitment to free trade. However, with enough awareness of the inhumane working conditions of today's struggling farmers, it is doubtful that much resistance will take place. Ensuring dignity and fair wages to our producers overseas is in no way a threat to free enterprise. On the contrary, it is our national duty.

In addition, farmers must cooperate with the United States to rid the world of this crisis. Farmers can do this by joining fair trade cooperatives with other farmers so that all of their crops will be guaranteed a fair price, and a fair trade organization can oversee their production. Also, farmers must work to diversify their products. This will make it possible for them to have an alternate source of income in case they are ever in need of one. Verena Stolcke, author and editor of the journal *Anthropological Theory*, says that the symbiosis of coffee with food crops even has the additional advantages of reduced labor costs and cost flexibility (80). On the down side, crop diversification can be problematic because other crops, like fruits, often make much lower profits than coffee and cannot be easily grown on the same terrain as coffee beans (Scholer par. 28). However, in a cooperative, a coffee farmer could join with a fruit harvester in a mutually beneficial relationship, eliminating this problem altogether.

30    Lastly, the American people as a whole must take a stand on the issue by being socially conscious buyers. This means paying the few extra cents for fair trade products. This also means being a voice for coffee farmers by urging Starbucks, Folgers, and the like to purchase their coffee at fair prices. Consumers have the ultimate leverage, after all: purchasing power.

Each person involved in the coffee trade, from farmer to roaster to seller to consumer, plays a part in the injustice that farmers face across the globe. Therefore, it is up to each of us to reverse this injustice. Fortunately, it can be done. If NGOs can organize and give media attention to coffee trade issues, if consumers can be persuaded to buy some fair trade products, if coffee corporations in the United States can sell even a little more coffee at fair trade prices, if the U.S. government can support the battle, and if coffee farmers are willing to cooperate with us, many of the problems can be solved. In the near future, perhaps big-name coffee companies will have a slight change of heart, perhaps Joaquín Franco will send his children to school, and perhaps consumers like me will be able to sip their coffee with ease. Perhaps one day the "best part of waking up" will be even better than we had imagined. We just have to take a step in the right direction.

## WORKS CITED

Brown, Grace H. "Making Coffee Good to the Last Drop: Laying the Foundation for Sustainability in the International Coffee Trade." *Georgetown International Environmental Law Review* 16.2 (2004): 247–80. Print.

"Coffee Crisis." *International Coffee Organization*. International Coffee Organization, Sept. 2004. Web. 26 Oct. 2004.

"Coffee Scorecards." *Make Trade Fair*. Oxfam, 20 Oct. 2004. Web. 26 Oct. 2004.

"Environmental Benefits." *Fair Trade Certified*. Transfair USA, 2004. Web. 28 Nov. 2004.

"Fair Trade Coffee." *Global Exchange: Building People-to-People Ties*. Global Exchange, 26 Oct. 2004. Web. 26 Oct. 2004.

Gareau, Brian J. "Use and Exchange Value in Development Projects in Southern Honduras." *Capitalism, Nature, Socialism* 15.3 (2004): 95–110. Print.

"Going Bust." *Make Trade Far*. Oxfam, 22 Nov. 2004. Web. 29 Nov. 2004.

James, Deborah. "Fair Trade Not Free Trade." *The Global Activist's Manual: Local Ways to Change the World*. Eds. Mike Prokosch and Laura Raymond. New York: Thunder's Mouth/Nation, 2000. 221–26. Print.

MacQuarrie, Bryan. "Bitter Feelings Over Coffee Bean Prices." *Boston Globe* 18 Nov. 2003: B1. Print.

Morrow, Caron Ann. "The Coffee/Conscience Connection." *St. Anthony Messenger* Feb. 2004: 28–33. Print.

**Proposals**

"President George W. Bush: President Bush on Foreign Affairs." *U.S. Department of State: International Education Programs.* U.S. Department of State, 21 Nov. 2004. Web. 21 Nov. 2004.

Schoenholt, Donald N. "The Economy of Coffee: Supply Gut, Crashing Prices, Desperate Farmers: What's the Solution?" *Whole Earth* (Summer 2002): 12–14. Print.

Scholer, Morten. "Bitter or Better Future for Coffee Producers?" *International Trade Forum.* International Trade Center, Oct. 2004. Web. 26 Oct. 2004.

Stolcke, Verena. "The Labors of Coffee in Latin America: The Hidden Charm of Family Labor and Self-Provisioning." *Coffee, Society, and Power in Latin America.* Eds. William Roseberry, Lowell Gudmundson, and Mario Samper K. Baltimore: Johns Hopkins UP, 1995. 65–93. Print.

"What Is Fair Trade Certification?" *Fair Trade Certified.* Transfair USA, 2004. Web. 22 Nov. 2004.

## Reading to Write

1. In this proposal, Katy Kreitler explains many problems related to the coffee industry: environmental issues as well as troubles for producers and consumers. One way that she handles such a large amount of material is by using clear transitions between sentences, paragraphs, and sections. What transitional devices (for example, repeating words and phrases, or showing a sequence of ideas by numbering them) does Kreitler use? Which ones do you find most effective?

2. Kreitler and Andrew Skogrand (p. 170) wrote their proposals in response to similar assignments given by the same professor. They both offer clear solutions to the problems they describe, and both make use of sections to structure their arguments and proposals for change. In what other ways are these proposals similar? How do they differ?

3. Write a proposal on a social issue that includes, but goes beyond, the United States. As Kreitler does, use sections and pay particular attention to transitions as you organize your argument and propose a solution to the problem you detail.

# 6

## ASSESSING TEXTS
## Evaluations

**W**hat trends, websites, films, television shows, or products interest or perplex you? Is there something that you find problematic or disturbing that others enjoy—or something that others disdain that you value? Whether you're assessing the efficacy of satire in a television show or film, as Antonia Peacocke and Emily Mousseau-Douglas do, or making a judgment about the messages sent by a website, as Jennifer Dietz does, evaluations allow you to make an assessment and to convince others of your informed opinion.

The primary purpose of an evaluation is to communicate your assessment, your informed judgment, of whatever it is you're analyzing. That assessment comes through in both the language you choose to describe your topic (note, for example, the way Holly Roland in her poem "Lucille" uses dark imagery to describe a lighthearted comedy) and in a more straightforward articulation of your position (Lauren Tyrrell, in her evaluation of the *Gilmore Girls*, asserts in her thesis statement that the patterns of communication in the show fail to demonstrate gender equality).

You'll also need to articulate the criteria for your judgment and provide support for your opinion. Tyrell, for example, uses outside sources on gendered communication patterns to define the criteria for her assessment and refers to these sources as she analyzes a particular episode of the *Gilmore Girls*. Antonia Peacocke quotes others to show the objections some have to *Family Guy*, a television show she admires, and she analyzes scenes from the show to argue for the value of the type of humor it presents. Both writers also respond to counterarguments, acknowledging and responding to the views of others, even as they strengthen and modify their own positions.

As you read the selections in this chapter, pay attention to how the writers articulate their positions, delineate the criteria for their judgments, and support their assessments. As you write your own evaluation, consider the following questions: What criteria will you use to judge your subject? What is your position? What sources will help you articulate and support your point of view? What counterarguments do you need to address to modify or strengthen your position?

# Lucille

## *Holly Roland*

*Holly Roland wrote this poem for her creative writing class, taught by Elizabeth Spires, at Goucher College in Maryland. Although she did not have a specific assignment for this poem, Roland says that her purpose was to use her evaluation of I Love Lucy to describe "the less glamorous aspect of fame." She explains that when she was a child she watched reruns of I Love Lucy and "was completely engrossed" in the world presented in the show; as she grew older, however, "that world appeared far too shiny, funny, perfect" as if it didn't "possess a darker side."*

I had always loved Lucy (as trite as that may be)
but love never gave way to envy, for
her corset choked her
and Ricky was far too busy
babalooing to care.                                                           5

Fred and Ethel had their laughs,
but beneath their façade lied an underlying
layer of static.
Hatred of her off-white pillbox hats
stacked infinitely in the closet.                                            10

Simplicity went astray, as nobody noticed
that late-night jingle was sharp
by a key. Lucille Ball
lived her life in black and white pixels,
a colorless motif:                                                            15

# Evaluations

where the sky was always bland
and smiles never gleamed,
where love came in one color
as drab and lifeless as her rosiest of cheeks.

## Reading to Write

1. In this poem, Holly Roland writes about a television show that origi-nally aired in the 1950s. She writes that "Lucille Ball / lived her life in black and white . . . / a colorless motif." What other images does she use, not only to reflect the time period in which this show aired, but also to convey her critique? What is she critiquing?

2. Roland plays on the title of the show I Love Lucy by including forms of the word "love" three times in the poem. She also includes the word "hate." How does Roland's use of these opposing words and concepts affect you as a reader?

3. Write a poem in which you critique a television show. Use language and specific images that not only convey the time period in which the show aired but that also reflect your critique.

# The Reality of eDiets

## Jennifer Dietz

*Jennifer Dietz wrote this evaluation when she was a student at the University of New Hampshire. Her assignment was to write a detailed analysis of some element of popular culture and to explain how it affects individual and social identity. This evaluation first appeared in* Transitions 2006–07, *a collection of writing from the University of New Hampshire composition program.*

Grueling hours at the gym, tasteless food, and referring to diet as a four-letter word are out, thanks to the number one online diet site, eDiets. The site provides readers with all the information they need to meet their weight loss and management goals, and be both physically and emotionally healthier. Users can track the calories in the food they consume each day, find a diet that is customizable for their needs, and learn how to exercise effectively. In a society where the ideal body type is portrayed as a thin one, some feel eDiets is a dream come true. However, through the process of helping individuals achieve their weight goals, eDiets may be promoting dangerous diet habits.

When provided with information regarding current weight status and personal achievement goals, eDiets generates a customized diet plan for an individual. The diet strategies available range from the Atkins diet to a vegetarian plan, with anything and everything in between. Readers can choose to pay for a diet plan, or simply follow the tips posted by experts, try the recipes, and plug daily food intake into the calorie counter to achieve desired results. With an abundance of motivational stories and advice boards, the site serves as a dieter's paradise.

Evaluations

Tabs such as fitness, news, and recipe club make it effortless for users to find the information they are looking for and navigate eDiets with ease. Whether the goal is to maintain a certain weight, lose a few extra pounds, or shed the merciless weight that has crept on over the years, the site gives the low-down on what it takes to be skinny. Much emphasis is placed on how to look, feel, and be physically thin. The site makes the word "diet" seem simplistic, and the word "goal" seem attainable.

It is easy to see why readers recommend and ponder the eDiets website so frequently. The site uses catchy article titles such as "Look Thinner: The Secret!" and "Transform Your Life" to lure readers into the mindset that a physical transformation is the cure for all of life's troubles. Convinced that the secret to success has been revealed, readers are moved to browse links and related readings. Pictures of thin spokesmodels and muscular trainers spark dieters' interest in the site, as they are both appealing and persuasive. It is nearly impossible not to be captivated by the lean, bikini-clad bodies that the site portrays as achievable. Though the people in these articles are placed in different stories, clothing, and settings, they all have one thing in common: they are thin. From these images, viewers may infer that with the help of eDiets, they too can look and feel this way.

5          The question at hand is whether everything about eDiets is as positive as it appears. On the surface, it may be. But, when readers delve deeper, they may find that certain aspects of the site promote unhealthy ideas and behavior. Readers may quickly notice that many of the articles and sub-links suggest that the ideal body is not only one that is in a state of optimal well-being, but also a thin one. In the article "7 Secrets of Naturally Thin People," the editor of eDiets states that "There's no one diet or meal plan or exercise plan that's right for everybody. That's what is great about eDiets—it customizes thin" (Droze). It is excellent that eDiets' plans are customizable to fit anyone's needs, but the statement "it customizes thin" suggests that this is the site's sole purpose. It is as if diet and thin go hand in hand, which is not the case. Many people log onto the diet site because they want to maintain a weight level

or lose excess weight, to learn to be conscious of what they are putting into their bodies, or to reduce the risks of disease and diet-related illness, not necessarily to be skinny.

Thin seems to be an underlying theme of eDiets.com: "Look Thinner: The Simplest Secret," the "7 Secrets of Naturally Thin People," and "Slim Down, Shape Up Like Oprah" project the idea that right now, thin is in. Currently in the media, stars are becoming increasingly tiny. From the extremes—Lindsay Lohan, Nicole Richie, and Mary-Kate Olsen—to those taking it slow, such as Oprah, lately more so than ever, the big thing is to be small. The eDiets site, whose goal is to push health and fitness, may actually be giving readers the impression that everyone should strive to be this "thin," which may be not only unrealistic, but also dangerous.

In addition to giving readers the impression that thin is the ideal, the website advertises a number of fad diets. Healthy eating and exercise diets, such as the "Subway Diet," Weight Watchers, and Jenny Craig are viable ways to set goals and stick with them. But available alongside these wholesome plans are more controversial ones such as the "Hollywood 48-Hour Miracle Diet" and the "5-Day Miracle Diet," both of which are clearly referenced on the eDiets website, and both of which have a number of negative characteristics associated with them.

Fad diets appeal to those who want to lose weight quickly, but the diets are not necessarily healthy. They are restrictive in caloric intake, unrealistic in that they cannot be followed for long periods of time, and are for temporary weight loss. The "5-Day Miracle Diet" is no miracle; it is sheer undernourishment. Dieters are drawn to its appeal: its promise of quick weight loss. Of course low-calorie, low-nutrient-based meals given at certain times of the day are going to result in weight loss, but for how long ("5-Day")? It only gets worse with the "Hollywood 48-Hour Miracle Diet," which tells users to simply drink the "amazing" fruit juice throughout the day. No calorie counting, measuring servings, or thought required. The trick is that this is all the intake users are allowed for two entire days ("Hollywood"). Food is cut out of the diet completely, causing dieters to basically starve themselves. Effective?

Temporarily. Healthy? Absolutely not. Diets such as these may lead to unhealthy eating patterns and sporadic weight loss.

Whether it is because of a fad diet, a healthy eating regimen, or to take a deeper look at what exactly is being put into the body, dieters tend to focus on nutritional information. The eDiets site makes this process simple with its free nutrition tracker. Members can scroll through organized lists of thousands of foods, or simply type a food name into the search box. The site supplies a comprehensive analysis of the calories, nutrients, and substances that make up the food item. The tracker allows users to input as many meals and snacks as they consume, then tallies each into a list of daily values, allowing dieters to see how much their intake changes from day to day. In addition, eDiets warns users when their intake of certain nutrients is too low or high, and congratulates them when it is the correct amount. This program is so convenient and accurate, what objections could possibly arise?

10    The major concern with the nutrition tracker may not be in relation to the information it generates, but rather to how frequently someone logs on to use it. Three meals and two snacks means five website logins. Add in the time they spend on their own making food choices and debating about which calories are worth setting in writing, and the result is constant thought of calories and food choices. The user's mind is constantly weighing options, possibly even feeling pride in low calorie tallies or regret after a day when he or she pushed the limit. Quickly a fun and informative hobby becomes compulsive behavior.

For Pat Melillo, dieting turned into a life-threatening obsession. After suffering from stomach complications, Pat was recommended by her doctor to go on a low-fat diet. Quickly, her healthy approach to cutting increments of fat from her meals took a turn for the worse. Pat stated that she "was trying to eat healthy. That's what I thought I was doing. I was told to stay away from fats and little by little there was just no more fat in my diet" (Van Sant). WebMD recommends, for a 2,000 calorie-based diet, an average of 27 grams of fat per day, making up approximately 25 percent to 30 percent of daily caloric intake. The body needs fats to stay healthy and energized ("USDA"). Pat's "diet" slowly robbed her body of fat completely. CBS reported that "she became obsessed with what she thought was the perfect diet" to which Pat admitted, "It just started to become a game . . . not realizing it was like a death wish" (Van Sant). When done too excessively, nutritional tracking can go far beyond what was at one time just an enjoyable and healthy habit.

It may be hard to see where the downfall lies when it comes to free fitness tests, tools, and advice. In a nutshell, eDiets Fitness contains all the information one needs to become physically fit. In a short period of time and with minimal stress, members receive a diet profile, then follow the exercise plan provided. Those looking for more flexible plans that are low in commitment can skip the profile and instead choose to customize their own workouts by following the articles, techniques, and advice provided by other members. All of the options, available resources, and motivational stories are pleasing to the eye, but they may be the source of more extensive problems. As the pounds come off, the workouts become longer and more complex. As the intensity rises, exercise can turn from a healthy fascination to an addiction.

When speaking of exercise as an *addiction*, what is meant is not a physical dependency, but rather an emotional "just one more pound" attitude. Even after losing the recommended or desired amount of weight, eDieters have found it hard to ease up on extensive exercise regimens once they are part of their daily routines. Take Erin, for example. Once weighing 227 pounds, she shed 79 pounds and a total of 50 inches from her body using eDiets. Now, at 148 pounds and looking fantastic, Erin has no intention of stopping herself. As described on the eDiets website:

> She always makes time for working out. She has her exercise schedule planned out a month ahead of time. The mindful mom even uses the childcare center at the gym so she won't miss a workout. "I exercise six days a week," she says. "Some days I exercise an hour. Some days I exercise two hours. I don't make excuses. Monday I either run or do the elliptical trainer. Tuesday I do weight training in the morning and kickboxing in the evening. Wednesday

## Evaluations

I do kickboxing. Thursday I weight train and run for 45 minutes. Friday, I run 45 minutes to an hour. Saturday I weight train and do 45 minutes of cardio. Sunday is my day of rest." Don't get the wrong idea. Erin isn't obsessed with exercise. Exercise has simply become a passion for Erin. ("I Lost")

Erin has become dependent on exercise, to the extreme of laying it out on the table a month in advance so she does not miss an opportunity to work out. Maybe it is possible that Erin views this routine as a passion, but it is easy to see why others may consider it a full-blown addiction. Because eDiets has the power to change peoples' lives in such a positive way, it also has the power to lead them down the road to an unsafe fixation.

Success: the defining moment in a dieter's journey when the scale numbers tip back instead of forward and a sense of accomplishment is felt. It is one of the best feelings in the world and undeniably leaves dieters wanting more. An eDieter's calorie-counting-gym-routine-which-plan-should-I-try-next-attitude becomes more than just a diet, but rather a way of life. The site gives members such an array of new tips and techniques that they could surf for hours on end. But amidst the stories of success and the positive results left to be achieved are a number of underlying issues. Because of its addictive qualities and promises of fast weight loss, eDiets, a site aimed at helping people diet healthily, may actually be a source of dangerous habits.

### WORKS CITED

Droze, Kim. "7 Secrets of Naturally Thin People." *eDiets.* 12 Feb. 2006. Web. 13 Feb. 2006.

"5-Day Miracle Diet." *eDiets.* 12 Feb. 2006. Web. 13 Feb. 2000.

"Hollywood 48-Hour Miracle Diet." *eDiets.* 12 Feb. 2006. Web. 13 Feb. 2006.

"I Lost 79 Pounds, Lowered My Risk!" *eDiets.* 12 Feb. 2006. Web. 13 Feb. 2006.

"USDA Food Guide." *WebMD*. WebMD, 2005. Web. 12 Feb. 2006.

Van Sant, Peter. "Dangerous Extremes." *CBS News*. CBS Broadcasting,
12 July 2004. Web. 12 Feb. 2006.

## Reading to Write

1. In order be persuasive, an evaluation needs to be fair, acknowledging both the strengths and weaknesses of what is being judged even as the author takes a particular stand. For example, Jennifer Dietz points to the ease of navigation and the value of motivational stories on eDiets, even though she claims the site "may be promoting dangerous diet habits." What other positive elements of the site does she mention? How does she show that these seemingly positive elements might lead to dangerous habits?

2. The criteria for Dietz's evaluation are implied, rather than directly stated. What are the implied criteria she uses to assess eDiets?

3. Write an evaluation of some element of popular culture. Write a fair assessment, acknowledging both the strengths and weaknesses of the element you're analyzing, but take a stance and support a clear position.

# Gilmore Girls: A Girl-Power Gimmick

## Lauren Tyrrell

*Lauren Tyrrell wrote this evaluation for her Writing and Cultural Studies class at Marywood University in Pennsylvania. Her assignment was to "make an argument connected to gender, race, ethnicity, age, or class" in order to evaluate "whether a particular television show or movie provided positive, negative, or mixed messages." Tyrrell began by writing about Gilmore Girls, which was her favorite television show. In the process of her research, though, she changed her assessment. She says that during her research and analysis, she "learned about the subtle ways in which stereotypes are infused in the mass media, and—perhaps most importantly—about the importance of an open mind when researching a topic." Her teacher, Laurie McMillan, nominated Tyrrell's piece for the way she "builds an interesting and complex argument while using the engaged voice and public persona of a cultural studies essay."*

I t was the moment fans had been waiting for.

"Raincoats and Recipes," the final episode of season four of the WB's hit TV drama *Gilmore Girls*, promised in its trailer to resolve several of the major storylines in the series, including the grand opening of Lorelei's self-owned Dragonfly Inn, the admission of her attraction to best friend Luke Danes, and the romantic reunion of her daughter Rory with ex-boyfriend Dean Forester.

Along with thousands of other fans, I was anxious to discover how the mother-daughter duo would handle these events. A new fan of the show, I had been able to immerse myself quickly in the Gilmore world thanks to daily reruns on cable. I was in high school at the time and admired young, single mother Lorelei Gilmore and her disarmingly beautiful and intellectually intimidating adolescent daughter, Rory. For me, these women represented a new breed of leading ladies who struggled against, and generally triumphed over, a male-dominated world. Their female empowerment is particularly apparent in the script, which is noted for its fast-paced humor and almost inconceivable comebacks.

Now, watching a rerun of this highly anticipated season finale, my naivete has faded. Lorelei and Rory were not shattering stereotypes; instead, the girls were shattering my own idealistic belief that they embodied the essence of women's empowerment. By the end of the show, the twosome had slipped wordlessly into the arms of their respective love interests, abandoning their characteristic banter and with it their long-running "girl power!" gimmicks. By first examining the importance of dialogue to the series and to Lorelei's and Rory's female empowerment, and then by comparing the Gilmore girls' normal speech habits to their subsequent inarticulate attempts with the men they love, I conclude that the patterns of communication in the *Gilmore Girls* series illustrate that the duo fails to manifest the gender equality that they seem to support. The inconsistency displayed by this twosome, who so many idolize as powerful, contemporary women, can have profound consequences for young women who may consider, as I once did, the Gilmore girls to be suitable role models.

My initial approbation of the mother-daughter duo no doubt had     5
much to do with their clever and articulate dialogue, a feature of this TV drama that truly distinguishes it during primetime. *BuddyTV* senior writer Oscar Dahl accurately summarizes the importance of conversation to the drama. "*Gilmore Girls* is dialogue," he writes; "that is the basis of the show." Indeed, with a script which totals fifteen to twenty pages more than that of any other series, *Gilmore Girls*, unlike most other shows, focuses more on communication than on action. This "signature verbosity," continues Dahl, embraces "a signature rhythm and cadence, specific to its main characters." Rory and Lorelei's distinct communication patterns, therefore, set this series apart from others.

*Gilmore Girls* uses this foundation of the communication habits of two attractive women in order to shatter traditional stereotypes about the typical speech styles of females, for these conventions describe habits in which the girls typically do not engage. In *Gendered Lives*, Julia T. Wood explains that female speech is often characterized by "tentativeness" along with equalizing phrases, expressions of support, and personal relativity (126–27). Susan A. Basow in *Gendered Stereotypes and Roles* adds that women exhibit their lack of assertion and aggression through the use of tag questions such as "don't you agree?"; qualifiers such as "maybe" or "I think"; and "compound requests" such as "you love me, don't you?" (58). The humorous and high-speed dialogue on *Gilmore Girls* allows little room for such verbal apprehension. In fact, Lorelei and Rory more often display characteristics associated with male communication, which include, according to Wood, the establishment of control and power in the conversation, focus on accomplishing a specific goal, and direct assertions (128–29). Because their speech habits cross these gender lines, conversation becomes a crucial element in the Gilmore girls' promotion of feminist ideals.

This promotion of female empowerment is particularly apparent when the two female protagonists communicate with men. The tentative, indirect speech by which Basow and Wood characterize feminine conversation is nonexistent when the Gilmore girls are speaking to men with whom they are not romantically involved. For example, in the season four finale, Lorelei flaunts her conversational prowess before Tom, a contractor who has failed to furnish doors for the guests' rooms in time for the inn's opening:

TOM: Relax, I'm trying to track them down.

LORELEI: Tom, guests are showing up here any second. They have no doors. People will have to get very friendly very quickly. ("Raincoats and Recipes")

Not surprisingly, Lorelei receives a call seconds later from Tom who, unable to top her retort, brusquely informs her that the doors have arrived. Here, Lorelei does not simply establish her authority to a male employee, she does so with humor and finesse. Her firm insistence made the contractor realize that she wanted not his masculine reassurances but his immediate obedience. By engaging in assertive, effective, and typically masculine speech, Lorelei defines herself as a female powerhouse, a woman with influence and also the confidence to utilize it.

Lorelei's daughter Rory seems to have inherited this same conversational aggression. Though she plays the role of the village sweetheart, Rory often demonstrates her capacity for the same sharp-witted speech as her mother. For example, after several awkward run-ins with her ex-boyfriend, Rory decides to confront the recently married Dean Forester about his attitude. Thinking he is mad at her, she is able to assert herself. "I left you three messages. You didn't answer any of them," she rants. "You blew me off at Luke's today. You won't look me in the eye . . . Why are you so mad?" ("Raincoats and Recipes"). Rory's candor during this confrontation contradicts the stereotypes Basow explores, including the general assumption of females "to be deficient in assertiveness" as well as their preference to "let men dominate conversations" (70). In this scene, just the opposite holds true, as the younger Gilmore confidently accuses and demands, and Dean, playing the traditionally female role, stutters and makes excuses. Teenagers who struggle to string together coherent sentences around their crushes can only admire Rory's straightforward approach with boys. This example shows that, daughter, like mother, deceives audiences with self-assured speech that seems to break gender stereotypes and promote feminism.

This empowerment vanishes, however, when the Gilmore girls get involved romantically; the presence of a potential lover transforms their conversational style from girl power to girl interrupted. Remember the invincible Lorelei, who so easily laid down the law about her missing doors? She takes on a different attitude around Luke Danes, her longtime friend, and at the conclusion of season four, her most recent romantic interest. Throughout the episode, Lorelei's failure to have vocal confidence characterizes her conversations with Luke. When he presents her with a bouquet of flowers at the Dragonfly's grand opening, her only comeback is a flustered, "Oh my God, they're

10

beautiful. Thank you. I was—um—well, okay, so, we should get you all—uh—checked in. And that's—uh—over there" ("Raincoats and Recipes"). Her flustered response to Luke, a man for whom she has feelings, plainly contrasts with her earlier dialogue with Tom, for whom she fosters no such affection.

Her dialogue with Luke is consistent with conventional interactions between men and women who are romantically involved. Basow explains that in traditional heterosexual relationships, there exists a "dating script," the lines of which have become so prevalent in society that in a survey, nearly all participants were in "strikingly high and strikingly gender-stereotyped" agreement (213). This script clarifies men's and women's expected conduct in heterosexual relationships. For example, while men should initiate the encounter, "women can signal their interest in indirect, flirtatious ways" (213). Men should not express their feelings much, though women should be emotional and adoring (214). Finally, according to Basow, heterosexual romantic relationships traditionally emphasize male dominance. A study of over 200 dating couples in Boston found that power imbalances were "usually in the direction of male dominance" (216). Lorelei's conversation with Luke exhibits exactly the qualities enumerated by Basow: his assertion of feelings—the flowers—is certainly more direct than her gushy, stammering speech. The formerly invincible Lorelei becomes just another woman who is head-over-heels in love.

Lorelei exhibits this switch again later in the episode, when Luke draws close to Lorelei to execute the kiss that viewers had been anticipating since the show's conception. Lorelei steps back from his advances, frightened, her face bewildered, a clear and classic portrayal of feminine modesty:

LORELEI: What are you doing?

LUKE: Will you just stand still? ("Raincoats and Recipes")

Here, Luke's tough, rugged reply to Lorelei's fearful—and trite—tentativeness establishes for the audience exactly who has control of the situation. Luke yanks her into his embrace, and without another word, Lorelei surrenders. How stereotypically romantic, and how inconsistent with the female empowerment that *Gilmore Girls* supposedly promotes.

Again, Rory mimics her mother in this regard; stuttering and half-completed sentences replace her usually direct and articulate speech when love is a factor. Her earlier confrontation with Dean leads him to regard her romantically once again; when she recognizes his turn-around, her words fail right along with her defenses. Her conversational deterioration is evident in the script. At first, she stands her ground, reminding Dean of his present marital status. He explains that it's not working, and with noticeably less assurance, Rory suggests, "Maybe you could, um, go see a counselor or, go away together." Her speech continues to fail as Dean insists his marriage is over until, as he pulls her into his arms, she cannot even finish her thought: "I can't believe this is ... that we're ... " ("Raincoats and Recipes"). Though her sentence is never completed, the stereotype is revealed. Rory Gilmore, whose assertive dialogue serves as a model for women's equality, sinks into her female typecast via her wordlessness when romantically involved. The switch is evident between the witty and self-assured Rory, dealing with a man who she thinks is mad at her, and later the submissive, speechless Rory, surrendering to a man who loves her.

In particular, Rory's sexual encounter exhibits the stereotype that 15 Wood describes as "women as victims and sex objects/men as aggressors." Females, she writes, must convey "beauty, sexiness, passivity, and powerlessness," the latter two being evident in Rory's communication breakdown. These "qualities women are encouraged to develop ... contribute to objectifying and dehumanizing them," Wood explains (265). Furthermore, Basow notes that men see assertion in women as an unattractive quality. "Thus," she concludes, "women who act assertively may be seen as violating sex role norms and may experience social disapproval for their assertive behaviors. No wonder some women might hesitate to engage in such behaviors" (70). Adhering to these inane cultural norms, Rory surrenders all the communicative confidence she had displayed in the speech competitions, roommate conflicts, and relationship rivalries of previous episodes in order to seal Dean's affection for her in their lovemaking scene. Tracing the footsteps of her mother, Rory displays an abandonment of previously promoted feminist ideals through the change in her speech pattern from assertive to silent—how sad that this driven adolescent feels her strongest aptitudes to be a detriment in earning romance.

In these examples, the Gilmore girls exhibit, via their failure of words around the men they love, the very stereotypes they had seemed to be refuting. Though the distinction between their dialogue before and after the intrusion of dominant males in their lives plainly illustrates the failure of this mother and daughter to manifest gender equality, some might wonder, don't all women lose themselves a little when involved in a romantic relationship? Wouldn't the Gilmore girls seem completely heartless if they didn't allow their men to take the reigns in the relationship? However, these counterarguments illustrate exactly the extent to which gender stereotypes have become ingrained in our society. If gender equality existed on the series, love would affect the speech and behavior of Luke and Dean as well; however, these men retain their communicative faculties, while the Gilmore girls exhibit flustered speechlessness. Believing that women naturally lose themselves while men naturally remain impassive is a fallacy.

So maybe this episode of *Gilmore Girls* was misleading in its representation of female characters—does one bad apple ruin the whole crate? In this case, yes; the season finale was the last depiction of Lorelei and Rory that viewers got for several months. According to the recency effect, the last image is the one that sticks the most. Fans flocked to *TV.com* and raved about the episode; however, none of the fan reviews commented on Lorelei's grandiose entrepreneurial achievement in the opening of her Dragonfly Inn, nor on Rory's successful completion of another year at an Ivy League university. Smaller subplots in the script, like the marital problems between Rory's grandparents and the deterioration of Lorelei and Rory's tight bond, are mentioned only in passing. What viewers want to recount and relive are those mushy moments, and maintaining a sense of female empowerment during them is especially crucial. Sadly, it is during these same romantic scenes that the Gilmore girls ditch their feminist ideals.

The fans, of course, were ecstatic about the portrayal of romantic relationships during this episode. One member, under the name of GilmoresRock5, wrote that she loved how Lorelei got "so klutzy" around Luke, and deems perfect "the moment when [Luke and Lorelei] kiss." Another member, Samstar 148, was pleased "that Rory isn't so good-girl anymore." Celectialdreams, summarizing the episode, focuses on Luke "yanking" Lorelei toward him for their first kiss. "This whole scene couldn't have been written better," she wrote. Audience remarks such as these demonstrate that fans not only noticed the switch in the girls' behavior, but preferred it—a frightening find.

Frightening, but perhaps not surprising, considering the prevailing influence that television has in our society. According to Wood, "the average 18-year-old has watched 19,000 hours of TV"—that totals well over two years of TV time (256). Depictions of men and women bombard children and adolescents constantly; typically, the men are "independent, aggressive, and in charge," while the women "reflect long-established cultural stereotypes" (258–59). Though *Gilmore Girls,* for the most part, contradicted these norms by portraying a dominating mother/daughter duo, the show failed in this season finale to uphold its previous standards. I think we must not underestimate the significance of a season's worth of female empowerment that concludes with the duo falling, without protest, into the arms of their men; ultimately, it is these men who have, quite literally, the final say.

Through changes in conversational patterns with men and with each other displayed in this episode, the *Gilmore Girls* does not uphold the equalizing ideals it pretends to endorse. Sadly, it was not only the moment that fans had been waiting for, but also the one they would remember the best: when mother and daughter, Lorelei and Rory, lose their words for two men who—let's face it—don't even make it through season five. *Click!* 20

Evaluations

## WORKS CITED

Basow, Susan A. *Gender Stereotypes and Roles.* 3rd ed. Pacific Grove:
    Brooks/Cole, 1992. Print.
Dahl, Oscar. "Gilmore Girls and Its Undervalued Dialogue." *BuddyTV.* Buddy
    TV, 4 Dec. 2006. Web. 23 Mar. 2007.
"Raincoats and Recipes." *Gilmore Girls.* WB. Scranton, 18 May 2004.
    Television.
"Raincoats and Recipes." *TV.com.* CBS Interactive, 26 Mar. 2007. Web.
Wood, Julia T. *Gendered Lives: Communication, Gender, and Culture.*
    7th ed. Belmont, CA: Thomson Wadsworth, 2007. Print.

## Reading to Write

1. Lauren Tyrrell establishes the criteria for her evaluation of gender
   role stereotypes in the *Gilmore Girls* by including scholarly research
   on gendered language use. She also incorporates fans' responses to
   the episode she analyzes. How does Tyrrell's use of these different
   sources contribute to the strength of her argument?

2. Tyrrell develops her argument by comparing and contrasting the
   main characters' ways of communicating in different kinds of relationships (Platonic and romantic). She also includes and responds to
   counterarguments—"that the Gilmore girls would seem completely
   heartless" if they didn't respond to their love interests in a particular
   way, and that their ways of communicating in one episode do not
   undercut the feminist ideals portrayed in other episodes. How does
   Tyrrell respond to these counterarguments? How does she then support her own position?

3. Choose a film, television show, or play to evaluate in terms of the
   messages it sends concerning gender, race, ethnicity, age, ability, or
   class. Use scholarly sources to establish the criteria for evaluation.

# Family Guy and Freud: Jokes and Their Relation to the Unconscious

## Antonia Peacocke

*Antonia Peacocke, a student at Harvard, began this evaluation as a newspaper column for her high school paper, The Zephyr. She later revised it as an essay, which was published in "They Say / I Say": The Moves That Matter in Academic Writing, with Readings. In reflecting on writing this piece, Peacocke says that she "began with a less nuanced thesis," arguing that "Family Guy was all wit and no offense." In the process of writing and revising, however, she learned "to acknowledge counterarguments" and to strengthen her evidence. She says that she especially enjoyed working with a variety of sources, including blogs, television shows, interviews, and articles.*

While slouching in front of the television after a long day, you probably don't think a lot about famous psychologists of the twentieth century. Somehow, these figures don't come up often in prime-time—or even daytime—TV programming. Whether you're watching *Living Lohan* or the *NewsHour*, the likelihood is that you are not thinking of Sigmund Freud, even if you've heard of his book *Jokes and Their Relation to the Unconscious*. I say that you should be.

What made me think of Freud in the first place, actually, was *Family Guy*, the cartoon created by Seth MacFarlane. (Seriously—stay with me here.) Any of my friends can tell you that this program holds endless fascination for me; as a matter of fact, my high school rag-sheet "perfect mate" was the baby Stewie Griffin, a character on the show. Embarrassingly enough, I have almost reached the point at which I can perform one-woman versions of several episodes. I know every website that streams the show for free, and I still refuse to return the five

## Evaluations

*Family Guy* DVDs a friend lent me in 2006. Before I was such a devotee, however, I was adamantly opposed to the program for its particular brand of humor.

It will come as no surprise that I was not alone in this view; many still denounce *Family Guy* as bigoted and crude. *New York Times* journalist Stuart Elliott claimed just this year that "the characters on the Fox television series *Family Guy* . . . purposely offen[d] just about every group of people you could name." Likewise Stephen Dubner, co-author of *Freakonomics*, called *Family Guy* "a cartoon comedy that packs more gags per minute about race, sex, incest, bestiality, etc. than any other show [he] can think of." Comparing its level of offense to that of Don Imus's infamous comments about the Rutgers women's basketball team in the same year, comments that threw the popular CBS radio talk-show host off the air, Dubner said he wondered why Imus couldn't get away with as much as *Family Guy* could.

Dubner did not know about all the trouble *Family Guy* has had. In fact, it must be one of the few television shows in history that has been canceled not just once, but twice. After its premiere in April 1999, the show ran until August 2000, but was besieged by so many complaints, some of them from MacFarlane's old high school headmaster, Rev. Richardson W. Schell, that Fox shelved it until July 2001 (Weinraub). Still afraid of causing a commotion, though, Fox had the cartoon censored and irregularly scheduled; as a result, its ratings fell so low that 2002 saw its second cancellation (Weinraub). But then it came back with a vengeance—I'll get into that later.

5          *Family Guy* has found trouble more recently, too. In 2007 comedian Carol Burnett sued Fox for 6 million dollars, claiming that the show's parody of the Charwoman, a character that she had created for *The Carol Burnett Show*, not only violated copyright but also besmirched the character's name in revenge for Burnett's refusal to grant permission to use her theme song ("Carol Burnett Sues over *Family Guy* Parody"). The suit came after MacFarlane had made the Charwoman into a cleaning woman for a pornography store in one episode of *Family Guy*. Burnett lost, but U.S. district judge Dean Pregerson agreed that he could

"fully appreciate how distasteful and offensive the segment [was] to Ms. Burnett" (qtd. in Grossberg).

I must admit, I can see how parts of the show might seem offensive if taken at face value. Look, for example, at the mock fifties instructional video featured in the episode "I Am Peter, Hear Me Roar."

[The screen becomes black and white. Vapid music plays in the background. The screen reads "WOMEN IN THE WORKPLACE ca. 1956," then switches to a shot of an office with various women working on typewriters. A businessman speaks to the camera.]

BUSINESSMAN: Irrational and emotionally fragile by nature, female coworkers are a peculiar animal. They are very insecure about their appearance. Be sure to tell them how good they look every day, even if they're homely and unkempt. [He turns to an unattractive female typist.] You're doing a great job, Muriel, and you're prettier than Mamie van Doren! [She smiles. He grins at the camera, raising one eyebrow knowingly, and winks.] And remember, nothing says "Good job!" like a firm open-palm slap on the behind. [He walks past a woman bent over a file cabinet and demonstrates enthusiastically. She smiles, looking flattered. He grins at the camera again as the music comes to an end.]

Laughing at something so blatantly sexist could cause anyone a pang of guilt, and before I thought more about the show this seemed to be a huge problem. I agreed with Dubner, and I failed to see how anyone could laugh at such jokes without feeling at least slightly ashamed.

Soon, though, I found myself forced to give Family Guy a chance. It was simply everywhere: my brother and many of my friends watched it religiously, and its devoted fans relentlessly proselytized for it. In case you have any doubts about its immense popularity, consider these facts. On Facebook, the universal forum for my generation, there are currently 23 separate Family Guy fan groups with a combined membership of 1,669 people (compared with only 6 groups protesting against Family Guy, with 105 members total). Users of the well-respected

## Evaluations

Internet Movie Database rate the show 8.8 out of 10. The box-set DVDs were the best-selling television DVDs of 2003 in the United States (Moloney). Among the public and within the industry, the show receives fantastic acclaim; it has won eight awards, including three primetime Emmys (IMDb). Most importantly, each time it was cancelled fans provided the brute force necessary to get it back on the air. In 2000, online campaigns did the trick; in 2002, devotees demonstrated outside Fox Studios, refused to watch the Fox network, and boycotted any companies that advertised on it (Moloney). Given the show's high profile, both with my friends and family and in the world at large, it would have been more work for me to avoid the Griffin family than to let myself sink into their animated world.

With more exposure, I found myself crafting a more positive view of *Family Guy*. Those who don't often watch the program, as Dubner admits he doesn't, could easily come to think that the cartoon takes pleasure in controversial humor just for its own sake. But those who pay more attention and think about the creators' intentions can see that *Family Guy* intelligently satirizes some aspects of American culture.

Some of this satire is actually quite obvious. Take, for instance, a quip Brian the dog makes about Stewie's literary choices in a fourth-season episode, "PTV." (Never mind that a dog and a baby can both read and hold lengthy conversations.)

[*The Griffins are in their car. Brian turns to Stewie, who sits reading in his car seat.*]

**BRIAN:** *East of Eden?* So you, you, you pretty much do whatever Oprah tells you to, huh?

**STEWIE:** You know, this book's been around for fifty years. It's a classic.

**BRIAN:** But you just got it last week. And there's a giant Oprah sticker on the front.

**STEWIE:** Oh—oh—oh, is that what that is? Oh, lemme just peel that right off.

BRIAN: So, uh, what are you gonna read after that one?

STEWIE: Well, she hasn't told us yet—damn!

Brian and Stewie demonstrate insightfully and comically how Americans are willing to follow the instructions of a celebrity blindly—and less willing to admit that they are doing so.

The more off-color jokes, though, those that give *Family Guy* a bad    10
name attract a different kind of viewer. Such viewers are not "rats in a behaviorist's maze," as *Slate* writer Dana Stevens labels modern American television consumers in her article "Thinking Outside the Idiot Box." They are conscious and critical viewers, akin to the "screenagers" identified by Douglas Rushkoff in an essay entitled "Bart Simpson: Prince of Irreverence" (294). They are not—and this I cannot stress enough, self-serving as it may seem—immoral or easily manipulated people.

Rushkoff's piece analyzes the humor of *The Simpsons*, a show criticized for many of the same reasons as *Family Guy*. "The people I call 'screenagers,'" Rushkoff explains, ". . . speak the media language better than their parents do and they see through clumsy attempts to program them into submission" (294). He claims that gaming technology has made my generation realize that television is programmed for us with certain intentions; since we can control characters in the virtual world, we are more aware that characters on TV are similarly controlled. "Sure, [these 'screenagers'] might sit back and watch a program now and again," Rushkoff explains, "but they do so voluntarily, and with full knowledge of their complicity. It is not an involuntary surrender" (294). In his opinion, our critical eyes and our unwillingness to be programmed by the programmers make for an entirely new relationship with the shows we watch. Thus we enjoy *The Simpsons*' parodies of mass media culture since we are skeptical of it ourselves.

Rushkoff's argument about *The Simpsons* actually applies to *Family Guy* as well, except in one dimension: Rushkoff writes that *The Simpsons*' creators do "not comment on social issues as much as they [do on] the media imagery around a particular social issue" (296). MacFarlane and company seem to do the reverse. Trusting in their viewers' ability to analyze what they are watching, the creators of *Family Guy* point out the weaknesses and defects of U.S. society in a mocking and sometimes intolerant way.

Taken in this light, the "instructional video" quoted above becomes not only funny but also insightful. In its satire, viewers can recognize the sickly sweet and falsely sensitive sexism of the 1950s in observing just how conveniently self-serving the speaker of the video appears. The message of the clip denounces and ridicules sexism rather than condoning it. It is an excerpt that perfectly exemplifies the bold-faced candor of the show, from which it derives a lot of its appeal.

Making such comically outrageous remarks on the air also serves to expose certain prejudiced attitudes as outrageous themselves. Taking these comments at face value would be as foolish as taking Jonathan Swift's "Modest Proposal" seriously. Furthermore, while they put bigoted words into the mouths of their characters, the show's writers cannot be accused of portraying these characters positively. Peter Griffin, the "family guy" of the show's title, probably says and does the most offensive things of all—but as a lazy, overweight, and insensitive failure of a man, he is hardly presented as someone to admire. Nobody in his or her right mind would observe Peter's behavior and deem it worth emulation.

15      *Family Guy* has its own responses to accusations of crudity. In the episode "PTV," Peter sets up his own television station broadcasting from home and the Griffin family finds itself confronting the Federal Communications Commission directly. The episode makes many tongue-in-cheek jabs at the FCC, some of which are sung in a rousing musical number, but also sneaks in some of the creator's own opinions. The plot comes to a climax when the FCC begins to censor "real life" in the town of Quahog; officials place black censor bars in front of newly showered Griffins and blow foghorns whenever characters curse. MacFarlane makes an important point: that no amount of television censorship will ever change the harsh nature of reality—and to censor reality is mere folly. Likewise, he puts explicit arguments about

censorship into lines spoken by his characters, as when Brian says that "responsibility lies with the parents [and] there are plenty of things that are much worse for children than television."

It must be said too that not all of *Family Guy's* humor could be construed as offensive. Some of its jokes are more tame and insightful, the kind you might expect from the *New Yorker*. The following light commentary on the usefulness of high school algebra from "When You Wish Upon a Weinstein" could hardly be accused of upsetting anyone—except, perhaps, a few high school math teachers.

> [*Shot of Peter on the couch and his son Chris lying at his feet and doing homework.*]
>
> **CHRIS:** Dad, can you help me with my math? [My teacher] says if I don't learn it, I won't be able to function in the real world.
>
> [*Shot of Chris standing holding a map in a run-down gas station next to an attendant in overalls and a trucker cap reading "PUMP THIS." The attendant speaks with a Southern accent and gestures casually to show the different road configurations.*]
>
> **ATTENDANT:** Okay, now what you gotta do is go down the road past the old Johnson place, and you're gonna find two roads, one parallel and one perpendicular. Now keep going until you come to a highway that bisects it at a 45-degree angle. [*Crosses his arms.*] Solve for x.
>
> [*Shot of Chris lying on the ground next to the attendant in fetal position, sucking his thumb. His map lies abandoned near him.*]

In fact, *Family Guy* does not aim to hurt, and its creators take certain measures to keep it from hitting too hard. In an interview on *Access Hollywood*, Seth MacFarlane plainly states that there are certain jokes too upsetting to certain groups to go on the air. Similarly, to ensure that the easily misunderstood show doesn't fall into the hands of those too young to understand it, Fox will not license *Family Guy* rights to any products intended for children under the age of fourteen (Elliott).

However, this is not to say that MacFarlane's mission is corrective or noble. It is worth remembering that he wants only to amuse, a goal for which he was criticized by several of his professors at the Rhode Island School of Design (Weinraub). For this reason, his humor can be dangerous. On the one hand, I don't agree with George Will's reductive and generalized statement in his article "Reality Television: Oxymoron" that "entertainment seeking a mass audience is ratcheting up the violence, sexuality, and degradation, becoming increasingly coarse and trying to be . . . shocking in an unshockable society." I believe *Family Guy* has its intelligent points, and some of its seemingly "coarse" scenes often have hidden merit. I must concede, though, that a few of the show's scenes seem to be doing just what Will claims; sometimes the creators do seem to cross—or, perhaps, eagerly race past—the line of indecency. In one such crude scene, an elderly dog slowly races a paraplegic and Peter, who has just been hit by a car, to get to a severed finger belonging to Peter himself ("Whistle While Your Wife Works"). Nor do I find it particularly funny when Stewie physically abuses Brian in a bloody fight over gambling money ("Patriot Games").

Thus, while *Family Guy* can provide a sort of relief by breaking down taboos, we must still wonder whether or not these taboos exist for a reason. An excess of offensive jokes, especially those that are often misconstrued, can seem to grant tacit permission to think offensively if it's done for comedy—and laughing at others' expense can be cruel, no matter how funny. Jokes all have their origins, and the funniest ones are those that hit home the hardest; if we listen to Freud, these are the ones that let our animalistic and aggressive impulses surface from the unconscious. The distinction between a shamelessly candid but insightful joke and a merely shameless joke is a slight but important one. While I love *Family Guy* as much as any fan, it's important not to lose sight of what's truly unfunny in real life—even as we appreciate what is hilarious in fiction.

## WORKS CITED

"Carol Burnett Sues over *Family Guy* Parody." *Canadian Broadcasting Centre* 16 Mar. 2007. Web. 14 July 2008.

Dubner, Stephen J. "Why Is *Family Guy* Okay When Imus Wasn't?" Web log post. *Freakonomics: The Hidden Side of Everything* 3 Dec. 2007. Web. 14 July 2008.

Elliott, Stuart. "Crude? So What? These Characters Still Find Work in Ads." *New York Times Online* 18 June 2008. Web. 14 July 2008.

Facebook. Search for *Family Guy* under "Groups." Web. 14 July 2008.

Freud, Sigmund. *Jokes and Their Relation to the Unconscious.* 1905. Trans. James Strachey. New York: Norton, 1989. Print.

Grossberg, Josh. "Carol Burnett Can't Stop Stewie." *E! News* 5 June 2007. Web. 14 Jul. 2008.

"I Am Peter, Hear Me Roar." *Family Guy.* Prod. Seth MacFarlane. Twentieth Century Fox. 28 Mar. 2000. Web. 14 July 2008.

Internet Movie Database. *Family Guy.* Ed. unknown. Last update date unknown. Web. 14 July 2008.

MacFarlane, Seth. Interview. *Access Hollywood.* Online posting on YouTube. 8 May 2007. Web. 14 July 2008.

Moloney, Ben Adam. "*Family Guy*—The TV Series." British Broadcasting Corporation. 30 Sept. 2004. Web. 14 Jul. 2008.

"Patriot Games." *Family Guy.* Prod. Seth MacFarlane. Twentieth Century Fox. 29 Jan. 2006. Web. 22 July 2008.

"PTV." *Family Guy.* Prod. Seth MacFarlane. Twentieth Century Fox. 6 Nov. 2005. Web. 14 July 2008.

Rushkoff, Douglas. "Bart Simpson: Prince of Irreverence." *Leaving Springfield: The Simpsons and the Possibility of Oppositional Culture.* Ed. John Alberti. Detroit: Wayne State UP, 2004. 292–301. Print.

Stevens, Dana. "Thinking Outside the Idiot Box." *Slate* 25 Mar. 2005. Web. 14 Jul. 2008.

## Evaluations

Weinraub, Bernard. "The Young Guy of 'Family Guy': A 30-Year-Old's Cartoon Hit Makes an Unexpected Comeback." *New York Times Online* 7 Jul. 2004. Web. 14 July 2008.

"When You Wish Upon a Weinstein." *Family Guy.* Prod. Seth MacFarlane. Twentieth Century Fox. 9 Nov. 2003. Web. 22 July 2008.

"Whistle While Your Wife Works." Family Guy. Prod. Seth MacFarlane. Twentieth Century Fox. 12 Nov. 2006. Web. 14 July 2008.

Will, George F. "Reality Television: Oxymoron." *Washington Post* 21 June 2001. A25. Print.

---

## Reading to Write

1. Antonia Peacocke defends the television show *Family Guy*, arguing that its humor provides valuable satire, even though that humor has been critiqued by others as base and lacking social value. What evidence does she provide in support of her claim? Which points do you find most effective?

2. Although Peacocke provides a positive assessment of *Family Guy* and its use of humor, she also acknowledges that it does sometimes cross "the line of indecency." What is the effect of her inclusion of counterarguments? Does it strengthen or weaken her overall argument? Explain why.

3. Write a positive assessment of something that others see as negative, or a largely negative assessment of something others see as positive. Be attentive to alternate points of view, even as you support your own position

# What's So Funny? Comedy in America

## Emily Mousseau-Douglas

> *Emily Mousseau-Douglas wrote this piece for her University Writing class, taught by Robin Kirman, at Columbia University. This piece first appeared online in Columbia University's* Undergraduate Writing Program Journal. *Mousseau-Douglas says that one valuable part of writing this piece was that it went through several drafts and workshops, explaining, "This workshop process was hugely beneficial to me in refining the goals and tone of my paper."*

ased on reviews and articles I had read about the new faux documentary *Borat: Cultural Learnings of America for Make Benefit Glorious Nation of Kazakhstan*, I expected that when I actually saw it, I would be disgusted. I imagined sitting low in my theatre seat, covering my eyes, horrified by what I saw on the screen. When I finally got to see the movie, I was disappointed at my lack of disgust and horror. It was not nearly as outrageous or offensive as all those articles had promised it would be. My disappointment made me think about my extensive exposure to vulgar comedy and the nature of comedy in America. Perhaps I have been desensitized to bodily functions and nudity, especially when they are presented in the name of comedy. Perhaps years filled with movies like *American Pie* and *Scary Movie*, capped by the summer of raunchy sex farces like *Wedding Crashers* and *The 40-Year-Old Virgin*, have made it hard for me to be shocked and appalled by anything, even the scene of a hairy naked man wrestling a fat naked man, which constitutes the climax of the Borat movie.

## Evaluations

For those who have not seen the movie, the idea is as follows: a journalist from Kazakhstan named Borat drives an ice cream truck across America hoping to meet the woman of his dreams, Pamela Anderson. Because Borat is new to America and knows nothing of American decorum or tradition, he unwittingly does and says things to the locals along his path that both infuriate them and show them at their worst. Take for example the man working at a rodeo who, trusting the seemingly simple foreigner, tells Borat that America is currently working on making it acceptable to "string up" homosexuals. The concept of lulling unsuspecting locals into a false sense of confidence so that they will reveal their innermost prejudices may sound cruel and potentially humiliating for all involved, but the movie has been very well received in America, debuting at number one and keeping the top spot for the following week as well. It is difficult to find an unfavorable review of the film, and the "comic elite" in America is calling creator and star Sacha Baron Cohen a "revolutionary" (Stein, Rottenberg). Still, despite the positive reception from critics, Borat has caused worldwide controversy, which made me wonder, what is it exactly that separates those who hate the movie from those who love it? Is it just that people who hate it don't "get it"?

Due to his performance as Borat, Cohen has been compared to Andy Kaufman, called a "Johnny Knoxville with a sense of humor," and a Dadaist (Stein, Rottenberg). His performance blurs the line between the "wildly surreal and the all-too-real" as he allows his subjects no "comforting recourse to ironic detachment" (Rottenberg). It is reported that during filming, Cohen was extremely dedicated to the project, refusing to break character between the time he woke up and the time he went to bed. The mustache was real, the suit remained unwashed to make him smell more "foreign," and all promotional interviews were conducted with Cohen in character (Rottenberg). This kind of ultra-real comedy, in which unwitting targets do not realize they are part of the joke, is a new trend emerging with the release of *Borat*. Referred to as "street comedy," it relies on extreme absurdity, well-placed realism (such as the authentically smelly suit), and little-to-no money (Stein). It is a descendent of *Jackass* and Stephen Colbert, but without the "twinkle in [the] eye" (Rottenberg). The look of *Borat*—the grainy, cheaply shot footage—is intentional, as is the fact that Borat hails from a real country. As British comedian David Baddiel points out, "If it had been an older comedian, Borat would have been from Stupidlandia" (Stein).

It is in the spirit of this new brand of guerrilla comedy that the faux documentary is so successful as a genre. *Borat* simply would not work as either a social commentary or a shock-filled comedy if a viewer felt that everyone on screen was in on the joke. The genuine reactions to Borat deliver most of the laughs, and it is knowing that these people are revealing their true selves, their innermost thoughts and beliefs, that allows the film to comment on American society and culture.

When considering some of the most famously disgusting comedic outlets, such as *South Park, Team America: World Police*, and even *Mad* and *Cracked* magazines, it seems obvious that even if the public is sure to be disgusted, comedy just has to go as far as it can go. Comedians revel in the challenge to make audiences cringe. With this in mind, consider how a group of the most respected comedians in America, following an advance viewing of Borat, shared a "sense of collective astonishment" (Rottenberg). In a group that included a *Simpsons* writer, Garry Shandling, and one of the creators of *Seinfeld* (the other, Larry Charles, actually directed *Borat*), there seemed to be a consensus that what they saw was "something totally original," and that Cohen had changed comedy in the same way that Marlon Brando changed dramatic acting after *On the Waterfront* (Rottenberg, Stein).

This new style of aggressive comedy is expected to horrify older viewers, namely those over the age of 35. Says journalist Joel Stein, "If you're over 35, you think you have the right to keep your regrettable moments private. If you're under 35, you realize that everything is public now." As one woman in the film tells Borat, when he asks her to clean him after using the toilet, "That is a very private thing." Nothing

5

is private for the younger generations. In the era of reality television and Internet video stars, everyone's idiocy or talent is on display for all to see. The notion of privacy as an assured right no longer exists, and everyone, at every moment, is at risk of revealing his or her true nature for the entertainment of others. At the Toronto Film Festival in September 2006, *Borat* "earned a rapturous reception," even though the projector malfunctioned midway through the movie. The festival is renowned for debuting future Oscar contenders, which *Borat* reportedly outshone (Rottenberg). The movie has also created a lot of buzz on college campuses as well as within the film industry. So it may be safe to assume that this type of movie, a colorful mix of vulgarity and supposed social commentary, is inevitably going to be more fervently anticipated, and finally received, by those Americans who are presumably more liberal, more open-minded, and more creative. Or is it just that this was the right time for the movie to be seen in America?

In his critique of the film, Professor Paul Lewis suggests that the latter may be the case, and the movie's reception internationally suggests it may be a cultural issue. Borat has definitely not been so welcome in Russia, or in his supposed homeland of Kazakhstan. The former has not banned the movie, as was reported, but its Federal Culture and Cinematography Agency, which is responsible for certifying films for distribution, has refused to certify *Borat* (Myers). The agency contends that its decision was based on the "potential to offend religious and ethnic feelings," although due to rampant illegal DVD production in Russia, the film will likely still be seen (Myers). Thus there may still be some demand for the movie, despite the belief by officials that it will offend many within the country, particularly Russia's large Muslim population.

*Borat* is the first movie to be refused certification for distribution in Russia since the collapse of Soviet censorship in the 1980s (Myers). Even Kazakhstan has not explicitly refused distribution of the movie, leading one to wonder whether Russia's choice to refuse distribution for Borat is based on cultural, ethnic, and religious considerations, or something else entirely. Daniil B. Dondurei, editor of *The Russian Art of Cinema* magazine, argues that the decision was motivated by politics. He cites "ethnic tensions, but also close relations between Russia and Kazakhstan, and a taboo in Russia against satirical depictions of national leaders or political systems"—a notable cultural difference from America, where leaders and politics are not only satirized publicly but also frequently, as for example on two intensely popular shows, *The Daily Show* and *The Colbert Report* (qtd. in Myers).

In Kazakhstan, where they were likely expecting a "major, if probably hysterical, hit to [their] image," the government went on the defensive in the wake of the release of *Borat*, taking out a four-page tourism advertisement in the *New York Times* and the *International Herald Tribune*, and producing television ads for distribution in America ("They Smell"). The print ad, described by journalist Josh Rottenberg as "unintentionally funny," tries to appeal to potential visitors with such tidbits as, "the country is home to the world's largest population of wolves" (Rottenberg). Initially, the government of Kazakhstan threatened legal action against Cohen, but it has now invited him to visit. Cohen is considering going to Kazakhstan (in character, of course), and he sees it as the "ultimate opportunity to conflate his made-up character with reality" (Stein).

So, Russia does not find Borat funny; Kazakhstan does not find    10
Borat funny (although they are beginning to adopt the adage, "if you can't beat 'em . . . "); and Jordan, Kuwait, Barhain, Oman, and Qatar, all of which have "barred distribution of the film" due to predominantly Muslim populations, do not find Borat funny (Myers). Then why does America seem to find him so funny?

The answer to this question appears to lie in an interesting cultural conglomeration: Borat, both the movie and the man, embodies everything that Americans find humorous. He is a combination of highbrow satire, lowbrow sight gags, extreme and inaccurate caricature—he creates in the average viewer, through his own inadequacies, a quiet feeling of superiority. This recipe has proven successful in so many of

Evaluations

America's most popular comedic outlets: *The Simpsons* most notably; network sitcoms like the 1980s hit *Perfect Strangers*, which capitalized on the inherent humor of a foreigner trying to start a life in America; even *The Daily Show*, which earned its extreme popularity by emphasizing for a delighted audience the constant foibles of politicians and other public figures.

America, it seems, has a history of humor based on patronization of the other, satire based upon stereotypes, beginning with the caricature of Yankee Doodle during the American Revolution (Stein). Yankee Doodle was depicted as a country "bumpkin," the opposite of the perception of the British as sophisticated, and was originally created as an "ignorant clodhopper [to] appeal to the British soldiery as an apt caricature of the rustic rebels" (Shuckburgh). Eventually, the character of Yankee Doodle was proudly adopted by American soldiers to emphasize and proclaim their difference and independence from the British (Shuckburgh). These exaggerated characters generally develop into recognized facsimiles of a given ethnic or economic group, as Yankee Doodle came to symbolize patriotic Americans, and are then embraced in the culture. Such is the case with Borat.

One trick, Rottenberg argues, that makes Borat (and Cohen) so successful is that he is playing on the average American's inherent notion of a "foreigner" and an almost guaranteed lack of geographical knowledge (Rottenberg). Cohen, Rottenberg says, capitalizes on the average American's willingness to believe even the most absurd things about how people live and behave in foreign countries. Because Kazakhstan represents one of the "many gaping holes in the average American's shaky knowledge of geography," anything that Borat says about the country will go unchallenged by his subjects (Rottenberg). As Stein says, Cohen preys on the "fear, fascination and, most of all, patronization of the other—the foreigner" (Stein). The irony is that while Cohen plays the "clueless, desperate-to-fit-in, optimistic foreigner" that has become a comedy staple, Borat's "attempts to be American pinpoint exactly how the world sees us: garish, violent, nouveau riche, a land of Donald Trumps and 50 Cents" (Stein).

Cohen simultaneously plays a "leering, filthy, poor, and opinionated foreigner and a confidence man who triumphs over the shills who fall into his lap," creating a caricature of a foreigner, and emphasizing the true feelings of his subjects (Lewis). Borat's success lies in the audience's knowledge that he may be fake, but the targets are very real. This duality allows the audience to laugh both at him and with him, and seamlessly combines the film's use of both exaggeration (satire) and reality (documentary).

According to journalist Carina Chocano, Borat's encounters with average Americans are "gems of fish-out-of-water buffoonery" and test some "surprisingly ambitious sociological theories." But to what end? Borat's main target appears to be bigotry within the United States, particularly in the South. Lewis claims that audiences, by assuming a position of "imagined superiority" over both Borat and his subjects, "take an angry pleasure in the appalling statements he brings out of others" (Lewis). By revealing these people's darker sides, Borat is giving the viewer a "shot of security and a double infusion of enhanced self-esteem" (Lewis). Viewers are given some sense of pride and the idea that things could be worse: they could be the person on-screen, being made into a fool for all to see. 15

Also, the indiscretions of the people on-screen are a novelty in our politically correct society. As Jay Roach, director of *Austin Powers,* says, "Political correctness has led to a more civil society because people with racist attitudes have taken them underground" (qtd. in Rottenberg). Until now. Borat reveals the true feelings of his subjects, much to the horror of the audience. But there is something compelling about hearing beliefs and ideas that are normally not allowed in a public forum. Particularly because it is socially unacceptable to publicly reveal one's prejudices and hostilities, *Borat* is both a window and a mirror, allowing people who do not share the opinions of those featured in the movie to see what others really think, and letting those who do share these beliefs to see themselves represented in popular culture for better or worse. This onscreen candor creates something akin to a car crash: even if people hate what they are seeing, they can't turn away. Of course, the fact that Cohen's antics as Borat create humor within the spectacle makes it palatable to a wider audience, horrifying viewers some of the time and making them laugh the rest of the time.

Satire as a form of humor is pervasive throughout American comedy, and it is seen as a highbrow alternative to parody or irony, intended to "attack vice, and promote virtue" (Granger). Tony Hendra defines satire as an "intellectual judo, in which the writer or performer takes on the ideas and character of his target and then takes both to absurd lengths to destroy them" (qtd. in Turner 55). Throughout his travels, Cohen (as Borat) challenges his subjects, creating situations in which they can either receive him well or not. Take, for example, the men on a New York City subway that Borat attempts to greet with a kiss. There is nothing overly aggressive or intrusive in the way in which Borat approaches the men; he only tries to kiss them on each cheek, in a way that is common in many European countries. More often than not, he is met with harsh language and the threat of bodily harm. This simple experiment reveals much about these men: homophobia, ignorance regarding other cultures, distrust, disassociation from the people around them, and probably even fear. The movie is full of similar incidents and similar people, all of which are startling in their hostility. Because the events on the screen are shocking and uncomfortable for the viewer, it becomes both natural and necessary to laugh to alleviate the uneasiness. Also, given the prevalence within American society of the traits exhibited by the men on the subway, the men become instantly recognizable to the audience, who "laugh along because [they] see [them]selves . . . and to face up to this sort of unvarnished, unpleasant reality is a powerfully subversive thing" (Turner 56). Unexpectedly, these men become representative of everything that is wrong with our society, and it becomes not only acceptable but obligatory to find the humor in their ignorance. How could we not? Suddenly we are aware that it is all around us, all the time.

In his book *Planet Simpson: How a Cartoon Masterpiece Defined a Generation*, Chris Turner notes that satire often emphasizes the "blazing hundred-foot-high neon gap between What Is and What Should Be," or the difference between how people know things to be and how they want them to be (57). He explains further, saying that this idea is particularly important in comedy in America because "America's ideals are so central to its society and so celebrated in its history and culture" (58). America prides itself on being welcoming, open-minded, and accepting. But Borat's experience certainly does not confirm this notion. In actuality, the people that he meets are the exact opposite. This is usually so, says Louis D. Rubin Jr., who asserts that American comedy arises out of a gap between a "cultural ideal" and fact, with the ideal usually being revealed as "somewhat hollow and hypocritical, and the fact crude and disgusting" (qtd. in Turner 58).

In addition to the more subtle comic devices Borat uses to get a laugh, there are displays of all levels of comedy in the movie, as described by Turner: sight gags, catchphrases, referential humor, and sophomoric humor—the previously mentioned bodily functions (59). Through the use of many levels of comedy, Borat is able to appeal to all types of viewers, and the movie never feels heavy with pretension. A child could watch the film and laugh. The sight gags and slapstick humor combined with the more subtle social satire create comedic stimulation for all the senses. The catchphrases ("High five!") act as both an effective marketing tool and an easy way for people leaving the theatre to feel that they can actively participate in the movie. Just because the show is over does not mean that you have to stop talking like Borat.

The referential humor in *Borat*—though limited—creates cultural 20 cohesion, another potential reason that the film has been so successful in the home of its main cultural reference: *Baywatch*. The references to the culture in Kazakhstan are quite obviously the fruits of Cohen's imagination and are, for the most part, unspoken. Borat's history and habits are never explicitly tied to Kazakhstan specifically, but instead embody most Americans' notion of a foreigner. The choice of Kazakhstan as Borat's home is effective because it "blends into all the other 'stans' we don't understand" (Lewis). But the American people and references are real. As Cohen himself says "The joke is not on Kazakhstan. I think the joke is on people who can believe that the Kazakhstan that I describe can exist" (Strauss). It is America that is *Borat's* punch line, and it was also American audiences who turned test screenings into "tent revivals, with audiences convulsing with laughter" (Rottenberg).

So is it that Borat just happened to be the right movie at the right time in America? Can timing, and America's general taste for vulgarity and satire, account for the movie's phenomenal success here? Paul Lewis calls *Borat* the "perfect ethnic joke for post-9/11 America," capitalizing on America's fear of foreigners as potential terrorists and turning it into laughter and fascination at the foibles of a naive newcomer. It is probably true that, before 9/11 and the country's increased fears of terrorism, Borat would not have received the hostile reaction he did from the people he met throughout his journey. And, without their prejudices caught on tape, the film would not be the shocking glimpse into American intolerance that it has become. It is because of this fact in particular that *Borat* is such a fascinating lesson in American self-awareness. It reveals much about the American character, and says much about the way that America is viewed by foreigners (and Cohen is one), but Borat has still been embraced by the very people that it criticizes. Despite the unfortunate truths that may be revealed through the Borat movie, America must be commended for its ability to laugh at itself, loudly and enthusiastically.

## WORKS CITED

Chocano, Carina. "Borat, the Film for 'Make Benefit' Insights into U.S." *The Age*. The Age Company, Nov. 2006. Web. 15 Nov. 2006.

"They Smell a Borat?" *Editor and Publisher*. Nielsen Business Media, Sept. 2006. Web. 15 Nov. 2006.

Granger, Bruce Ingham. *Political Satire in the American Revolution, 1763–1783*. Ithaca: Cornell UP, 1960. Print.

Lewis, Paul. "'Borat Tells Us Much About Ourselves." *News Tribune*. Tacoma News, Web. 15 Nov. 2006.

Myers, Steven Lee. "Borat Is Not Approved for Distribution in Russia." *New York Times*. New York Times, Nov. 10 2006. Web. 15 Nov. 2006.

Rottenberg, Josh. "Beyond the Cringe." *Entertainment Weekly*. Time Inc., 20 Oct. 2006. Web. 15 Nov. 2006.

Shuckburgh, Richard. "Songs and Oaths: Yankee Doodle." *Ben's Guide to U.S. Government for Kids*. U.S. Government Printing Office, Nov. 2006. Web. 15 Nov. 2006.

Stein, Joel. "Borat Make Funny Joke on Idiot Americans! High Five!" *Time*. Time Inc., 29 Oct. 2006. Web. 15 Nov. 2006.

Strauss, Neil. "The Man Behind the Mustache." *Rolling Stone*. Jann Wenner, Nov. 2006. Web. 30 Nov. 2006.

Turner, Chris. *Planet Simpson: How a Cartoon Masterpiece Defined a Generation*. Cambridge: Da Capo, 2004. Print.

## Reading to Write

1. Emily Mousseau-Douglas writes an evaluation of humor in America through examining not only a particular genre (the comedic faux documentary) but also a particular film, *Borat*. She claims that *Borat* "embodies everything that Americans find humorous" (satire, sight gags, caricature). What examples does she provide to support her argument? Which examples and sources do you find most convincing?

## Evaluations

2. Both Mousseau-Douglas and Antonia Peacocke (p. 217) examine the relationship between vulgarity and social commentary, and between expressions of prejudice and satire. In what ways are their evaluations of satire as a form of humor similar? How do they differ? Is one more effective to you than the other? Why?

3. Write an evaluation of a larger issue, trend, or concept by examining a specific example, as Mousseau does when she evaluates humor in America with an analysis of *Borat*. For example, you might evaluate college students' attitudes toward privacy by examining a few pages of a social networking site and interviewing those who represent themselves on the site.

# 7

## APPROACHING LITERATURE
### Analyses

Consider a literary text that interested, moved, or affected you in some other way. What themes do you notice? What literary conventions does the writer use? What are the effects of those choices? Are there other texts or theories that influence your interpretation? If, for example, you are doing a close analysis of a poem originally written in another language, as Michael Kauffmann and Melanie Subacus do in "Cynthia Holds Her Wine," or considering the ways in which historical context and critical theory illuminate a message, as Anne Hart and Lindsey Arthur do in their approaches to a novel, such literary analyses allow you to present and support an interpretation, one that provides a deeper understanding of the literary text.

As you develop a thesis for your literary analysis, pay close attention to the details of the text you're analyzing—the words, themes, metaphors, images, uses of sound, and other literary conventions. You might, for example, pay attention to the repetition of words as Kauffmann and Subacus do in their translation of a Propertius poem, repeating "woe" four times within four lines. Or you might analyze the ways in which other literary conventions help create meaning, as Stephanie Huff does when she considers the significance of metaphors in a Percy Bysshe Shelley poem, and Jason Rose does when he analyzes characterization and dialogue in Don DeLillo's novel *White Noise*. You can also include historical context or other outside information to support your interpretation, as Hart and Arthur do in their analyses of Jeffrey Eugenides' novel *The Virgin Suicides*.

## Analyses

As you read the selections in this chapter, consider the themes, patterns, and literary conventions the authors analyze. Note the ways they articulate their theses and support their claims. As you write your literary analysis, consider the following questions: What conventions seem most important and effective in the literary piece you're analyzing? What themes or patterns do you notice? Is there a critical theory that helps you understand the patterns or themes within the text? What historical or contextual information helps you better understand the text and support your interpretation?

## "Cynthia Holds Her Wine"
## *Propertius 2.33B*

### *Michael Kauffmann and Melanie Subacus*

> *Michael Kauffmann and Melanie Subacus wrote this translation of Propertius's poem when they were students at Saint Joseph's University in Pennsylvania. They recognized that translation, like any literary analysis, involves multiple critical choices. Kauffmann, who writes poetry, and Subacus, who has a background in Latin literature, collaborated in choosing "whether to remain literal to the language and syntax of the original, to aim for fluid expression of broader ideas . . . or to loosely echo the original, creating an almost entirely different text." Subacus explains the initial process of translation: "I first rendered the poem into a very literal prose translation, highlighting repetitions of words, and making notations concerning syntax, meter, wordplay, and the use of other literary devices." Kauffmann then used the literal translation and notes to write a sonnet, thematically based on the original. They revised together. Kauffman notes that collaboration was the only way this translation was possible; he says that Subacus "was able to make a dead language seem alive" to him. This translation originally appeared in* The Crimson & Gray, *SJU's student literary magazine.*

Cynthia, what time is it? Do not laugh!
Midnight! Your wallet, it thins; cup—empty!
You fill it again, a glass and a half,
Not tired at all, raising stakes plenty . . .

## Analyses

5　He must have wasted away, who first found
Grapes, distilled to nectar of truth and sin.
Woe to man, slave to the vine, twisting round,
And woe to beauty that the grape wastes thin,
Woe to a woman who mistakes her man,
10　And woe to me, as my world starts to spin . . .

But drink! You are beautiful, and you can.
Wine does not waste you, though you lose or win.
Drench the table! Bring the best from the store.
Free your speech, so from your mouth my poems pour.

---

### Reading to Write

1. Michael Kauffmann and Melanie Subacus chose in their translation to stay true to the emotion of the original poem, yet to use a different poetic form. Reread the headnote for this selection and consider the options they weighed in translation. What choice would you have made? Why?

2. List the words and images most repeated in this sonnet. How does this use of repetition affect your interpretation of the poem?

3. Kauffmann and Subacus worked together, each bringing unique perspectives and skills to translating this poem. Work with a classmate to write either a translation of a poem or a literary analysis of a text that you've read for class. As you prepare, discuss the perspectives and skills each of you brings to the project.

# Metaphor and Society in Shelley's "Sonnet"

## Stephanie Huff

> Stephanie Huff wrote this analysis in her Literary Theory class at
> Wright State University in Ohio. It first appeared in The Norton
> Field Guide to Writing. Huff says of writing this piece, "I wanted to
> examine not only what metaphors were used" in Shelley's poem, "but
> also the weight given to each. Number of references to the metaphor
> became important, as did intensity of words." The process of writing
> this paper taught her to "look beyond what a metaphor means to how
> and why it was constructed."

I n his sonnet "Lift not the painted veil which those who live,"
Percy Bysshe Shelley introduces us to a bleak world that exists
behind veils and shadows. We see that although fear and hope both
exist, truth is dishearteningly absent. This absence of truth is exactly
what Shelley chooses to address as he uses metaphors of grim distortion and radiant incandescence to expose the counterfeit nature of
our world.

The speaker of Shelley's poem presents bold assertions about the
nature of our society. In the opening lines of the poem, he warns the
reader to "Lift not the painted veil which those who live / Call Life"
(1–2). Here, the "painted veil" serves as a grim metaphor for life. More
specifically, the speaker equates the veil with what people like to call
life. In this sense, the speaker asserts that what we believe to be pure
reality is actually nothing more than a covering that masks what really
lies beneath. Truth is covered by a veil of falsehood and is made opaque
with the paint of people's lies.

Analyses

This painted veil does not completely obstruct our view, but rather distorts what we can see. All that can be viewed through it are "unreal shapes" (2) that metaphorically represent the people that make up this counterfeit society. These shapes are not to be taken for truth. They are unreal, twisted, deformed figures of humanity, people full of falsities and misrepresentations.

Most people, however, do not realize that the shapes and images seen through the veil are distorted because all they know of life is the veil—this life we see as reality only "mimic[s] all we would believe" (3), using "colours idly spread" (4) to create pictures that bear little resemblance to that which they claim to portray. All pure truths are covered up and painted over until they are mere mockeries. The lies that cloak the truth are not even carefully constructed, but are created idly, with little attention to detail. The paint is not applied carefully, but merely spread across the top. This idea of spreading brings to mind images of paint slopped on so heavily that the truth beneath becomes nearly impossible to find. Even the metaphor of color suggests only superficial beauty—"idly spread" (4)—rather than any sort of pure beauty that could penetrate the surface of appearances.

5      What really lies behind this facade are fear and hope, both of which "weave/Their shadows, o'er the chasm, sightless and drear" (5–6). These two realities are never truly seen or experienced, though. They exist only as shadows. Just as shadows appear only at certain times of day, cast only sham images of what they reflect, and are paid little attention, so too do these emotions of hope and fear appear only as brief, ignored imitations of themselves when they enter the artificiality of this chasmlike world. Peering into a chasm, one cannot hope to make out what lies at the bottom. At best one could perhaps make out shadows and even that cannot be done with any certainty as to true appearance. The world is so large, so caught up in itself and its counterfeit ways, that it can no longer see even the simple truths of hope and fear. Individuals and civilizations have become sightless, dreary, and as enormously empty as a chasm.

This chasm does not include *all* people, however, as we are introduced to one individual in line 7 who is trying to bring to light whatever truth may yet remain. This one person, who defies the rest of the world, is portrayed with metaphors of light, clearly standing out among the dark representations of the rest of mankind. He is first presented to us as possessing a "lost heart" (8) and seeking things to love. It is important that the first metaphor applied to him be a heart because this is the organ with which we associate love, passion, and purity. We associate it with brightness of the soul, making it the most radiant spot of the body. He is then described as a "splendour among shadows" (12), his purity and truth brilliantly shining through the darkness of the majority's falsehood. Finally, he is equated with "a bright blot / Upon this gloomy scene" (12–13), his own bright blaze of authenticity burning in stark contrast to the murky phoniness of the rest of the world.

These metaphors of light are few, however, in comparison to those of grim distortion. So, too, are this one individual's radiance and zeal too little to alter the warped darkness they temporarily pierce. This one person, though bright, is not bright enough to light up the rest of civilization and create real change. The light simply confirms the dark falsity that comprises the rest of the world. Shelley gives us one flame of hope, only to reveal to us what little chance it has under the suffocating veil. Both the metaphors of grim distortion and those of radiant incandescence work together in this poem to highlight the world's counterfeit nature.

## Reading to Write

1. Stephanie Huff analyzes not only the metaphors Shelley uses in his poem but how often those metaphors, which suggest either darkness or light, are used. How does this "weighting" of metaphor and imagery affect her argument? Point to places in her analysis where she supports this aspect of her argument.

## Analyses

2. Huff uses quotations from Shelley's poem to support her interpretation. Consider the quotations she uses and her interpretation of those lines and metaphors. Is your interpretation similar to or different from Huff's? Are there places where you would extend or modify her analysis?

3. Write an analysis of a poem or another short piece of literature in which one literary convention (such as metaphor, the repetition of a particular word or image, rhyme, or some other repetition of particular sounds) is especially related to the meaning or effect you observe. Use specific examples from the literary text to support your thesis.

# Technology as a Simulacrum of God in White Noise

## Jason Rose

*Jason Rose wrote this analysis for the course in American Literature since 1865 at Louisiana State University. His teacher, Jean Witherow, asked students to focus on a "literary technique, examining choices the author makes to shape a work so that it expresses an experience or elaborates a theme." Rose chose to examine the ways that Don DeLillo connects modern technology and spirituality in White Noise, a theme that interested him on his first reading of the novel but that he came to understand in more depth through writing this analysis.*

Don DeLillo's 1985 novel *White Noise* is based on the idea of simulacra—simulations replacing realities that no longer exist. The novel uses this theme to explore several postmodern issues such as the homogenization of culture and identity, the subsequent loss of identity, and the nature of simulacra. At the same time, *White Noise* reevaluates several timeless questions from a postmodern view such as the nature of God, the meaning of death, and the value of truth. These themes mesh and mix together within the context of the novel and, as a result, produce some interesting observations. For example, by confronting the issues of death, the fear of death, and the loss of individual and cultural identity to consumerism, all in the context of Technology, DeLillo is able to show how Technology attempts to replace God as a simulacrum on all levels in the postmodern world. In this essay, I will examine how DeLillo uses characterization and dialogue in *White Noise* to show how, in a postmodern world, Technology attempts to replace God as the giver and taker of life, as the source of hope and despair, and as a uniting cultural entity.

## Analyses

Throughout the novel, DeLillo presents Technology as the source of life and the bringer of death simultaneously, a role previously thought to be reserved for God. In the postmodern, secular world of *White Noise*, that power comes from man-made Technology, though it remains frighteningly out of mankind's control. The phenomenon of "white noise," the novel's namesake, is often used in the book as a symbol for the embodiment of active, intrusive Technology. It is unsurprising, then, that the characters in the novel feel that white noise also carries an element of death. In a conversation on the subject, Jack Gladney and his wife, Babette, exchange their views of death:

> What if death is nothing but sound?
>
> Electrical noise.
>
> You hear it forever. Sound all around. How awful.
>
> Uniform, white. (189)

In this way, DeLillo encourages the reader to view Technology as carrying the power of death.

The most startling example of this is the centerpiece event in the novel—the airborne toxic event. The billowing cloud of the man-made chemical Nyodene Derivative is described by the narrator, Jack Gladney, in mythical terms as the manifestation of death itself: "The enormous dark mass moved like some death ship in a Norse legend, escorted across the night by armored creatures with spiral wings" (124). Jack's comparisons of the cloud of Nyodene D to a Viking "death ship" and of the helicopters around it to flying "armored creatures" aptly illustrate DeLillo's comparison of Technology to mythical or supernatural incarnations of death.

Jack makes the comparison between Technology and God explicit when he says, "Our fear was accompanied by a sense of awe that bordered on the religious. It is surely possible to be awed by the thing that threatens your life, to see it as a cosmic force, so much larger than yourself, more powerful, created by elemental and willful rhythms" (124). Here, Jack refers to the cloud of chemicals in an almost reverent way. His description of the cloud is similar to God as the "cosmic force" in charge of life and death.

In the novel, Technology does not merely appear to be death    5
incarnate—it truly does carry that power. DeLillo openly associates
Technology with death in the passage where Jack wonders about his
son's receding hairline: "Man's guilt in history and in the tides of his
own blood has been complicated by technology, the daily seeping
falsehearted death" (22). Here, DeLillo, through Jack, plainly tells us
that technology not only has the power of death—Technology is death,
"daily seeping" and "falsehearted."

We see this again at the beginning of Chapter 9. Here, Jack relates
that "they had to evacuate the grade school on Tuesday. Kids were
getting headaches and eye irritations, tasting metal in their mouths.
A teacher rolled on the floor and spoke foreign languages" (35). In earlier times, these sorts of events would have been attributed to the supernatural or religious—speaking in tongues is still a part of many
religions today. In the postmodern world of *White Noise,* however, the
source of these events is Technology, which is, unfortunately, nearly
omnipresent. DeLillo humorously makes this clear when Jack notes,

> Investigators said it could be the ventilating system, the paint or
> varnish, the foam insulation, the electrical insulation, the cafeteria
> food, the rays emitted by the microcomputers, the asbestos fire-
> proofing, the adhesive on shipping containers, the fumes from the
> chlorinated pool. (35)

Furthermore, just as people had no way of dealing with supernatural problems except with supernatural answers, the people in the novel
have no way to combat this problem other than with more Technology.
DeLillo uses more humor to point out the obvious irony of fighting
Technology with Technology:

> Denise and Steffie stayed home that week as men in Mylex suits
> and respirator masks made systematic sweeps of the building with

> infrared detecting and measuring equipment. Because Mylex is
> itself a suspect material, the results tended to be ambiguous and a
> second round of more rigorous detection had to be scheduled. (35)

DeLillo makes a final nod to the irony of Technology being used to stop
Technology when Jack hears a rumor about "a man dying during the
inspection of the grade school, one of the masked Mylex-suited men,
heavy-booted and bulky. Collapsed and died, went the story that was
going around, in a classroom on the second floor" (40). In this way, we
can see how DeLillo portrays people as at the mercy of their Technology,
just as people in an earlier time had been at the mercy of God.

People in a postmodern society replace God with Technology as the
source of death, so they must also attempt to replace God with Technology as the source of life. However, in this respect, Technology is not
quite able to replicate God's position. A good example of this is the
adult class that Babette, Jack's wife, teaches at the Congregational
Church, where "she is teaching them how to stand, sit, and walk" (27).
It is no coincidence that Babette is offering them this pseudoscientific
hope of a healthy life in a church. Jack comments, "It isn't clear to me
why they want to improve their posture. We seem to believe it is possible to ward off death by following rules of good grooming" (27). Jack
seems to recognize the absurdity of relying on good posture alone to
stave off death, but these people have lost God as a source of that hope.
With Technology unable to offer anything to improve their spiritual
lives, they can only take lessons on how to improve their natural
health. This, of course, does little to help their spiritual anxiety.

The fear of death as the ultimate unknown is a powerful problem
inherent in the human condition, and so it is a universal theme in works
of fiction. In the past, religion was a powerful source of psychic comfort
and a primary shield against spiritual despair. God was viewed as both
the source of death and the cure for the fear of death. The idea that a
good man need not fear death, because there was an afterlife for good
people, was an example of this. God was thought to be the ultimate
arbiter of life and death, and through his will death was understood to

be an acceptable thing, a necessary thing. In *White Noise*, DeLillo taps into this powerful theme in the context of postmodernism—in a highly secularized world where Technology is seen as the source of life and death, Technology must also become the source of hope and despair. Once again, however, Technology is not able to completely replicate God.

When Jack goes to the ATM to check his bank account balance, 10 DeLillo shows us how people like Jack, who lack a source of identity and spiritual comfort, can get some sort of hope and security from Technology in the absence of God:

> I went to the automated teller machine to check my balance. I inserted my card, entered my secret code, tapped out my request. The figure on the screen roughly corresponded to my independent estimate, feebly arrived at after long searches through documents, tormented arithmetic. Waves of relief and gratitude flowed over me. The system had blessed my life. I felt its support and approval. The system hardware, the mainframe sitting in a locked room in some distant city . . . The system was invisible, which made it all the more impressive, all the more disquieting to deal with. (46)

Like God, the "invisible system" of Technology has "blessed" Jack's life and given his existence affirmation. However, it is significant to note that this affirmation is not really a cure for Jack's despair. The system is unable to truly ground Jack's identity or tell him who he is—it can only simulate it.

Technology in *White Noise* is also able to mimic God's ability to instill the fear of death in someone or to alleviate it. After Jack is exposed to Nyodene Derivate, he is told that the substance is potentially fatal and he will die from it. Jack says, "I'm tentatively scheduled to die. It won't happen tomorrow or the next day. But it is in the works" (192). Thus, DeLillo has literally had Technology place the fear of death inside Jack. Similarly, a major plot line in *White Noise* has Technology used to combat this fear of death. Dylar is a pill that "specifically interacts with neurotransmitters in the brain that are related to the fear of death" (190).

Babette sleeps with a man in exchange for the drug, because she cannot get over her fear of death and can think of no other way to help herself other than Technology. From these two examples, it can be seen how the fear of death is deeply rooted in Technology—Technology gives Jack the fear of death and attempts to give Babette relief from that fear, just as God used to. Of course, it is telling that DeLillo notes that Dylar does not seem to work. Just as Jack's life-affirming experience at the ATM does not actually help with his identity crisis, Dylar cannot actually alleviate Babette's fear of death. It is a simulacrum—a poor copy which no longer has an original.

Technology in *White Noise* also imitates the belief in God's presence as a uniting cultural entity. In a postmodern world, a belief in God cannot be assumed, and Technology attempts to fill that role. Mass media and mass consumerism attempt to homogenize and unite the world as a global culture. The tabloids that Babette reads to Old Man Treadwell illustrate Technology's attempt to replace belief in God as a source of cultural unity. Religious myths sometimes serve a purpose of both maintaining a culture and relieving worries about life though tales of the holy or supernatural. Tabloids attempt to serve the same purpose— they are filled with absurd and fantastical stories about UFOs, God, and celebrities. They are the mythologies of mass media. They, too, maintain American culture and offer people like Old Man Treadwell some kind of relief from heavy, worrisome thoughts.

In *White Noise*, the character Murray often serves as a spokesman for the view that supermarkets, television, and advertising are the world's new sacred temples and the new mysticism. For example, in the supermarket, Murray talks to Babette about the Tibetan view on death. He then adds, "That's what I think of whenever I come in here. This place recharges us spiritually, it prepares us, it's a gateway or a pathway. Look how bright. It's full of psychic data ... Here we don't die, we shop. But the difference is less marked than you'd think" (37–38). While DeLillo probably does not intend for the reader to take Murray completely seriously, he does highlight the similarities between the temple and the supermarket. Supermarkets appear to be Technology's version of a temple or church, though obviously they cannot give their visitors a true "spiritual recharge," as Murray puts it; rather, supermarkets are a postmodern imitation of real temples, just as Technology is a simulacrum of God.

Another conversation with Murray leads to the semi-spiritual properties of television. He tells Jack that he will sometimes be "watching TV into the early hours, listening carefully, taking notes. A great and humbling experience, let me tell you. Close to mystical" (50). It appears that television, in Murray's view, offers people a gateway to a new kind of spirituality. He says it produces "chants. Like mantras. '*Coke is it. Coke is it. Coke is it.*' The medium practically overflows with sacred formulas if we can remember how to respond innocently and get past our irritation, weariness and disgust" (51). Murray's references to the "mystical," "spiritual," and "sacred" show, according to him, how television replicates the unifying effects of religion. However, given the absurd context of the character and the book, DeLillo is writing Murray as a spokesman for Technology. Given the characters' spiritual and psychological issues, mass media is Technology's failed attempt at replacing real religions.

In the postmodern society in *White Noise*, the idea of God (the original) has *not* been fully replaced by Technology (the simulated), though the simulacrum has made every effort to do so. Technology has the power of death, but it cannot fully mimic the power of life. It is able to instill the fear of death and is able to give false hope to people, but cannot truly bring them peace. Finally, Technology functions successfully as a uniting cultural entity in the form of mass media and globalization, but it fails to provide the uniting psychic relief that the belief in God was able to bring for centuries. This is in line with the theme of the novel: simulacra attempt and fail to fully replicate and replace the originals. Through the characters and their dialogue, DeLillo shows how Technology as a replacement for God is merely a simulacrum, a lesser copy in the absence of the original.

15

## WORK CITED

DeLillo, Don. *White Noise*. New York: Penguin, 1999. Print.

Reading to Write

1. Jason Rose capitalizes the word "technology" in this analysis. Why do you think he made that choice? How might this unconventional use of capitalization relate to his argument? What effect does that choice have on you as a reader?

2. Consider Rose's thesis statement, his claim that "Technology attempts to replace God as the giver and taker of life, as the source of hope and despair, and as a uniting cultural entity" (paragraph 1). Throughout the paper—and especially in the final paragraph—Rose makes an argument about the efficacy of technology in replacing the supernatural. Where in this analysis does he shift from showing technology's "attempt" to "replace God" to evaluating its efficacy in doing so? How does this look at efficacy relate to his title and the notion of a "simulacrum"?

3. Rose analyzes characterization and dialogue to support his claim about a particular theme in *White Noise*. Choose an important theme to trace in a novel or another literary text you're reading for class. Use your analysis of one or two literary conventions to support and illustrate your claim about that theme.

# Televisuality in *The Virgin Suicides*

## Anne Hart

*Anne Hart wrote this analysis for her writing course American Dreams, Gothic Landscapes at Duke University. Her assignment was to use "previous research on postwar suburban culture as a critical lens" for an analysis of Jeffrey Eugenides' novel* The Virgin Suicides. *Her teacher, Keith Wilhite, nominated Hart's essay for the way it shows her "sophisticated understanding of U.S. suburbia and its relationship to the emergence of 'televisual' culture after WWII" and the way Hart "uses this context to provide an insightful interpretation of the novel's narrative technique."*

S ince the emergence of television and suburbia as characteristic staples of American life, the relationship between them has become increasingly complex. Originally, the two entities became linked through their dual powers of influence on the beliefs and culture of American society. Television proscribed a "better" way of life for viewers to emulate, and suburbia became the perfect setting for fulfilling personal fantasies prompted by television programs. Suburbia, in addition, facilitated television's popularity; because of the physically fractured nature of suburbs in relation to their surroundings, people were more likely to stay at home and be entertained by their televisions. As time went on, television became an even more important cultural mainstay. The heavy flow of news, information, and entertainment into American households made possible by television increasingly framed the way people viewed the world, and as such, it greatly influenced their lives. Television is, in essence, one of the most significant cultural influences present in today's and yesterday's societies.

## Analyses

Jeffrey Eugenides' novel *The Virgin Suicides* revises television's central role in American suburbia by transferring the medium's function onto the interactions between the Lisbon family and their neighborhood community. Eugenides first establishes the dominance of television in suburban lives through his depiction of various families' television habits. He then builds upon this foundation by constructing a relationship of reciprocal gazing between the Lisbons and their neighborhood; in effect, the Lisbons are being watched by their neighbors as if they were a television program, and they watch their neighbors in the same way. In doing these two things, Eugenides first confirms and then twists ideas held about the role of television in suburbia.

Both George Lipsitz and Lynn Spigel argue that television earned its lasting role in Americans' lives through its influence over the ideologies of viewers. Television shows exemplified the "right" or "perfect" way of life and suggested to audiences that, in pursuing these examples of life, one could find happiness. All aspects of sitcoms—from the mother's outfits to the types of family interactions depicted—were subtle suggestions to viewers that if one's life matched that featured on screen, one would be more accomplished and content. Through this power, television gained a central role in both the household and in viewers' minds. The fact that the medium is close at hand during many salient moments in the plotline shows television's central role in the characters' lives in the novel. Just after Cecilia's suicide, the narrator notes the contrast between the city and their suburb, saying that "up close, yellow house lights [were] coming on, revealing families around televisions" (35). Eugenides emphasizes television's overwhelming importance in the lives of the characters by pairing its presence with this poignant moment. By joining the two things, he makes an association between television and an earth-shattering event: a young girl's suicide. At this point, the neighborhood has not yet found out about the suicide, showing how oblivious they are to reality. If television did not have such a constant presence in suburban life, people might have noticed something like an ambulance blaring down their street. But barely anything could interrupt the families' total focus on the continuous electric flow of the television.

In another instance, following Cecilia's funeral, Mr. Lisbon does nothing but watch baseball games on television, even when visitors come to offer their condolences (49). Here the idea of television as a central force is exhibited in Mr. Lisbon's dependence on the appliance, and it is also furthered by being turned into a kind of compassionate presence within the household. Mr. Lisbon is not very receptive to neighbors visiting after his daughter's funeral, and so he focuses un-waveringly on the television. It becomes a kind of emotional crutch; it is a way for him to deal with his pain. Eugenides' portrayal of the television in these two functions—as a central focus and supportive crutch—therefore brings together not only the ideas of Lipsitz and Spi-gel, but also those of Marsha Cassidy. Cassidy shows that television's initial influences came in great part from its companionate, pseudo-social interactions with viewers through daytime participation pro-grams. By offering viewers a venue of contact with the outside world from their own suburban homes, the television was able to seamlessly enter the domestic sphere as a member of the family with which to connect. It is through this relationship that Mr. Lisbon is able to gain a kind of comfort—no matter how strange—from the television. As a part of the family, both as an appliance and a companion, the televi-sion has earned the family's love and trust through its assertive and supportive role.

Aside from the characters' actual television watching, there is a televisual relationship in the reciprocal gazing between the Lisbon girls and the rest of their neighborhood. The narrators provide the most apparent and excessive example of the neighborhood's voyeurism. The boys constantly watch the Lisbon girls, monitoring their every activity and recovering every possession of theirs that they can. The boys' surveillance of the household and the girls defines an immense portion of their lives. They have watched the girls since they were young children, like a favorite old television show that they never tired of.

5

## Analyses

When re-entering their old tree house as adolescents, they discover that "the oblong window we'd cut with a handsaw years ago still looked onto the front of the Lisbon house" (202). Their obsession is a common bond that has kept them friends after many years; while everything around them changed as they grew older, the girls remained a constant. In their homes, the constant focus on the Lisbon family continued. The narrators mention that "around dinner tables, our conversations inevitably turned to the family's predicament" (171). The role of the Lisbon family as a program of sorts continues in other neighborhood households. Neighbors discuss the most recent happenings in the Lisbons' lives as if they were talking about what happened on the most recent episode of a beloved television show. Toward the end of the novel, the boys actually venture up close to the household and describe how "the light inside the house made us invisible outside, and we stood inches from the window but unseen, as though looking in at Lux from another plane of existence" (208). To them, Lux, and everyone else inside the household, does indeed seem to come from another dimension of reality; the characters in their program are real but somehow inaccessible. They are unknowable and untouchable, but they exist right in front of them.

The boys' relationship with the Lisbon girls demonstrates Lipsitz and Spigel's ideas about the centrality of television. They argue that television became a necessary and desired facet of suburbia by combining entertainment for all ages with the legitimization of consumerism through shows and commercials, all compounded by suburbia's physical structure, which made television the go-to source for entertainment. In fact, the importance of television is exaggerated because the Lisbon family is always "on." The plot of their show is constantly developing, because these girls are alive in reality; they are not a television show, but instead take on a program's function in the lives of the boys. This is, perhaps, why the boys have become so obsessed with them: if they ever stop watching, they might miss something, so as a result they spend much of their time observing them. The girls are—as television is in suburban culture as a whole—dominant in the boys' thoughts and lives. The boys' strong desire not to miss a moment of the girls' lives comes from an endeavor to know them. These beautiful, powerful girls are like a mystery for which they must gradually collect all of the clues. As is the case on television, they reason that they can piece the solution together by collecting artifacts and intensely observing the girls' actions.

The Lisbon girls gaze back at the boys just as they are being gazed upon. However, in their case, the neighborhood "program" holds a much different, non-televisual function. While they do watch neighborhood activities, it is not with the same desperate attention that the boys give to them. They are not obsessed with events outside their windows, but rather the girls watch because it is all they have as a connection with the outside world. The program of the neighborhood outside becomes the focus of their attention by default. With the girls in a world devoid of outside contact or entertainment, it is no wonder that the boys discover that "[the girls] had been looking out at us just as intensely as we had been looking in" (124). Again, there is a centrality of the neighborhood in the girls' lives that is akin to the preeminence of television in the suburbs. The girls watch not to gain knowledge, in this case, but rather to be entertained. In some instances, the girls may be looking for more than just entertainment in their neighborhood show. The narrators say that "we decided that the girls had been trying to talk to us all along, to elicit our help, but we'd been too infatuated to listen. Our surveillance had been so focused we missed nothing but a simple returned gaze" (199). Marsha Cassidy's ideas about television's role as a companion are applicable to the Lisbon girls. According to the boys, the girls were reaching out to them for help like they might to a friend. For the girls, the "program" of the neighborhood is to connect people and events in the world outside their homes, and with this attempt at connection, the girls hope for interaction and interference from the world they watch.

The televisual relationship between the narrators and the girls gradually transforms and intensifies throughout the course of the novel, showing that, for both groups, intent observation of others functions as a means of social interaction. Before the suicides, the boys watched the girls because they loved them and wanted to know every-thing about them. As the novel progresses, these motives remain, but they are also joined by a concerned interest in the girls' lives when the suicides begin. On the other hand, there is little evidence of the girls watching the boys before Mrs. Lisbon puts them on lockdown inside the house. Only once their mother begins heavily restricting their con-tact with the outside world do the girls focus their attention on the neighborhood outside their windows. Though it may not be the girls' expressed desire to learn everything about the boys and their neigh-borhood, it is through watching them that they discover the easiest, most direct, and most natural form of communication and interaction with them. It is through watching the other group's actions that both the girls and the boys feel like they are connected to and "know" them, and this knowledge is a form of contact.

By the end of the novel, the two-way surveillance has concluded. The boys' favorite show has finally had its series finale and is taken off the air. The ending demonstrates that the social contact made possible through surveillance is nowhere near strong enough to really interact with or help someone. The boys reach out by watching and document-ing, but take no tangible steps to help the girls until it is too late. They did not realize that watching would not be enough; when watching their own televisions, observation is more than enough to count as interaction. The model of social interaction the boys experienced with their televisions—what Cassidy described as a companionate relationship—does not successfully carry over into reality. Eugenides thus shows that examples set by television are, when applied to real-ity, anything but ideal. When cleaning out the Lisbons' old house, "the last thing Mr. Hedlie threw out was the empty television set" (228). The broken television signifies the collapse of the Lisbon program for the neighborhood—the show is truly over. Despite its end, one of the boys nonetheless picks up the set and takes it home with him as an-other artifact. This symbolic act shows that, even though they are no longer alive and can no longer be watched, the boys will never truly be finished observing and thinking about the Lisbon girls.

The novel distorts and plays with Lipsitz and Spigel's idea of television as a central and constantly emulated facet of suburban life. It certainly establishes the appliance as a fundamental part of life, both literally and figuratively. The Lisbon girls are arguably the most dominant presence in the neighborhood, yet—unlike television—nobody copies them. In this way, the girls diverge from the function of television discussed by Lipsitz and Spigel. Eugenides also lays bare the differences between the perfect suburban life as portrayed on television and the characters' suburban reality in a neighborhood outside of Detroit by projecting a sense of ineptitude on many neighborhood events. The fathers attempt to drag the fatal fence from its foundation, but after many unsuccessful attempts, they have to call a company to do it for them (55). The television version of this event would be completely different: it would feature strong, heroic fathers working together to remove the fence, and while they would exert manly effort, there would be no complications or failures. In another instance, the paramedics arrive on the first page of the novel moving "much too slowly," and the fat one says, "This ain't TV, folks, this is how fast we go" (3). From the beginning of the story, Eugenides contrasts reality with television, showing how real life can never measure up to the expectations projected onto it by a television-watching public.

Eugenides undermines the concept of television's function and influence in suburbia, showing that instead of a positive force, televisual effects can be quite damaging. The boys are misled by the dominant force they have been surrounded by their whole lives, and they have subconsciously incorporated television's function into their own minds. Since their televisions serve as supportive, companionate entities with which they can interact through observation, they transfer the same principles onto their interactions with the Lisbon girls. They believe that their form of contact with the girls, watching them, is a legitimate expression of outreach and interest. They treat the girls as if they were characters in a television show. At the end of the novel, the boys finally begin to see that, despite the countless hours and days spent watching and discussing them, they had never known the girls and "will never find the pieces to put them back together" (249). Eugenides thus shows that voyeurism is not a legitimate form of social interaction, and it is not a successful way to gain knowledge.

Eugenides uses his characters' experiences with television and televisual ways of looking to show that, overall, suburbia is an extremely dreary and depressing setting in which to live one's life, especially as a teenager. Teens need stimulation and social and physical room to grapple with and form their identities. In suburbia, this is hard to do in a literal sense, so—being creatures of adaptation—they find another venue in which to do so. For Eugenides, teenagers in suburbia need to experience excitement and challenges as part of their natural development. While the characters in his book do this with televisual voyeurism, suburban teenagers may find other potentially more dangerous ways to have these experiences. Read in this way, *The Virgin Suicides* could be seen as a call for suburban reform. Suburbanites can accept and embrace where they live, but they should also realize that harm could befall their children because of the lack of social and cultural stimulation found in suburbs. While suburbs are supposedly perfect and sterile, this novel shows that they could be much darker places and in need of change.

## WORKS CITED

Cassidy, Marsha. "The Dawn of Daytime: Reaching Out to Women Across America." *What Women Watched: Daytime Television in the 1950s.* Austin: U of Texas P, 2005. 27–48. Print.

Eugenides, Jeffrey. *The Virgin Suicides.* New York: Warner, 1993. Print.

Lipsitz, George. "The Meaning of Memory: Family, Class, and Ethnicity in Early Network Television Programs." *Cultural Anthropology* 1.4 (1986): 355–87. Print.

Spigel, Lynn. *Welcome to the Dreamhouse: Popular Media and Postwar Suburbs.* Durham: Duke UP, 2001. Print.

## Reading to Write

1. In her analysis of "televisuality" in *The Virgin Suicides*, Anne Hart analyzes literal references to television watching in the novel, the ways in which the Lisbon girls function as a figurative "show" for others, and the ways the Lisbon girls watch the neighborhood. How does Hart's use of outside sources support her analysis of these different aspects of "televisuality"?

2. Hart links her analysis of the role of television and voyeurism in Eugenides' novel to a larger critique of suburban culture. Do you agree with this critique? Why or why not?

3. Write an analysis of a novel or another literary text. As Hart does, use outside sources to contextualize and support your argument.

# The Domestication of Death: Preserving the Suburban Status Quo in *The Virgin Suicides*

## Lindsey Arthur

> *Lindsey Arthur wrote this literary analysis in her first semester of college at Duke University. Keith Wilhite, her instructor for* Writing 20, American Dreams, Gothic Landscapes, *asked students to use their "previous research on postwar suburban culture as a critical lens" in their reading of Jeffrey Eugenides' novel* The Virgin Suicides. *Arthur writes: "Learning how to synthesize different texts (a novel and several nonfiction research papers) as we did in this class is something that I believe has helped me write persuasive papers throughout college, not only in my English classes, but in any course that requires critical and creative thinking."*

T he idea that every day is ordinary is a common perception of suburbia. Every family in the homogeneous community lives according to well-established but unspoken rules of social etiquette, tending to their manicured lawns and decorating their freshly painted two-story homes with Christmas lights every December. Separated from the crime, poverty, and diversity of the city, the suburbs tend to exude a sort of calm, reflective of their apparent adherence to the status quo. Jeffrey Eugenides questions this stereotypical assumption in his novel *The Virgin Suicides*, drawing attention to what he considers to be the carefully concealed dark side of suburban culture. The novel suggests that this aspect of suburbia remains hidden largely as a result of the phenomenon of domestication, the communal consensus to "make the unthinkable ordinary" (Brown 86). It is not a total absence of tragedy, hardship, and adversity that enables this façade of perfection to exist. In fact, Eugenides sees the suburbs not as impervious to the trials of the outside world, but rather as simply less willing to acknowledge their existence in order to preserve the suburbs' image as utopian communities removed from the struggles of real life. This effort to take the inherent elements of instability and fear out of even the most incomprehensible tragedies pervades Eugenides' novel, suggesting that life in suburbia may be more complicated than it appears from the outside.

Although the community may try to eliminate hardship from suburban life by addressing difficult issues with "alert not alarm," it cannot fully erase life's inherent struggles from even the most insulated communities (Brown 78). The suicides of five teenage girls in a Detroit suburb exemplify the application and limitations of this carefully constructed veneer of perfection. The girls' actions shatter the stability of the traditional Lisbon family and draw the attention of the surrounding community. With little else to distract them, a number of adolescent boys become fixated on the lives of the girls and the motivation behind their suicides. The parents of these boys, in addition to much of the surrounding community, find themselves simultaneously intrigued and repulsed by the gradual disintegration of the Lisbon family. "Around the dinner tables, conversations inevitably turned to the family's predicament," as though the suicides are no different from any other form of neighborhood gossip (171). In this way, the suburban community seeks to dilute the issue through dinnertime banter while simultaneously distancing itself from the gravity of the Lisbons' problems. Because this response demonstrates that the primary concern of the majority is to preserve its own sense of security and the prestige that is associated with the "tony suburb known more for debutante parties than for funerals of debutante-aged girls," the domestication of the suicides appears to be an ideal solution (96).

In the aftermath of Cecilia's death, the neighbors begin to worry about the dangers of the Lisbon family's fence that Cecilia used to kill herself. Their focus on the fence illustrates a concern for the trivial elements of the suicide that can be easily handled, rather than the tragedy of the event itself and the underlying causes that are of actual significance. If they can address the issue of the fence, they believe, they can take concrete action and move away from the infinitely more complicated aspects of the situation with which they are not prepared to deal. This emphasis on measurable rather than meaningful action relates to the rationale behind domestication. Incomprehensible and overwhelmingly complicated situations cannot be deciphered quickly or easily because of the emotion, fear, and uncertainty that plague those who are involved. Domestication solves this dilemma in that it accepts and even encourages an oversimplification of the problem. The fence is therefore used as a scapegoat of sorts for Cecilia's act, symbolizing the uncontrollable violence, death, and unhappiness from which the community strives to separate itself. In order to erase the physical evidence of the suicide and uphold the high standards of sub-urban decorum, the neighbors decide to remove the fence. This becomes an almost patriotic endeavor, with "all those lawyers, doctors, and investment bankers locked arm in arm in the trench" creating "a moment [during which the] . . . century was noble again" (54). In this way, the community manages to turn the terrible misfortune of a local family into an activity that actually builds the morale of those involved and evokes a sense of confidence. This approach, while potentially comforting to the surrounding community, ignores the feelings and wishes of the Lisbon family, the true victims of the suicide.

Even when the community dares to address the emotional impact of the tragedy, they do so in a generalized way so as to "cleanse [it] of any fearsome element" (Brown 79). The principal of the school vaguely references the issue during convocation, acknowledging only that "it has been a long, hard summer for some of us here today. But today begins a new year of hopes and goals" (104). The nature of this brief reference, which further underscores the unwillingness of the community at large to bring the heart of the issue out into the open, is based upon the general assumption that even catastrophes of this magnitude can be overcome without difficulty. Rather than encouraging free and honest discussion, the brevity and intentional ambiguity of the principal's statement does nothing more than to increase the stigma around a subject that is already considered to be taboo. It is as if he believes that by euphemizing Cecilia's suicide, he can erase some of the horror from the minds of the Lisbon girls as well as their peers.

The "Day of Grieving," implemented by the school to send the mes-    5
sage that "grief is natural . . . [and] overcoming it is a matter of choice," creates a situation in which "the tragedy [is] diffused and universal-ized" (104). The words chosen to describe the event by the principal's wife, Mrs. Woodhouse, exude the essence of domestication, creating a trivial slogan of sorts to deal with the tragedy. If "grief is natural," but "overcoming it is a matter of choice," then the school is suggesting that the sorrow of the Lisbon family is voluntary and unnecessary (104). Given its later use for the advertisement of a diet product, this slogan domesticates the issue and clearly indicates that the grief and loss of the Lisbon family are not taken very seriously. If emotional recovery, like weight loss, can be achieved with hard work, then the Lisbon fam-ily's inability to recover is a result of their own laziness. Despite the statement's falsity, its implications resonate with the girls, causing them to withdraw from their peers and keep to themselves even dur-ing school hours. The Lisbon girls, for whom the day was supposedly designed, do not participate, perhaps because of the superficial nature of the event. The insincere and almost perfunctory approach of the school trivializes their suffering, thereby resulting in more harm than good.

This overgeneralization for the sake of controlling the "loaded emotionalism" of the issue appears once again in the newspaper arti-cles and television programs that attempt to deal with the suicides of the Lisbon girls (Ohles 216). Despite the significant amount of media attention, coverage of the suicides fails to go beyond the surface and explore the difficult and potentially cruel truths of the matter. Hardly mentioning the Lisbon girls at all, many of the articles simply "inform the readership of a common social danger" faced by teenagers as a whole (96). The use of statistics and an overview of "the causes of

Analyses

suicide in general" in place of specific names and meaningful details shift the focus away from the suburban home and eliminates any sense of personal relevance from the topic, thereby greatly decreasing the inherent element of fear (98). Even this minimal coverage, however, evokes negative responses from neighbors who claim to believe that the girls should be free to "rest in peace" (98). Mothers who do not want to imagine their own children taking their lives find any suggestion of such an eventuality to be both terrifying and offensive.

Instead of responding to the suicides of the remaining Lisbon girls with sorrow or even shock, much of the suburban community returns to its traditional lifestyle almost without hesitation. Summer continues as usual, and following a toxic spill at the River Rouge Plant, "debutantes [cry] over the misfortune of coming out in a season everyone would remember for its bad smell" (234). In typical suburban style, however, catastrophe is averted by simply avoiding the severity of the problem and domesticating the troublesome side effects. This accommodation comes in "the ingenious solution of making the theme of . . . Alice's debutante party 'Asphyxiation'" (234). Little consideration is given to the spill's destructive effects on the already compromised natural environment, an issue thought to lie beyond the concern and control of "guiltless" suburbanites. This sense of detachment directly parallels the generally apathetic response to the suicides. The narrators' parents, who "reacted to the final suicides with mild shock, as though they'd been expecting them or something much worse, as though they'd seen it all before," choose to view the events as something outside of and entirely separate from their safe and comfortable lives (231). Approaching the suicides with such inattention frees them from the pain that would come with any legitimate investment of energy, thereby enabling them to continue their seemingly untroubled lives without interruption. This sense of relief after the final suicides indicates not blindness to reality, but rather a carefully constructed manipulation of the facts to create a scenario more consistent with the "better, finer, more elegant patterns of life" inherent in the suburban "realization of the democratic dream" (Gutek 16).

Families assuage their fears evoked by the suicides by assuring themselves "with the notion that a dark force beset the girls, some monolithic evil [they] . . . weren't responsible for" (177). Accepting this simplistic conclusion, many seem to believe that the unidentified cause of the suicides can and should be contained behind the decaying walls of the Lisbon house. The general perception of the source of the suicides as a foreign, monolithic entity resembles the general view of Americans towards Soviet communism. Because of their classification of the Lisbon family as "different," the neighbors strive to separate themselves as much as possible. Just as the Red Scare and McCarthyism sought to prevent the communist infiltration of America, the community wants, above all, to quarantine what they identify as the virus emitted upon Cecilia's suicide. As it is often simpler and more popular to accuse than to strive to understand, the community follows in the path of Senator McCarthy by placing the blame on a single, easily identifiable facet of a much more complex problem. To adopt a monolithic explanation certainly hinders, and in some cases inhibits, any true understanding of the matter. Though such an explanation undoubtedly makes the suicides easier to accept, neither the Lisbon girls nor the source of their apparent grief can be fully comprehended when viewed through such a narrow lens, thereby preventing the administration of any form of valuable recovery or aid. In this way, the concern of the neighbors appears to stem more from a desire to keep the ugly truth outside of their peaceful suburban homes than from a genuine concern for the Lisbon family.

The Lisbon family, obedient to the wishes of Mrs. Lisbon, applies these same generalizations to the surrounding community. Despite the general unwillingness to acknowledge the existence of problems within their own communities, suburbanites recognize the threats posed by the outside world and grow increasingly wary of associating with anyone outside of what they consider to be their comfort zone. In fact, these suburban dwellers may be excessively concerned about what they perceive to be the dangers of "the mix of classes and racial and ethnic groups that characterize urban areas," given their decision to insulate among those who share their general lifestyles, views, and socioeconomic status (Miller 394). This exaggerated fear of "outsiders," exemplified by Mrs. Lisbon's attempt to confine her daughters within their home, manifests itself in the bomb shelter she creates in the basement. Initially intended to store "an abundant supply of canned goods downstairs, as well as fresh water and other preparations against nuclear attack," the bomb shelter is ultimately used as a means of storing the items necessary to enable the Lisbon family to remain within the house at all times (163). The utilization of the bomb shelter to facilitate the imprisonment of the girls and "protect" them from any and all potential dangers implies a great faith in the material world. It is as though Mr. and Mrs. Lisbon believe that all problems can be solved within the home with the use of the appropriate tangible goods, and this faith in consumer products is in itself a form of domestication. Viewing the suicide of their daughter Cecilia as a simple crisis that can be resolved with canned foods and bottled water, the Lisbon parents do not take into account the complexity of the grief faced by their daughters. Trapping them within the four walls of their house cannot shelter them from the hardships of life, particularly given the presence of tragedy within their very family. This clearly indicates that the separation of the Lisbon family from the surrounding neighborhood is a mutual initiative. The failure of the Lisbons and their neighbors to understand one another parallels the Cold War relationship between the United States and the Soviet Union. In both cases, each prefers to remain detached in order to retain their preconceived notions. They view the world in terms of black and white in order to avoid the complex but more enlightening shades of gray that exist somewhere in between. This enables them to remain complacent in the comfort of their beliefs rather than forcing them to reassess their thinking.

10      The practice of domestication may initially appear to be harmless or even therapeutic in situations of distress. While this is perhaps true in the short term, the passage of time illuminates the weaknesses of such an approach. Selective vision does not eradicate the most

harmful elements of a problem, but rather merely disguises them behind an "eligible scapegoat" (Ohles 216). Although the suicides clearly
signify a larger problem, the general unwillingness to delve into the
murky and potentially frightening origins of the girls' actions renders
no discovery possible. The narrators lament that they "will never be
able to find the pieces [of the puzzle that is the girls' suicides] to put
them back together," yet this defeat is not inevitable. Instead of accepting the suicides as the result of a collection of unknown events outside
of their control, the community has the alternative of exploring the
matter in pursuit of a greater understanding of the reasons behind it. It
is, ultimately, not the suicides of five teenage girls, but rather the communal response of the majority that is of the utmost importance. The
"demise of [the] . . . neighborhood" after the girls' suicides could perhaps have been prevented had the community been willing to consider
the possibility that the suicides reflected the limitations of Grosse Point
and the need for change (243–44). Even today, the suburban dream
possesses the capacity to both inspire and to blind. In this way, Eugenides suggests not that suburban culture is inherently unhealthy,
but rather that the unwillingness of suburbanites to evaluate themselves and their established norms can impede the evolution necessary for society.

## WORKS CITED

Brown, JoAnne. " 'A is for Atom, B is for Bomb': Civil Defense in American
    Public Education, 1948–1993." *Journal of American History* 75.1 (1988):
    68–90. Print.

Eugenides, Jeffrey. *The Virgin Suicides*. New York: Warner, 1993. Print.

Gutek, Gerald. "Unsolved Problems of the 1960s: A Legacy of the Depression
    of the 1930s." *Peabody Journal of Education* 43.1 (1965): 13–17. Print.

Miller, Laura. "Family Togetherness and the Suburban Ideal." *Sociological
    Forum* 10.3 (1995): 393–418. Print.

Ohles, John. "What Is Behind the Criticism of the Schools?" *Peabody Journal
    of Education* 36.4 (1959): 214–18. Print.

## Reading to Write

1. "Domestication" is a key word in Lindsey Arthur's analysis of *The Virgin Suicides*. She defines domestication by quoting an outside source in her first paragraph. Trace her use of forms of this word throughout the analysis, noting the specific manifestations of "domestication" she identifies in the novel. How do the examples Arthur provides expand and reinforce the initial definition she gives of "domestication"?

2. Both Lindsey Arthur and Anne Hart (p. 255) consider an aspect of suburban culture in their analyses of the same novel. In what ways are their analyses similar? In what ways do they differ? Do you find one more effective than the other? Why?

3. Get together with a small group to discuss a literary text you've read for class. Pay attention to differences and similarities in your interpretations. Discuss the passages (and perhaps secondary sources) that support your interpretation. Either collaboratively or on your own, write a literary analysis. Consider using a key term, as Arthur uses "domestication" and Hart uses "televisuality," to make your argument.

# 8 ～

## MIXING GENRES
## Lyrics, Collages, Braids

W hat do you want to accomplish with your writing? Do you want to make connections, create scenes in your reader's mind, delight, inform, persuade, or provide a context for reflection? What genre will best allow you to achieve your goals? These questions encourage you to consider purpose and its relation to genre. You might already be aware of genres that help you inform or persuade your reader, but which genres allow readers to meditate on a concept or consider a paradox? Which genre might best help a writer express the pressures of college life or create a particular mood?

There are times when, in order to achieve your purpose, it's appropriate to use the conventions of more than one genre, as Kristin Taylor does in her braided essay "Freeing the Caged Bird: My Conversations with Maya Angelou," or when you need to see the conventions you have been taught ("avoid sentence fragments") as fluid rather than fixed, as Amy Ho does in "The Yin and the Yang of Things." All of the pieces in this chapter contain autobiographical elements, but they move beyond the constraints of linear narrative or the conventions of a single genre.

Mixed genres that might, at first, seem unfamiliar draw from familiar generic conventions—whether from literary or visual arts. In composing *braided essays*, for example, writers employ the conventions of three separate genres in order to create an artistic whole. *Lyric essays* blur the lines between poetry and prose, demonstrating an attention to language, image, white space, sound, and rhythm. Just as visual artists create collages, bringing together disparate images for a unified effect, writers of *collage essays* assemble seemingly disparate experiences, topics, or ideas, integrating them through repetition, intentional juxtaposition, or some other pattern.

In linking your purpose to genre, it helps to think about how you might organize your essay: spatially, architecturally, chronologically, by a pattern of images, or through repetition. When choosing the appropriate genre for your writing, one starting place is to think visually. What, for example, might be the writer's purpose in creating a text that resembles a mosaic, stairs, two lines intersecting, parallel lines, or a spiral? A mosaic might contain a collection of vignettes, definitions, perhaps even visual images—all arranged to create a larger picture. An essay represented by intersecting lines might consist of three sections: one section about one person or experience, a section about a different person or experience, and a third in which the two come together. Thinking visually (architecturally, geometrically, or cinematically) will provide options beyond familiar generic structures, but those familiar structures—the conventions you already know—can also aid in achieving your purpose.

As you read the poem and essays in this chapter, consider the ways in which each writer's mixing of generic conventions helps reveal and accomplish purpose. Then consider your own purpose for a piece you will write and decide which generic conventions will best suit that purpose.

# Nana's

## John Buonomo

> John Buonomo wrote "Nana's" in a poetry workshop at Saint Joseph's University. In this poem, he offers a collage of words that help create a larger picture of a particular place. Buonomo explains that he "tried to convey an environment through . . . images that can be read . . . in any order," demonstrating "the versatility of language use."

pottery          vegetables          old hands
sky              tea steeps           leafy chatter
whiskers         yes                  bumblebees
this is how it seems.

---

### Reading to Write

1. What senses are evoked in this collage of words?

2. How does the last line of the poem—"this is how it seems"—affect your understanding of the images that precede it?

3. Think about a particular person or place that is important to you and make a list of sensory details you associate with that person or place. Write a collage poem or essay that includes those details. If you choose to write an essay, use the items on your list as section titles.

# The Yin and the Yang of Things

## Amy Ho

*Amy Ho wrote "The Yin and the Yang of Things" for an Advanced Composition class at the University of Arizona. Her teacher, Tammie Kennedy, nominated this piece as "a stellar example of the lyrical essay." In her assignment, Kennedy provided this guidance: "The essay should be alive and full of new spaces in which meaning can germinate. It should invite mediation rather than provide answers. Focus on the quest, not the destination." Ho says that she kept the sections of this essay brief to provide readers "room for reflection and interpretation." In writing this essay, she "learned to let go of the apprehension of revising and losing, and found that with the changes came new dimensions."*

I n lightness there lies darkness, and in the dimmest corridors of darkness lies a hint of light, a hint of truth. Opposing yet inseparable, the forces of the Yin and Yang are all-encompassing, pervasive. Manifesting themselves in all forms, the forces are present in all that we breathe, all that we see, all that we do, and quite simply, all that there is.

## 梦 DREAMS

Quiet solitude, burning, agonizing memories. The reason for damp salty tear-soaked pillows. Paralyzed legs, silent screams. Could be's, should be's, would be's, won't be's. Unresolved issues crawl and burrow into your ears, gnawing their way to your eye sockets. Eyes wide open, I can't even travel to that place. I'm too nauseous to fall asleep.

# 花 FLOWERS

Bundles and bundles of roses and carnations strewn upon caskets. Unseen, unsmelled, and unappreciated. Stop and smell the flowers, they say. It's a shame we don't get enough of them when we're still alive and breathing.

# 变化 CHANGE

The pigmentation of soundless autumn leaves transforms, ominous thunderclouds dissipate, icicles surrender their glorious forms. Stars collide. The seasons change; we change. Resist it or seize it, change is inevitable. Change is indispensable. Change is revolutionary.

# 無常 IMPERMANENCE

A gust of callous wind, extinguishing the flicker of a candle. Where flames once raged and danced, only ashes remain. The plummeting of the last rose petal upon the bed of sun-dried soil. The languid decay of that petal. The pattern of sand after the crashing of each tide, slightly reallocated with each thrust. The celestial liquid of the sky stops seeping through the crevices of the clouds. Revelries end, curtains close, and we return home to our lukewarm beds, drifting around the currents of time. Here today; gone tomorrow.

5

# 孤独 SOLITUDE

Away from the crowds. Away from the clamor, those ear-piercing cacophonous roars. Away from the stench of people, reeking of ignorance, apathy, carelessness, and greed. A safe haven for autonomy, a sanctuary for unadorned silence. Freer than a droplet in the ocean, freer than a particle in the Milky Way. Escape from criticism, from interpretation, from judgment. Clear mind. Clear thoughts.

# 死 DEATH

The ship reaches the dock of the mystifying shore, the plane departs for its last flight of the day, the soul embarks on the ultimate journey of life. The turning of the last page of the last chapter. Reconciliation, ultimate peace. Tranquility that cannot be bought. As the last breath is drawn, and the eyelids are sealed, the final awakening begins.

# 自杀 SUICIDE

The cessation of loneliness; the cessation of pain. Unfettered from the chains of scrutiny, emancipation from the grips of suffering. As the shackles of agony loosen, for once, that blade, that bullet, that lethal dose of morphine, offers a savior. Liberation never felt that good. I am free.

# 迷恋 INFATUATION

Can't sleep, can't walk, can't think, can't talk. Can't eat, can't feel, can't see, can't breathe. Sleepless nights, dream-filled days. What a beautiful insomnia. Gravity loses its steadfast grip; like a moth drawn towards the flame, I am summoned by an enigmatic radiance and warmth. Peripheral vision narrows, perceptions become skewed. Intoxicated by its luminosity, I flutter too close, and linger too long. Wings singed, the dust of disenchantment drifts downward. Soaring is never the same again.

# 爱 LOVE

10    See above.

# 昨天 YESTERDAY

When dreams were still unshattered, jumbo pink erasers could fix any mistake, and Barney band-aids cured all pain. When boys had raging cooties, bonds of friendship were stronger than the grip of epoxy glue, and living unhappily ever after was simply inconceivable.

# 今天 TODAY

Can't stop worrying about plans for tomorrow.

# 明天 TOMORROW

Always tomorrow. I'll take care of it tomorrow. I'll see you tomorrow. But sometimes, we don't. Can't wait till tomorrow. Bright and glorious, another chance. Yet sometimes the promise of tomorrow is as cheerful as discovering a tumor. A malignant one. Eyes closed, fingers crossed, secretly praying *I hope I don't wake up. But the sun still rises.*

---

## Reading to Write

1. Lyric essays often blur the line between poetry and prose. What poetic conventions—for example: imagery, simile, and repetition—do you recognize in Amy Ho's essay? Which conventions does she use most successfully? Provide specific examples as support.

2. In many places, Ho uses sentence fragments instead of full sentences. Why might she have made that choice? What is the effect on you as a reader?

3. In what ways does Ho's essay—through its content, form, and style—illuminate the philosophical concept of yin and yang that she introduces in the opening paragraph?

# Five Fridays

## *Hang Ho*

> *Hang Ho wrote "Five Fridays" in an Advanced Composition class at the University of Arizona. Her teacher, Tammie Kennedy, assigned a personal essay, asking students "to move beyond straightforward first-person narrative by experimenting with form in new and creative ways." Ho says that her experiment with form allowed her not only to "reflect on the conflicts involved" in her pursuit of a medical career, but also to communicate "emotion, motive, and voice" in more nuanced ways.*

### I. A FRIDAY TO-DO

My advisor gazes at me appraisingly from across the maple desk in her office. She tells me, "If you intend to seriously pursue admission into a medical school, these are the things you need to do." As she recites the list, she taps each finger on her left hand with her right index finger:

*Index:* Volunteer at hospitals.
*Middle:* Volunteer at private practices.
*Ring:* Volunteer to work in a lab.
*Pinky:* Shadow physicians.
*Index:* Get a mentor.
*Middle:* Get letters of recommendation.
*Ring:* Get a good GPA.
*Pinky:* Get involved in your major.
*Index:* Join clubs.
*Middle:* Join the medical fraternity.
*Ring:* Join study groups.
*Pinky:* Find a better reason to be a doctor.

*Index:* Find a method for studying for the MCATs.
*Middle:* Find a good date to take the MCATs.
*Ring:* Do well on the MCATs.
*Pinky:* Improve your interview skills.
*Index:* Take fewer classes to maintain a solid GPA.
*Middle:* Take eighteen extra credits of upper division life sciences.
*Ring:* Take General Chemistry, Organic Chemistry, Cellular
Biology, Evolutionary Biology, General Chemistry Lab,
Organic Chemistry Lab, Cellular Biology Lab, and Evolutionary
Biology Lab.
*Pinky:* Be aware of how much work is involved.

She finishes ticking the list off on her fingers and continues to gaze appraisingly at me. I wonder if she has that beady look in her eyes because she thinks I'm intimidated.

"You need to be aware that choosing to go into medicine is a lifestyle choice. It involves giving up a lot of time and energy. You will have to sacrifice time with your friends and your family. You will have to truly devote yourself to reaching that goal."

I take a breath. And, intoxicated with supreme confidence that I can do all that and more, I nod and smile and say, "I understand."

## II. MARGARITA NIGHT

I say:
Oh, I'll definitely be there. This week totally sucked. I really need to go out and unwind. We've all turned into social hermits this year and that needs fixing. With margaritas. And tequila. And Captain. We'll be drunkies and it'll be amazing. Okay, let me take a shower and put some makeup on, and I'll give you a call later tonight.

I say:
Oh hey. What time is it? Actually, I fell asleep . . . Yeah, I'll probably still go . . . Crap, I guess I should start getting ready then, huh?

I say:

You know, I'm exhausted. If I go out tonight, I'll end up sleeping through all of tomorrow, and now that I think about it, I should really start studying for that test next week. I'm dying slowly in that class. I think maybe I'll just get some sleep tonight so I can study tomorrow. I know, I know, I'm boring. But I've been up until three every night for a week and I'll just fall asleep on the couch if I go. Maybe we can do lunch or something tomorrow instead? Okay, have fun. Drink my margaritas for me. We can Photoshop me into the pictures tomorrow and it'll be just like I was there. I'll definitely be there next Friday though. I can't miss out on that.

## III. GRANDMA SAYS

I don't like the idea of you driving in the dark. Maybe next time you should come home on Saturday and then you don't have to drive in the dark. A girl like you should take care of herself, make sure she doesn't put herself in vulnerable positions like that. Who would help you if something went wrong on the road? And have you been studying hard? Keep studying hard. That's the only way to have success. It's a hard life when you don't do well in school. That's the life we had in Vietnam. Working and working and everyone had to fight for every grain of rice. You were probably too young to remember. Your father was a doctor, you know, and he could barely afford a pack of cigarettes a week. You don't know what it's like to live a hard life. I remember how your parents worked in the old days when you first came over here from Vietnam. I remember when they had to count every cent they had. And they had to buy groceries with those stamps that the government gives poor people. Do you remember? Those were such hard times. They had three jobs. The kind of work they did. That's the kind of life you lead when you don't have an education, cleaning and groveling for other people. And your uncle had to help them. And look at how easy life got after they finished school. They did it for you. They want to see you succeed. You're all they've got. Make sure you do well for them. You're not like your cousins. They're just a bunch of rowdy boys. All they ever want to do is play. You're more like Suzanne. She was such a good student too. It's a shame she wanted to do television and now she's thirty and your aunt still has to give her money. Don't be like that. Your parents worked so hard for you. You should do well for them, take care of them when they get old. That's the way we do things, not like those Americans who have no respect for their elders and no proper sense of what hard work really is.


## IV. MOM, ON THE PHONE

Hi Mom. How was your week?
Good . . . How was yours? Did you have any tests this week?
A few. Bio. Statistics. Math.
How did you do?
I don't know yet.
How are your grades?
They're okay . . . I think they're okay.
(*pause*)
What are you going to do this weekend?
Study. Just study and do homework. I have a lot of homework. Oh, and I'm signing up for classes tomorrow.
How many credits will you take?
Seventeen.
That's a lot. Too many. Maybe you should take less. You can't handle that much.
I know it's a lot, but I can't take less, Mom.
(*pause*)
Are you coming home this weekend?
I wanted to, but I can't. I have too much work due next week. I don't think I'll have time to come home until the weekend after next.
That's too long. And do you realize that it's your Grandma's birthday? Can't you just make some time this weekend? She wants to see you.

I know, but I just can't, Mom. I'm sorry. I just don't have time. But maybe if I can get all my work done early, I'll come home next weekend. Okay? I'll really try.

## V. ANOTHER FRIDAY TO-DO

10 –O-Chem Exam: Ch. 4–7.5

*well that was a complete waste of a week and a half of frantic studying I might as well have just not taken that but hey at least now I get to breathe grab some coffee on the way back to the dorm drive up to Tempe early go to dinner with Ian get nothing accomplished this weekend but lounge around in bed smile at those green eyes curl up in his button-downs sleep with my nose pressed against his shoulder a good morning kiss when I wake up but wait can't forget how much stuff is due next week I really should get back to Tucson early this time can't afford to slack off any more than I already have I need to get a head-start on all that work that's the only way it'll get done hold on wait I forgot I have to go see*

–Laura Berry @ Honors College @ 10am

*oh I suck at scheduling that's only ten minutes to walk across campus I guess I'll just have to run put off that coffee for a few minutes I'll do my nails when I'm done and pack oh and a shower can I fit that in between one and three shave the legs and put on some fresh makeup even if Ian does say that I look good without it he says such sweet things and it's funny he seems to actually mean them maybe I'll wear a dress that little black one that he likes so much with the leather peep-toe flats and that rose necklace oh and on the way back to the dorm I can turn in the*

–Statics HW: Body Equilibrium Problems 2, 3, 4, 6, 14, 19, 21, 27, 34, 49, 60, 62, 81, 87, 93, 113, 115; Truss analysis problems 4, 8, 9, 11, 35, 43, 54, hdout 9A, hdout 9B (5pm)

*glad that's done at least but still need to turn it in by three Civil Engineering's on the way I think it's somewhere between the Honors College and the dorm maybe I'll call Ian while I'm walking let him know when I'll be leaving Tucson tell him that I can't stay all weekend because I have to spend some time with my parents like I told them I would but before I leave I really should*

—Send Tony Cellular Analysis draft

*said I'd have it to him by Monday and there's no way I'll remember on Sunday night need to remember to get gas too I don't think three notches on the fuel gauge will get me from Tucson to Ian's even on cruise control I wonder if I left my extra contact lens case at his place I haven't seen it around oh I need to do laundry but I can do it on Sunday night when I get back in town I'm sure it'll be Sunday night even if I say right now that it'll be Sunday morning I don't have the time to stay that long but I know already that Mom will want to go out to eat Dad will want to check my car Grandma will want to remind me to study and I'll spend the entire afternoon at Ian's but hold on I still need to make sure I*

—Call Mike Frithsen re: Interview for Cancer Center North
(520) 694-0806

*before five this afternoon probably for the twentieth time this week maybe I should just switch my major and to hell with med school they really meant it when they said lifestyle choice when they said dedicate your life to it and I made my choice but still what a choice I just want to breathe to do nothing but sleep to keep wasting away my weekends and ambitions in Tempe with that guy what a wonderful guy I've got who says all those sweet distracting things who I really do . . . really do love . . . Love him . . . love him . . . but no hold on that's not right. When will I ever have time to really love him?*

---

## Reading to Write

1. Hang Ho uses lists extensively in this essay. Which list do you find most effective? Why?

2. Ho represents several different people through the ways that they speak. Consider the strategies she uses to represent each individual's speech (fragments, lists, simple sentences, and so on). How do these conventions help Ho develop character in this essay?

3. Write a personal essay structured by lists. Just as Ho does, use your title to clue readers in on the structure.

# Dead Ends

## *Brandon Derrow*

> *Brandon Derrow wrote "Dead Ends" in Tammie Kennedy's Advanced Composition class at the University of Arizona. Like Amy Ho, Derrow was answering an assignment to write a lyric essay—to, as Kennedy explains—employ a "poetic sensibility concerned more with language, imagery, sound, and rhythm over the more linear demands of narrative." Derrow says that although he wrote this essay "out of a need to wrangle some personal issues, namely isolation from family," he learned that "you can write something personal that isn't self-indulgent or a therapy session on paper."*

On a dirty and otherwise empty bookshelf lies a vintage video recorder, choked with dust, neglected and alone. There is a videotape in it, contents unknown. All the same, it's someone's past, life, ruin, last flash of happiness, shame, regret. It is, in its own right, the Shroud of Turin, the Dead Sea Scrolls, a Rubik's Cube, Jack the Ripper.

1. A family vacation. Galveston, Texas. A boy stands in the Gulf of Mexico, holding a dead fish. Two girls etch their names in the sand with tiny fingers while the waves slowly erase each letter. A woman rolls up her pant legs and splashes the kids with her feet. Off to the far left a man stands, smoking, staring at the emptiness of the distant sea, where the waves cease and the water turns into painted cardboard against lavender and orange juice sky. Man and woman stand together for a snapshot before it is time to leave. She smiles as if she has not been happy for a long time, and may not even be happy right now, but it's the closest she's gonna get to it for a while. He does not smile, just

smokes, eyeing the camera like a gunfighter, twists the cigarette into the sand with his shoe. This would be one of many signs of things to come. The act would continue, half-assedly, for the viewer's pleasure. It becomes a boring commercial for something no one would buy. Later the man would go off to perpetually circle a black hole no one would visit: the satellite no longer transmitting, released of its contract. This would come as no surprise and would have very little effect on all involved parties. The natural order of things: build, decay, release.

2. A birthday party. Louisiana humidity feels like being cloaked in a steaming hot towel, mummified. Some kind of reptile petting zoo, which seems like a terrible idea and a hotbed for lawsuits. Holding baby crocodiles. Maybe they were alligators. They snap their jaws like bear traps, exposing ivory fangs. They seem so primordial, dangerous, petrifying. Mudcake paths laced with poison ivy lead to the bayou. The swamp is as mysterious, foreboding, and ghostlike as it is in the brochures, movies, dreams. Nightmares.

3. A lake somewhere in the Blue Ridge Mountains. Continuous flooding has turned it into a phantasm of what it once was, the rusted rotting amusement park that falls in on itself next to some Midwestern highway. It's one of those places that can be assumed to be haunted by some mountain man or beast of folklore, snatching up unattended kids and teenagers in cars with foggy windows. It's not. It's an escape. It's a hiding place. It's where you go to disappear, when you've made a mistake and want to bury yourself, to drink warm beer and throw the cans into the water with a hollow splash, hoping they've forgotten about you or what you've done. A bit down the dust and gravel road is a dam. This place is, in fact, haunted. This is where you go if you want to die and want no one to know about it. Four suicides in one summer. The roads through the mountains never end, always lead someplace different, always some dead end. Driving fast with no headlights. You can feel the tires give way to the gravel, feel yourself slide toward the edge, toward the ravine, splitting the car open on timber and can opener

rocks. This doesn't happen, but it feels like it should. This is why people come here. It's a burial ground.

5    4. Christmas morning, year unknown. Everyone is accounted for and no one has to make an excuse for not coming. A museum exhibit. A train set, a talking doll, space shuttle, bicycle, bloody nose, broken arm. This does not happen anymore. There is also a natural order to this: a scattering of the parts. The occasional phone call that is mostly silence. Yeah we're doing just fine.

5. A drive from Ohio to Arizona. Rural Indiana is a relic preserved in amber: slaughterhouses, farmhouses, pastoral fields all smothered in fog. Old machines rest on dewed grass, rusted firm to the frozen fertile ground. Missouri, or Misery? Endless fields meet endless sky. If heaven existed you could see it from Kansas. Or Oklahoma. Tornado Alley is a lonesome stretch and a bad idea for someone with a lot, or nothing, to think about. The radio is broken. Beware of gusty areas. Do not drive into smoke. Caution: high winds. Trucks please use caution on downgrades. Emergency stop ahead. The world's largest McDonald's arches over both sides of the highway like the Leviathan straddling the ocean. Santa Fe seems as if it is suspended in midair. The *Hagia Sophia* of the Midwest. There is a shortcut in New Mexico where every horror movie involving a desolate stretch of highway is filmed. Here semis pass in a procession of souls. So it seems. Thunderstorms bring clouds of black that are impossible to see through. Driving through them is like cheating death, sliding near the ravine, down into a ditch that ends at the middle of the earth. The buzz of fluorescent lights in truckstop bathrooms resembles a dentist's drill.

6. A funeral. Black suit jackets with blue jeans and long dresses glide from room to room. A casket floats on an altar. A low machine-like buzz drones in the background. The faces carry a slight smile behind masks of acknowledged loss. Outside, smokers talk about the farm, the

crops, machine shops, anything but dying. Her face never reflected the pain of cancer eating her bones. A young man approaches the dead, studies her face outlined by gentle spotlights. Build, decay, release: this happens to everyone. We know this because she is still smiling. He runs out, gets in a car, drives fast through the fog and wet air. The tires lazily grip the loose gravel. No one close to him has ever died.

7. A confession. A man sits on a bed in a poorly lit room. Ancient country music comes from another room: the kind written by the eternally heartbroken and whiskey-wired. It sounds like a small FM transistor, one used for camping or feeling sorry for yourself. He's been drinking, which explains the uninhibited honesty. He's never been like this. His life is actually nice: nice house, nice job, family, friends, vacations, cars, health. He's only like this when he thinks of someone he has never met but knows to exist. He doesn't think of this much because he equates it with failure. Failure to connect. People are often forgotten. Some go for walks across a dam at midnight and never come back. Some take drives across the country and never make it to B from A, thrust into the ravine, lost for weeks. "I'm sorry I never got to meet you; I'm sorry it's not different." He sobs so heavily the words become inaudible and he shuts off the tape. He will make this tape hundreds of times and will never send it. It is for himself.

8. Vacation. Texas. The Alamo is a skeleton remembered because its slogan is "Remember the Alamo." We remember the Alamo in the same way we remember to brush our teeth, pick up milk, go to work, check the mail, lock the door, wash our clothes. The Alamo is a reminder of something cloudy, something that seems to be a representation, one side of a multi-sided story. We like comeback stories. One against many. Standing your ground. Troy's 300 against Xerxes' horde of millions, an ordinary woman refusing to go to the back of a bus, French peasants armed with pitchforks and brooms versus the aristocracy, William Wallace, Joan of Arc, and so on.

10    Galveston. The beach is different. Dirty. Seaweed, dead fish, tropical storm leftovers turn the water into old soup. The boy stands mo-
tionless in the ocean, dead fish and seaweed brushing against his legs.
The girls do not write their names in the sand; they sit on a bench,
faces resting on their hands, let down. Disappointment hangs on all
the faces, not as a mask but as a reflection of something faced for the
first time. This beach is not what a beach should be and the family is
not what a family should be. The woman still smiles and the man still
smokes from afar and he still stares like a gunfighter refusing to smile.
Bang Bang he shoots them down. But it's not his fault.

9. Birthday party. The swamp. The swamp seems like a good place to
bury yourself. To look for lost lovers. To find people who never came
back from a war. To go out walking after midnight. The swamp seems
like it would hold all of the world's secrets, all of the things people say
and promise to take to their grave. This is where you go to look for
something you lost, something you will never find. A place to make a
confession. Feet punching through the thick mucus of mud and water.
Weeping willows stretch their arms into the water, a midnight bap-
tism. Mourning birds and humming insects call out to no one and
everyone. How to disappear completely.

10. A lake. The Blue Ridge Mountains. It always seems as though you
are being followed when you come here. It's all the things you're dragging there with you: the corpses, the skeletons, regrets, the things you
are going to throw in the lake. On the other side of the mountain, on a
hill riddled with thistle and brush, is a family burial plot. It is marked
with wooden crosses made of kindling, painted white. A Civil War leftover. No one is buried here anymore. Most of the graves are for children. The people that live in the mountain are buried here as well.
Buried in that they will never leave. They have cabins at the end of dirt
roads lined with rusted barbwire and full of deep pockmarks. They
probably just want to be left alone. Forgotten. They stay up at night,
listening to old country music, crying. They listen to the hum of the

woods, indistinguishable howls, the wind whipping the firs like those people who walk through the streets, whipping themselves with barbed ropes, praying for penance. They are eternal martyrs, anchorites, anchoresses. Like Jesus. He is another underdog story. Jesus and his disciples versus Pontius and his army of nonbelievers. They suffer for themselves, for unforgivable sins, for unrecoverable loss.

11. Christmas morning. Mourning. Families go through the motions like actors practicing for gigs they never wanted. A hemorrhoid cream commercial, home shopping network spokespeople, the extra using a pay phone in the background. No one wants to be there, but everyone thinks they should. This is what a family should be. There are no presents, no slippers, no coffee mugs, no Burl Ives. This will be the last supper, and it will go out with a whimper, not a bang. The slight smiles and silence are appreciation for ones before, when it still mattered, when people still cared and didn't want to be somewhere else. The notion was being buried. There was no grand funeral, no procession through the cobblestone streets. Everyone nods, shakes hands, hugs, and scatters quietly.

12. A long drive. She reads to me as I stare at the rain hitting the windshield, making veins across the glass. Tucumcari, Las Cruces, Springfield, Truth or Consequences, Amarillo, Indianapolis. Along the panhandle of Texas we realize we are equal but separate. Smile, hug, scatter quietly.

None of this happened because the camera still sits on the bookshelf. Dead air space. The tape is empty. Nothing but hiss static and black space. It didn't happen because we forgot to remember. Remember the Alamo. Remember the natural order of things. Remember to lock the doors. Build decay release rebuild. Everything can be a dream if you choose to remember it that way. You can drive through the mountain, listening to rocks ping the undercarriage, broken radio, feeling the car pull like a magnet toward the sloping edge, knowing it will never happen. Dead ends. 15

## Reading to Write

1. Both Amy Ho (p. 276) and Brandon Derrow wrote lyric essays in response to the same assignment. In what ways are these essays similar? How do they differ?

2. One aspect of both lyric and collage essays is the repetition of images to create coherence. Which images does Derrow repeat in his essay?

3. Write a 5- to 7-page lyric essay, paying close attention to language, image, and the rhythm of your prose. Try repeating images throughout the text of your essay.

# Freeing the Caged Bird: My Conversations with Maya Angelou

## Kristin Taylor

*Kristin Taylor wrote "Freeing the Caged Bird: My Conversations with Maya Angelou" for her African American Literature class at Columbus State University in Georgia. Her teacher, Noreen Lape, asked students to write a braided essay, to "weave the three strands of the braid: the personal, literary, and scholarly/research strands." Taylor says that as she shaped her "traumatic experiences into a narrative form, while also exploring them in conjunction with Angelou's similar experiences," she "became a living example of the healing and restorative powers of language." Taylor explains further that writing this braided essay helped her learn how Angelou uses "narrative to untangle her self-blame," a process that brought Taylor healing as well.*

———

Too much was taken from me that night, though at fourteen, I didn't know it. In hindsight, the imperceptible transformation from my old self to who I am now began with him. Still, I can't help but wonder how my life might be different had I been anywhere else that night. At first, I tried to quiet the nagging question of changeability by pretending that it didn't really happen—not to me, not with my friend's father. But in trying to make the memories disappear, I forgot where they led me. I didn't notice how one ghost only invited another until they all came back haunting, and I found there were more of them than I had ever tried to forget. There was no escape from the haunting, except in remembering, but to remember was to relive.

There I am, sitting at the black upright Steinway, eager to let him hear that I have finally learned the sixteenth-note runs of Mozart's "Rondo Alla Turca." For the longest time, I would skip that part, satisfied with my mastery of the octave runs that precede it; he has no idea that I have learned it for him. I finish playing. "Try it again, Joy," Damien says, calling me that name I love, "this time without the pedal." I play the Rondo again. "A world of difference," I hear him say, and knowing he is pleased, so am I.

I slide my legs around the piano bench, turning to face whoever is entering the room. In comes Anne, Damien's daughter, and Emma, both of whom are my friends and schoolmates; Emma's mother follows them. "Play it again, Kristin; let them hear." I play the Rondo once more, but there is only one person I'm playing it for, only one person I want to notice the way my back sways with each crescendo and decrescendo. I do not know that in a year when the relationship ends, it will take me months to play again. Finishing, I suggest that I should probably call my mother to tell her where I am and when I'll be home. Leaving the room, I do not notice Damien follow me.

Anne's mother is on the phone, and thinking I will simply have to wait until she is finished to call my mom, I turn back toward the piano room only to hear Damien say, "Come with me. You can use the car-port phone." Following him, I have not taken two steps onto the hard cement when I drop the portable phone, the thin plastic battery cover coming free from its notch, and I see the phone, the cover, and the battery lying at my feet. "I am so clumsy sometimes." I cannot help but say it, though I will later regret it, as I stoop to pick up the phone and its pieces that could not withstand the fall. After placing the battery back inside and securing the protective cover, I begin to dial.

5            "Hey, Mom, I just wanted to tell you that I'm . . . um." I feel his arms engulfing me; he pulls me so close to him that I can feel the chest hair underneath his white tee shirt against my cheek. I can smell him, the man and the scent of his rude clay. "Um. At the Millers'. Um." I feel his face just above the top of my head. Over and over, he kisses my brown hair. "Um. Emma's mom wanted to bring them some. Um." He is one constant motion that my sense of touch is feeling and yet not feeling. The hands of a fifty-year-old man slithering along my body are more than my fourteen-year-old mind can comprehend. "Cheesecake. Um."

His hands, those same hands that play the piano as I long to play, are up and down my neck and back, reaching just low enough on my waist to make me ponder his intentions and just high enough to remove the question. "I'll be home. Um. In a little while. Um." No sooner has he begun than he leaves me standing alone in the carport. "I love you too."

It took little time for my parents to prevent me from visiting the Miller home again, yet my own understanding of the ramifications of what happened that night took much longer. I was left to sort through my seemingly senseless responses to Damien. On one hand, feelings of being wronged began to surface subtly, until finally in my desperation, I began to wish he had simply raped me. At least then, I reasoned, my reactions would be warranted. For who was I to feel so violated when his lingering caress could have easily been an innocent action I had misconstrued? But on the other hand, I suddenly felt that I loved him and desired the sense of belonging that his lingering caress had provided.

The first time I read Maya Angelou's *I Know Why the Caged Bird Sings*, I was a junior in high school. My parents had recently discovered that I had been secretly communicating with Damien for nearly a year, even though they had forbidden any further contact with him. At that time, I pored through the pages of Angelou's childhood autobiography, seeing myself in her guilt-ridden responses to her relationship with Mr. Freeman. I could think of no other logical reaction, for I too felt I was to blame for my part in my relationship with Damien.

Now, at nineteen, I curl up in a chair with *Caged Bird* once more, but this time Angelou and I have a different understanding of each other, a different conversation, if you will. While my experiences are certainly not identical to Angelou's, I still see myself in young Ritie. As I read her story this time, I long to speak to Ritie through the page and tell her she is not the one to blame, but to alleviate Ritie of her self-blame means to do the same for myself. Now I understand the true nature of Mr. Freeman's relationship with her and Damien's relationship with me, but more importantly, I understand that she and I are not the ones to blame. As I am empowered by Angelou's work and take comfort in knowing that I am not alone in my feelings of self-blame, I am left to ponder the psychological complexities of sexual abuse. Primarily, why does sexual abuse lead so many victims to blame themselves, rather than their abusers?

In deciphering abuse, it is crucial to understand that the violation wreaked by men such as Damien and Mr. Freeman "is based on important differences in maturity levels" between the offender and the child; therefore, the child "has no idea of the offender's intentions, no way to know that the affection expressed isn't genuine, and no recognition of the techniques used to manipulate him or her" (Salter 67). In Ritie's case, her vulnerability in this regard is exacerbated by her socialization, having been raised according to the Southern ways of Momma, who teaches her to respect adults unquestioningly. Prior to her rape, Ritie knows that she "didn't want to touch that mushy-hard thing again, and [she] didn't need him [Mr. Freeman] to hold [her] any more" (Angelou 65). Yet despite her desires and intuition to disobey Mr. Freeman, she still responds to him as an authority figure, saying "No, sir, Mr. Freeman" (65). As she tries to make sense of the rape, she says,

> It was the same old quandary. I had always lived it. There was an army of adults, whose motives and movements I just couldn't understand and who made no effort to understand mine. There was never any question of my disliking Mr. Freeman, I simply didn't understand him either. (62)

Ritie's confused rationale attests to her vulnerability because of the age difference between her and Mr. Freeman. As a young girl who is unable to realize that she has been violated, Ritie faults herself for not making sense of Mr. Freeman's behavior, translating her perceived inability to understand the actions of all adults into her failure to comprehend his actions as well.

10    As is typical of childhood victims of sexual abuse, Ritie feels an immediate sense of emotional connection with Mr. Freeman after he molests her, saying, "I began to feel lonely for Mr. Freeman and the encasement of his big arms. Before, my world had been Bailey, food,

Momma, the Store, reading books and Uncle Willie. Now, for the first time, it included physical contact" (Salter 66; Angelou 62). Because Ritie desires Mr. Freeman, she views herself as a willing accomplice when he later rapes her. She feels guilty for what she sees as her equal participation in the relationship, initiating the feelings of self-blame that dominate Ritie's life throughout *Caged Bird*.

Unfortunately for young Ritie, she is unable to understand that the absence of a true father figure in her life leaves her with an emotional emptiness that Mr. Freeman, consciously or unconsciously, is able to exploit (Challener 24–25). Ritie admits that she "felt at home" in Mr. Freeman's arms (Angelou 61). She even goes so far as to say, "This was probably my real father and we had found each other at last" (61). When Ritie's desires for Mr. Freeman surface, they are a result of her longing for a paternal relationship, but Mr. Freeman contorts her innocent desires into sexual ones. Ritie, however, cannot comprehend the complexities of Mr. Freeman's abuse or that it is possible for her to desire physical contact and emotional intimacy without enjoying his exploitative behavior. Not realizing the true cause of her attachment to Mr. Freeman or her emotional vulnerability, of which he has taken advantage, Ritie only knows to blame herself, just as I only knew to blame myself for my attachment to Damien.

Ritie's self-blame intensifies in court when she denies having had contact with Mr. Freeman prior to the rape. In her opinion, to tell the truth is to admit that she enjoyed Mr. Freeman "holding [her] precious," meaning her family will respond with anger and disappointment in her (63). Yet Ritie fails to foresee the dire consequences of speaking truthfully. Following the trial, only Ritie knows that she has lied in the courtroom, and soon after, her family is told that Mr. Freeman is dead. Because Ritie's childhood perception forces her "to make [a] cause-and-effect lea[p]" between the two actions without understanding the "true logic" which links them, Ritie believes that Mr. Freeman is dead because she lied (Brodzinsky, Schechter, and Henig 47). Ritie now blames herself not only for desiring Mr. Freeman and lying about her encounters with him but also for bringing about his death.

# Lyrics, Collages, Braids

Ritie's descent into self-blame is further perpetuated by silence, both externally and self-imposed. This trend is initiated by Mr. Freeman, who threatens Ritie's brother, cautioning Ritie, "If you ever tell anybody what we did, I'll have to kill Bailey" (Angelou 62). By silencing Ritie, Mr. Freeman communicates to her the unspeakable, and therefore shameful, nature of their encounters. Yet even when Mr. Freeman is no longer present in Ritie's life, her family continues the silencing. Following the trial, Grandmother Baxter tells Ritie and Bailey, "I never want to hear this situation nor that evil man's name mentioned in my house again" (72). While it is clear that the adults in Ritie's life blame Mr. Freeman for the rape, they simultaneously fail to explain to Ritie that Mr. Freeman is at fault and leave her without any understanding of what happened to her. Never having the opportunity to free herself from blame for the rape or Mr. Freeman's death, Ritie comes to fear the consequences of her words so strongly that she decides to stop talking altogether. As she slips into silence, she admits, "In the first weeks my family accepted my behavior as a post-rape, post-hospital affliction" (73). But when the doctor claims she is healed and she has not returned to her normal, pre-rape behavior, she is called "impudent and [her] muteness sullenness" (73). Rather than recognizing her silence as an effect of the trauma she has endured, her family views it as shameful, punishable behavior.

While Ritie silences herself verbally, I responded to my encounters with Damien by silencing myself musically. Damien had served as a father figure and piano mentor to me, encouraging me in my musical aspirations as a pianist, but his actions that night in his carport confused these established roles. In the months that followed, my inexplicable desires for Damien surfaced, and playing the piano became a way of kindling the emotional connection I wanted from him. When our relationship ended, my love for the piano was compromised; music was no longer a means of speaking the unspeakable, but rather the residual reminder that I was once held precious, to paraphrase Angelou. Just as Ritie determines that she "ha[s] to stop talking," too pained by the consequences of her words, I determined that I had to stop playing (73). But for Ritie, the effects of silencing go a step further.

As Quas, Goodman, and Jones explain, common responses to sexual abuse "may be exacerbated if family disruption (e.g., a child's removal from the home) occurs following discovery of abuse" (724). Finding herself and Bailey moving back to Stamps, Ritie assumes that her family "just got fed up" with her "grim presence," admitting "[t]here is nothing more appalling than a constantly morose child" (Angelou 74). For Ritie, being uprooted yet again at this crucial point in her childhood removes any remaining semblance of familial security and plays its own integral part in feeding her self-blame. The move to Stamps, combined with her inability to express her feelings and the shame imposed upon her for her silence, completes her devastation (Hyman, Gold, and Cott 295–96). Without the opportunity to heal, Ritie's self-blame cannot transform into the realization that she was abused, and it continues to haunt her in the years to come (Quas, Goodman, and Jones 724).

For victims of sexual abuse, "[t]heir earliest intimate experiences and relationships are fraught with exploitation and abusiveness. The result is severe damage to the child's interworkings, and too often the child carries the scars of abuse into adulthood" (Chop 297). The long-term consequences of Ritie's sexual abuse become evident in the lack of normality in her future relationships. When Tommy, one of her schoolmates, wants to be her valentine, her encounters with Mr. Freeman provide the only frame of reference through which she can evaluate any non-platonic relationship. Rather than responding like her friend Louise, who considers Tommy's letter a dismissible non-issue, Ritie's immediate reaction is to question his intentions, asking, "[W]hat evil, dirty things did he have in mind?" (Angelou 120). As her friend, Louise, explains that being Tommy's valentine simply means being "[h]is love," Ritie responds with disgust, saying, "There was that hateful word again. That treacherous word that yawned up at you like a volcano" (121). Finding herself caught between her inability to lie to Louise and her determination not "to freshen old ghosts," Ritie quickly evades the issue altogether (122). Yet, the ghosts are just as fresh as they have always been.

At sixteen, those ghosts continue to haunt Ritie, causing her to question her "normalcy" and preventing her from coming to a healthy understanding of her sexuality (241). As Ritie grows frustrated with her "sadly undeveloped breasts" and smooth armpits, she feels prevented from entering the world of womanhood and fears she is becoming a lesbian (233). Determined to resolve the internal conflict, she decides that a "boyfriend would clarify [her] position to the world and, even more important, to [her]self" (238). But sexual intimacy fails to remove her question of "normalcy," as she only finds the encounter disillusioning (241). Because her experiences with Mr. Freeman nine years prior cause her to equate love with sex, she anticipates "long soulful tongued kisses and gentle caresses" with the unnamed young man she tries to seduce but only experiences cold physicality—"laborious gropings, pullings, yankings and jerkings" (240). When she later finds herself pregnant as a result "of the strange and strangely empty night," her disillusionment becomes complete (241).

Still, Ritie's pregnancy and the birth of her son afford her the opportunity to begin coming to terms with her life thus far, ultimately giving the caged bird within her its reason to sing. The first night Ritie's son sleeps with her, she fears that she will "roll over and crush out his life" (245). Awakened by her mother, Ritie responds with "terror," immediately assuming she is at fault for somehow harming her son (246). Instead, she has been protecting her baby with her arm, even while sleeping. *Caged Bird* ends with the first step towards Ritie finding the ability to free herself from blame, as she accepts her mother's advice: "See, you don't have to think about doing the right thing. If you're for the right thing, then you do it without thinking" (246). While we do not see Ritie's self-integration come to fruition in *Caged Bird*, we know that Angelou, in her adulthood, calls her pregnancy "the best thing" and her son "[her] monument" (Powell 10). Ritie's resilience allows her to transform some of her darkest experiences into some of her most meaningful, shaping the self-empowered woman we see in Angelou today.

In telling her story of sexual abuse, Angelou explains that she longed to "tell a truth which might liberate [her], and might liberate others" (4). In an interview, she tells Dannye Powell:

> I have a file in my office filled with letters from women and men,
> mostly women, who read *Caged Bird* and somehow felt liberated
> enough to tell their mothers, or to confront their fathers or their
> uncles or their brothers, as grown women, and to say, "This was
> cruel, what you did to me." (4)

While I don't actually have a letter in Angelou's file, my story is still
there, merging with those of others who have been touched by Angelou's
work and found the strength to sing their songs. As Paul Laurence
Dunbar's poem "Sympathy" states, "the caged bird sings . . . not a carol
of joy or glee, / [b]ut a prayer that he sends from his heart's deep
core"—a cry for freedom that can come only after his imprisonment is
realized (lines 15, 18–19). *Caged Bird* gives abused women the opportunity to see that while "a pain still throbs in the old, old scars," coming
to terms with that pain is necessary to heal and free oneself from
blame (line 12). Yes, to remember is to relive, but it is only in remembering that the caged bird sings for freedom.

## WORKS CITED

Angelou, Maya. *I Know Why the Caged Bird Sings*. New York: Bantam, 1969.
Print.

Brodzinsky, David M., Marshall D. Schechter, and Robin Marantz Henig.
*Being Adopted: The Lifelong Search for Self*. New York: Doubleday,
1992. Print.

Challener, Daniel D. *Stories of Resilience in Childhood*. New York: Garland,
1997. Print.

Chop, Stephen M. "Relationship Therapy with Child Victims of Sexual Abuse
Placed in Residential Care." *Child and Adolescent Social Work Journal*
20.4 (2003): 297–301. Print.

Dunbar, Paul Laurence. "Sympathy." *The Norton Anthology of African
American Literature*. Eds. Henry Louis Gates Jr. and Nellie Y. McKay.
New York: Norton, 2004. 922. Print.

# Lyrics, Collages, Braids

Hyman, Scott M., Steven N. Gold, and Melissa A. Cott. "Forms of Social
    Support That Moderate PTSD in Childhood Sexual Abuse Survivors."
    *Journal of Family Violence* 18.5 (2003): 295–300. Print.

Powell, Dannye Romine. *Parting the Curtains: Interviews with Southern
    Writers.* Winston-Salem, NC: Blair, 1994. Print.

Quas, Jodi A., Gail S. Goodman, and David P. H. Jones. "Predictors of
    Attributions of Self-Blame and Internalizing Behavior Problems in
    Sexually Abused Children." *Journal of Child Psychology and Psychiatry*
    44.5 (2003): 723–36. Print.

Salter, Anna C. *Predators: Pedophiles, Rapists, and Other Sex Offenders.*
    New York: Basic, 2003. Print.

## Reading to Write

1. In this essay, Kristin Taylor "braids" a personal story, analysis of
   Maya Angelou's *I Know Why the Caged Bird Sings*, and research on
   sexual abuse. Locate the passages that correspond to each of these
   strands. How does she transition between and make connections
   among these strands?

2. What are the different conventions Taylor uses in each strand of this
   braided essay? That is, how do the conventions of narrative writing
   (such as description and dialogue) differ from the conventions of
   literary analysis (such as quoting and interpreting passages), and
   how does bringing in research on sexual abuse help Taylor interpret
   both her own experience and the experiences represented in Angelou's memoir?

3. Write an 8- to 10-page braided essay that weaves personal experience,
   analysis of something you've read in class, and outside research.

# One Writer's Process: Three Drafts

## Kaitlin Foley

*Kaitlin Foley wrote the following three drafts in her Composition II class at Johnson County Community College in Kansas. Her assignment was to write an argumentative research paper. The students in Foley's class chose on the first day of the semester to devote all papers and reading to the wide topic of media, and so their research papers had to pertain in some fashion to media. The goals for the final research paper included developing an academic voice in writing; practicing elements of argument such as assertion, support, and persuasion; and gaining skill with style, grammar, and mechanics. These documents show the development of Foley's argument over multiple drafts. Her revision process was guided by her teacher, Andrea Broomfield, whose selected commentary is also included here. Broomfield says that we see Kaitlin's "writing process is the real thing—a lot of hard work, many consultations, many peer review workshops, and improvements at each step." In reflecting on her development, Foley writes, "I originally began this persuasive research paper intending to research advocacy groups and grassroots movements within social networking. However, my thesis eventually changed to focus on the worldwide impact of online social networking itself." She continues, "Communication with my professor was a vital part of my writing experience. One important skill that I developed while working on this paper is the ability to pause, examine the paper from a different perspective, and determine how to best proceed."*

## Social Networking Websites and the Media: How the Internet Is Changing the World, and How the News Media Is Responding

From Facebook and YouTube to MySpace and Twitter, it's virtually impossible to escape the reach of popular websites. Finding people is their business, whether through search engines, emailed invitations, or simply word of mouth—or keyboard, as the case may be. In addition to these methods of publicity, which one might expect in a digital world, stories about popular networking websites are beginning to show up in a more traditional form of media: newspapers. The *New York Times* and the UK's *Guardian* have been publishing increasing numbers of Internet-related stories, and not just in the technology section. As interest in social networking websites grows, newspapers print more articles on them. At the same time, however, the articles themselves are fueling interest in such websites. This circular enthusiasm is not unique to popular websites, of course, but is exceptional because of the wide variety of subjects that relate to social networking. Technology writers report on the technical aspects and potential usefulness of new sites, of course, but those same websites are often analyzed by entertainment writers in opinion editorials and humorous articles, by financial experts from a business perspective, and even by general news reporters. As the Internet becomes a larger part of our lives, this is reflected in our newspapers. The news media's coverage of popular websites in a variety of topics illustrates a shift in worldwide culture, while at the same time actively fueling further interest in such websites and increasing social awareness.

### AN INTRODUCTION TO SOCIAL NETWORKING

The Internet is truly immense; within it, information can be found on almost any topic imaginable, and websites exist where one can find groups of people with interests from playing bagpipes to raising exotic hamsters. This paper will, however, center on just four of the largest and most popular websites: MySpace, Facebook, YouTube, and Twitter. In Robin Mason and Frank Rennie's book, the *E-Learning and Social Networking Handbook,* they note that a key value of social networking is the "gift culture"—a feature of an online community where users both provide and partake in the site's content. They add that "the primary focus in social networking is participation rather than publication . . . the essence of social networking is that users generate the content" (Mason and Rennie 3–4). Mason and Rennie's definition of social networking is accurate, and one might add that the use of these websites can range from casual to professional. From chatting high school students to enterprising businesspeople, social networking sites are utilized by a wide group of people who are, indeed, far more than simply an audience.

The four networking websites noted above are among the most mentioned in the news media, largely due to their popularity among users. MySpace is primarily a social website, where users can both contact old friends and make new connections, and then share notes, music, photographs, and videos with them. Services have expanded to include pages for bands, lists of events, and user-posted classified ads and job offers. Owned by Rupurt Murdoch's News Corporation, the site is primarily a business venture, and it has over 126 million users (Laughlin, Cox, and Segal pars. 1–4). Facebook is similar to MySpace—users here also find their friends and share personal information, news, and media with them, and the site (which originated for networking among college students) is also for-profit. Facebook boasts over 200 million users, about 70 percent of whom reside outside of the United States ("Facebook"). YouTube, on the other hand, is a different sort of social networking. It follows Mason and Rennie's idea, in that it exists primarily on user-generated content (and responses to this content, in the form of comments), but close interpersonal features are fewer. Registered or unregistered users can watch videos uploaded by people all over the world, and they can then share their own videos or discuss a video in a

"Comments" section on the same page. This conversation fosters interpersonal connections, but offers less intimate information than the two previous sites. Finally, Twitter, like YouTube, requires users to submit little personal information, but it adds the social aspects of MySpace and Facebook. Called "microblogging," Twitter members send "tweets," or short messages of under 140 characters, to answer the question "What are you doing?" Users follow each other's tweets and can then reply back, while a system of key words, or "tags," permits millions of updates to be sorted and searched. Varied as these websites are, they remain alike in their central purpose, which is to create opportunities for users to connect with each other while providing the site's content.

The newspaper industry has been quick to embrace the opportunities offered by social networking websites. Reading any article at the website of the *New York Times*, for example, will allow one to share the article with others via a wide variety of outside sites, including MySpace and Facebook, and often find the reporter's own blog. The newspaper has a profile on Facebook, and the 700,000 people following it on Twitter are constantly updated with news stories. There is also a *New York Times* video feed on YouTube, where clips related to recently published articles are uploaded. Not only do these networking websites allow the *Times* to provide readers with up-to-date information, but readers are able to actively respond to the news. Viewers of the paper's YouTube stream can converse in the "Comments" section below the video. The *Times* Facebook page currently has over 400,000 fans, any of whom are able to post their thoughts about breaking news without fear of repercussion. Meanwhile, writers and reporters are using the social networking phenomenon to their advantage as well, both as new outlets (with blogs and Facebook pages) and as news-generating sources. For example, in addition to traditional analyses in the technology section of the paper, reporters are also writing entertaining opinion pieces about social networking, such as Jemima Kiss's "Facebook. It's Just Gone Crazy" from the *Guardian*, in which Kiss gives a humorous explanation of what Facebook is in a question-and-answer format.

Even beyond the pop culture aspects of such social networking websites, however, reporters have found something else to write about: actual news stemming from these sites.

## SOCIAL NETWORKING WEBSITES IN THE NEWS MEDIA

In the article "Revolution, Facebook Style," Samantha M. Shapiro explores a series of protests led by young men and women in Egypt. These protests, she says, began as demonstrations against Israeli attacks on Hamas, and evolved into larger protests against the Egyptian government and President Mubarak (pars. 1–3). In her article, Shapiro focused on the way that these protests grew from Facebook groups—pages on the Facebook website that users can create to support causes or interests. Shapiro writes,

> Although there are countless political Facebook groups in Egypt, many of which flare up and fall into disuse in a matter of days, the one with the most dynamic debates is that of the April 6 Youth movement, a group of 70,000 mostly young and educated Egyptians, most of whom had never been involved with politics before joining the group . . . they have tried to organize street protests to free jailed journalists, and this month, hundreds of young people from the April 6 group participated in demonstrations about Gaza, some of which were coordinated on Facebook, and at least eight members of the group were detained by police. (par. 5)

Obviously, the conventional news here would be the protests, the participants, and the outcomes. However, Shapiro found a new angle. With dozens of languages available in countries worldwide, people anywhere with Internet access can join Facebook—and they do. They have the opportunity to form groups and meet people with opinions similar to theirs. By choosing to focus on the utilization of Facebook by these young men and women in the Egyptian protests, Shapiro has attracted a new readership—readers who are perhaps more interested in the technological and social aspects of April 6 than they are in the political aspects.

At other times, however, the news media may be too eager to integrate popular websites into their stories. For example, after the April 5 elections in Moldova, groups of citizens protesting the Communist Moldovan government gathered in Chisinau, culminating in violence from both sides. Newspapers were quick to attribute the display to Twitter. For example, in "Protests in Moldova Explode, With Help of Twitter," Ellen Barry wrote that the 10,000 young Moldovan men and women utilized Twitter to plan their April 7 protest in Chisinau (A1). Yet, as other news sources quickly pointed out, Twitter users were not the ones to organize the event—rather, bloggers and Facebook users did (Bennet pars. 21–22). Twitter was actually used for live updates from protester's phones—a key difference, as Mihai Moscovici mentioned in his Twitter feed. "Once again, Twitter didn't generate any revolution in Moldova. It was used as a tool to report about the protest in Chisinau, Moldova," he wrote on April 12. Moscovici was one of the protesters who kept up a constant report as the Moldovan government began cutting off local Internet and cellular services. His Twitter feed from April 7 includes posts such as "Presidency building is broken. The door is unlocked. Police use gas to resist protesters. Chisinau, Moldova." Here, the news media misinterpreted the use of Twitter; it was not a way of arranging the protest, but a way of documenting it, while other social networking sites were responsible for the enormous turnout (Applebaum par. 3). The media's swift willingness to label this a "Twitter revolution" illustrates a strong interest in social networking as it interacts with current events and, though Barry's facts were incorrect, the mere fact that it was a *New York Times* article generated publicity and interest in Twitter.

## ISSUES WITHIN THE SOCIAL NETWORKING SYSTEM

Because of the prevalence of social networking sites, the Moldovan protesters could plan and record the April 7 demonstration. They were also able to then share it with the world by uploading videos of police and protestors to YouTube, where they can still be viewed by almost anyone with Internet access, whether they live in Moldova or in the United

States (EUXTV). Some, however, are not as lucky. In "YouTube Being Blocked in China, Google Says," Miguel Helft writes that China has reportedly disallowed access to the entire YouTube website, possibly due to a video that appeared to have shown Tibetans being beaten by Chinese officers (pars. 2–4, 9). "China routinely filters Internet content and blocks material that is critical of its policies," writes Helft. "It also frequently blocks individual videos on YouTube" (par. 7). China's reaction to the website is an indication of alarm about not only the popularity of YouTube, but also the site's assumed influence on Chinese citizens. While the prohibition of web access by any group works against one of the key aspects of the Internet, freedom of information, the news coverage of this ban has actually worked to attract more international attention to YouTube, and to videos such as the very ones that China's government is supposedly attempting to conceal.

In another demonstration of the widespread nature of social networking websites, the news media has also reported on them from a business and financial perspective. Brad Stone and Miguel Helft reported in "In Developing Countries, Web Grows Without Profit" that Internet users in developing countries are using increasing amounts of bandwidth (particularly with photos and video), while providing the website owners with little return from advertisements. Companies are forced to consider such tactics as limiting access in such countries or compromising the quality of web access (pars. 4, 13–19). Financial issues such as this further complicate expansion of the Internet and social networking. The lack of equality in Internet access, when access is even available, is a large part of what has been termed the "digital divide."

The digital divide, a discrepancy in access to technology, is one of the major difficulties facing Internet growth. In developing countries, few people have access to computers, and fewer still have their own. According to Shapiro, only about one out of nine Egyptian citizens has access to the Internet, even with Internet cafés and public computer access (par. 3). In "Trends in Media Use," however, Donald F. Roberts and Ulla G. Foehr note that (depending on familial income) 29 to 93 percent of American families have access to the Internet in their own homes, in addition to a variety of out-of-home options. This trend of accessibility variance across economic and location factors is also echoed in Hiroshi Ono and Madeline Zavodny's study, "Digital Inequality: A Five-Country Comparison Using Microdata," where the authors state,

> In spite of the tremendous increase in [information technology] use in recent years, a pattern of "digital inequality," or differences in IT access and usage, persists both across countries and across certain socioeconomic and demographic groups within countries. In 2000, the 29 OECD member states contained 90 percent of all Internet users in the world, and there were more Internet users in Sweden than in the entire continent of Africa. (1135–36)

While there is no single factor in the digital divide, Internet access can, like many opportunities, be attributed to location and economic status. Computers and service providers are expensive; developing nations may not have the resources, while people in rural environments lack chances to connect to the Internet, and to then learn to use it. In *Digital Divide: Civic Engagement, Information Poverty, and the Internet Worldwide*, Pippa Norris goes further and separates the digital divide into the "global divide," inequality between nations in different stages of development, "social divide," a division between those rich and those lacking in information within countries, and a "democratic divide," a gap which depends on how one does (or does not) use the Internet (4–13). The attention of the general media is often on the first two of Norris's divisions—global and social, and more often than not is concentrated on rural and race groups in the United States, such as in Michael Marriott's "Digital Divide Closing as Blacks Turn to Internet," in which Marriott states that the "falling price of laptops, more computers in public schools and libraries and the newest generation of cellphones and hand-held devices that connect to the Internet have all contributed to closing the divide" (par. 3). It is difficult to find instances of the news media addressing the global issue of digital divide, perhaps because so many in our own country still lack access to information technology. Nonetheless, while it is vital to connect within our own countries, it is also important to help connect citizens of other countries, thus truly creating a World Wide Web.

## CONCLUSION

Social networking sites offer the news media an ever-increasing array of    10
stories, in topics from technology to business to entertainment. The Internet has become such an integral part of our lives that it can be considered to be "news" in itself, whether on its own or as an element of a larger story; newspapers respond to public interest in popular networking websites, and public interest increases with this information. Throughout the world, groups of people are doing new and innovative things with social networking websites—sometimes even spurring social change. At the same time, government censorship and the inequality of the digital divide are preventing many from using the Internet to reach out to their fellow people, whether across the street or across the world.

By taking current news stories and social issues and connecting them to modern technology, reporters and editors provide a new perspective to readers. The focus on social networking as a cause or a reaction to current events not only exposes readers to new technologies, but also introduces those familiar with technology to social and political issues. Popular websites are much more than a "hook" to attract readers to news articles; the websites are common to a wide variety of lifestyles and merit news in their own right. Social networking has become a central part of our culture and, to increase the interconnectivity of cultures across the world, care must be taken to reach those who lack access. The news media has both responded to the popularity of social networking websites, and has also helped them achieve their worldwide following.

## WORKS CITED

Applebaum, Anne. "The Twitter Revolution that Wasn't." *Slate*. Slate.com, 20 Apr. 2009. Web. 23 Apr. 2009.
Barry, Ellen. "Protests in Moldova Explode, With Help of Twitter." *New York Times*. New York Times, 7 Apr. 2009. Web. 18 Apr. 2009.

# One Writer's Process: Three Drafts

Bennet, Daniel. "The Myth of the Moldova Twitter Revolution." *Frontline*. Washington Post, 8 Apr. 2009. Web. 20 Apr. 2009.

EUXTV. "Protesters Storm Parliament in Chisinau: Realitatea TV." *YouTube.com*. YouTube, 7 Apr. 2009. Web. 20 Apr. 2009.

"Facebook Statistics." *Facebook*. Facebook, 2009. Web. 24 Apr. 2009.

Helft, Miguel. "YouTube Blocked in China, Google Says." *New York Times*. New York Times, 24 Mar. 2009. Web. 23 Apr. 2009.

Kiss, Jemima. "Facebook. It's Just Gone Crazy." *Organ Grinder Blog*. The Guardian, 6 June 2007. Web. 19 Apr. 2009.

Laughlin, Lauren Silva, Rob Cox, and Jeff Segal. "Shine of MySpace May Fade a Bit." *New York Times*. New York Times, 27 Apr. 2009. Web. 28 Apr. 2009.

Mason, Robin, and Frank Rennie. *E-Learning and Social Networking Handbook: Resources for Higher Education*. New York: Routledge, 2008. Print.

Marriott, Michael. "Digital Divide Closing as Blacks Turn to Internet." *New York Times*. New York Times, 31 Mar. 2006 Web. 22 Apr. 2009.

Moscovici, Mihai. "Moscovici on Twitter." *Twitter.com*. Twitter, 26 Apr. 2009. Web. 26 Apr. 2009.

Norris, Pippa. *Digital Divide: Civic Engagement, Information Poverty, and the Internet Worldwide*. New York: Cambridge UP, 2001. Print.

Ono, Hiroshi, and Madeline Zavodny. "Digital Inequality: A Five-Country Comparison Using Microdata." *Social Science Research* 36 (2007): 1135–155. *Pro Quest*. Web. 22 Apr. 2009.

Roberts, Donald F., and Ulla G. Foehr. "Trends in Media Use." *The Future of Children* 18.1 (2008): 11–37. *JSTOR*. Web. 23 Apr. 2009.

Shapiro, Samantha M. "Revolution, Facebook Style." *New York Times*. New York Times, 22 Jan. 2009. Web. 20 Apr. 2009.

Stone, Brad, and Miguel Helft. "In Developing Countries, Web Grows Without Profit." *New York Times*. New York Times, 26 Apr. 2009. Web. 27 Apr. 2009.

## INSTRUCTOR COMMENTS ON FIRST DRAFT

*Okay, so you're struggling a bit with this, and that's a really good thing for you—it means that you are seriously having to stretch yourself intellectually.*

*I think that at this point, you lack a convincing thesis. You have a lot of substance and excellent coverage of how social networking has altered traditional news reporting and how social networking itself is altering all sorts of sociopolitical dynamics, but you are not able as of yet to find a way to bring the two themes together in a compelling thesis.*

*I have blocked three passages in the paper itself, any one of which could be drawn out and made more prominent in the introduction. I'm going to give you those places and then ask you to determine which of them seems the best to use as a focal point (a newer, better thesis):*

¶ 2: "From chatting high school students to enterprising businesspeople, social networking sites are utilized by a wide group of people who are, indeed, far more than simply an audience."

*I like this a lot. What this statement does—if you could give it more prominence and thus focus the actual paper around this statement—is it allows you to use your examples from Egypt and from Moldova, at the same time that it allows you to discuss how other countries such as China recognize the threat and are trying to keep Internet access (particularly to sites like YouTube) controlled—and likely why they will fail in the attempt. In other words, this was really what you set out to do initially, and what I think you still ought to do for your final draft. You can use all the research you have, but you will need to rewrite the introduction and parts of the analysis in the body to make this thesis a focal point.*

*Here's another potential direction if you don't like the quotation from ¶ 2.*

¶ 7: "While the prohibition of web access by any group works against one of the key aspects of the Internet, freedom of information, the news coverage of this ban has actually worked to attract more international attention to YouTube, and to videos such as the very ones which China's government is supposedly attempting to control."

*This statement, refashioned as a thesis (i.e., made more general with China as an example), would allow you to write a paper arguing that irrespective of the global/digital divide, the power of news networking is only going to grow stronger, and governments are going to be increasingly helpless in how to control the dissemination of news. Taking this as a thesis would demand a much different paper than the one you have, however. It would mean that you are using some of your research, but you are rewriting much of the paper to discuss future scenarios when almost all people do have Internet access and governments cannot control information. This might be better for a future research paper.*

*The third possibility of a focal point is in ¶ 9:*

"Social networking has become a central part of our culture and, to increase the interconnectivity of cultures across the world, care must be taken to reach those who lack access."

*This statement is classic argument, and what you would have to do if this became the thesis is prove to us why care should be taken. Why should I care? Why should you? For that matter, why should a government such as Cuba's or China's care? Here, you would use research that you already have, but you would have to develop a more compelling justification for what you are currently treating as universal assumptions (i.e., "Well of course 'we' should care!").*

*What you probably want to get rid of is your point about how traditional news media report on new media. That point seems to be tangential to your real concerns, and it also seems to be a digression.*

*I hope that this all makes sense. You have work ahead of you of in trying to shape this paper, and that's kind of tough. Focus on rewriting the introduction. The easiest possibility for a thesis is probably that statement in ¶ 2. Let me know if I can help.*

## Social Networking Websites and the Future: How the Internet Is Providing Opportunities for Worldwide Connections

Social networking websites allow one to turn on a computer in the United States and immediately access the thoughts, feelings, videos, pictures, and breaking news stories of people on the other side of the world—virtually connecting people who will, with all likelihood, never meet face-to-face. Users of social networking sites actively control the content of the websites by responding to the work of others and uploading their own ideas. These websites—spanning the Internet from MySpace to Twitter—have been adapted by users to suit their needs as market researchers, movie producers, grandparents, and businesspeople. As the target audiences of networking sites have grown, so has the content, so that social networking sites have evolved into a medium in which users are more than an audience—users upload videos, write stories, and post pictures, not webmasters or professionals. As the Internet grows and spreads across the world, members of social networking websites are adapting the sites to suit their needs, from business to entertainment to political activism, and are not only receiving online information, but are also actively contributing to the online content available, thus creating a truly World Wide Web.

### AN INTRODUCTION TO SOCIAL NETWORKING

The Internet is truly immense; within it, one can find information on almost any topic imaginable, and websites exist for groups of people with interests from playing bagpipes to raising exotic hamsters. This paper will, however, center on just four of the largest and most popular websites: MySpace, Facebook, YouTube, and Twitter. In Robin Mason and Frank Rennie's book, the *E-Learning and Social Networking Handbook*, they note that a key value of social networking is the "gift culture"—a feature of an online community where users both provide and partake in the site's content. They add that "the primary focus in social networking is participation rather than publication . . . the essence of social networking is that users generate the content" (Mason and Rennie 3–4). Mason and Rennie's definition of social networking is accurate, and one might add that the use of these websites can range from casual to professional. From chatting high school students to enterprising businesspeople, social networking sites are utilized by a wide group of people who are, indeed, far more than simply an audience.

The four networking websites noted above are among the most popular worldwide, as demonstrated by their prominence in pop culture and news stories. MySpace is primarily a social website where users can both contact old friends and make new connections, and then share notes, music, photographs, and videos with them. Services on MySpace have expanded to include pages for bands, lists of events, and user-posted classified ads and job offers. Owned by Rupurt Murdoch's News Corporation, the site is primarily a business venture, and it has over 126 million users (Laughlin, Cox, and Segal pars. 1–4). Facebook is similar to MySpace—users here also find their friends and share personal information, news, and media with them, and the site (which originated for networking among college students) is also for-profit. Facebook boasts over 200 million users, about 70 percent of whom reside outside of the United States ("Facebook"). Beyond these two major networking sites, YouTube offers a different sort of connection. It follows Mason and Rennie's idea, in that it exists primarily on user-generated content (and responses to this content, in the form of comments), but close interpersonal features are fewer. Registered or unregistered users can watch videos uploaded by people all over the world, and they can then share their own videos or discuss a video in a "Comments" section on the same page. This conversation fosters interpersonal connections, but offers less intimate information than the two previous sites. Finally, Twitter, like YouTube, requires users to submit little personal information, but it adds aspects of MySpace and Facebook, as users provide each other with live updates about their plans, actions, thoughts, and interests. Called "microblogging," Twitter members send "Tweets," or short messages of under 140 characters, to answer the question "What are you doing?" Users follow each other's Tweets and can then reply back, while a system of key words, or "tags," permits millions of updates to be sorted and searched by any member. Varied as these websites are, they remain alike in their central purpose, which is to create opportunities for users to connect with each other while providing the site's content.

Social networking websites have long been viewed as virtual hangouts for teenagers and young adults. Recently, however, they have gained a more professional appeal, often as businesses and organizations attempt to reach out to younger audiences. NASA astronaut Mike Massimino plans to Tweet from space on his next mission, while surgeons at the Henry Ford Hospital have created similar interest by posting minute-by-minute Twitter updates during surgeries. Even austere newspapers are joining the Internet phenomenon—reading any article at the website of the *New York Times*, for example, will allow one to share the article with others via a wide variety of outside sites, including MySpace and Facebook, and often to find the reporter's own blog. The *Times* also has a Twitter feed with 700,000 followers, 400,000 fans on its Facebook page, and a YouTube stream with dozens of videos related to current news articles. Not only do these networking websites allow the *Times* to provide readers with up-to-date information, but readers are able to actively respond to the news. Viewers of the paper's YouTube stream can converse in the "Comments" section as Facebook users debate in public forums, and all are able to post their thoughts about breaking news without fear of repercussion.

From a business perspective, sites like MySpace, Facebook, Twitter, and YouTube provide one major attraction: free advertising. With a few simple clicks, companies can create profiles, research target audiences, and network with current and potential clients. For employees or jobseekers, however, the websites can create as many problems as possibilities. According to Mike Marusarz, "Most bosses search your name online before you even interview. One popular feature of Facebook

5

allows you to post and be 'tagged' in pictures, which can be a potential minefield for someone looking for a job" ("Finding a Job"). While the prevalence of social networking has allowed its use to expand into the workplace, care must be taken to avoid disadvantageous mixing of work and personal lives.

## HOW SOCIAL NETWORKING WEBSITES IMPACT THE WORLD

In the article "Revolution, Facebook Style," Samantha M. Shapiro explores a series of protests led by young men and women in Egypt. These protests, she says, began as demonstrations against Israeli attacks on Hamas, and evolved into larger protests against the Egyptian government and President Mubarak (pars. 1–3). Focusing on the way that these protests grew from Facebook groups (club-like pages that users can create to support causes or interests), Shapiro writes,

> Although there are countless political Facebook groups in Egypt, many of which flare up and fall into disuse in a matter of days, the one with the most dynamic debates is that of the April 6 Youth Movement, a group of 70,000 mostly young and educated Egyptians, most of whom had never been involved with politics before joining the group . . . they have tried to organize street protests to free jailed journalists, and this month, hundreds of young people from the April 6 group participated in demonstrations about Gaza, some of which were coordinated on Facebook, and at least eight members of the group were detained by police. (par. 5)

Here, networking on Facebook is demonstrated to have united young Egyptians by providing an uncensored environment in which they could discuss their views. The young men and women, who Shapiro describes as previously being almost politically apathetic, have been able to create an online atmosphere of political interest and, moreover, have expanded this virtual community into physical displays of activism.

Egypt is not the only country in which young citizens have utilized social networking websites to spur social change. In another example, after the April 5 elections in Moldova, groups protesting the Communist Moldovan government gathered in Chisinau. The protests culminated in violence from both sides. In "Protests in Moldova Explode, With Help of Twitter," Ellen Barry wrote that the 10,000 young Moldovan men and women utilized Twitter to plan their April 7 protest in Chisinau (A1). As other news sources pointed out, however, Twitter users were not the sole organizers of the event—bloggers and Facebook users were (Bennet pars. 21–22). Similar to the upheaval in Egypt, young, dissatisfied citizens used Facebook to organize a protest. Meanwhile, Twitter was actually used for live updates from protester's phones—updates read not only by Twitter users in Moldova, but by users across the world. Mihai Moscovici kept up a constant report during the April 7 events, even as the Moldovan government began cutting off local Internet and cell phone services. "Presidency building is broken. The door is unlocked. Police use gas to resist protesters. Chisinau, Moldova," he Tweeted. Succinct as his messages were, his moment-by-moment reports remain available for all to read. "Once again, Twitter didn't generate any revolution in Moldova. It was used as a tool to report about the protest in Chisinau, Moldova," he wrote on April 12. This is a key point, for it was the combination of multiple social networking websites that created power and publicity for the protesters. Twitter provided a way to document events as they occurred, while other social networking sites were responsible for the enormous turnout (Applebaum par. 3).

## ISSUES WITHIN THE SOCIAL NETWORKING SYSTEM

Because of the prevalence of social networking sites, the Moldovan protesters could plan and record the April 7 demonstration. They were also able to then share it with the world by uploading videos of police and protestors to YouTube, where they can still be viewed by almost anyone with Internet access—whether they live in Moldova, the United States, or many other countries (EUXTV). Some Internet users, however, are not as lucky. In "YouTube Being Blocked in China, Google Says," Miguel Helft writes that China has reportedly disallowed access to the entire

YouTube website, possibly due to a video that appeared to have shown Tibetans being beaten by Chinese officers (pars. 2–4, 9). "China routinely filters Internet content and blocks material that is critical of its policies," writes Helft. "It also frequently blocks individual videos on YouTube" (par. 7). China's reaction to the website is an indication of alarm about not only the popularity of YouTube, but also the site's assumed influence on Chinese citizens—it is quite possible that the Chinese government recognizes that social networking websites have extended beyond entertainment purposes to a position of prominence in social issues.

Censorship such as China's potentially prevents individuals from accessing information important to making informed decisions, and one must wonder how far government control can extend to the Internet. YouTube is by far not the only video sharing website. Even Facebook and MySpace allow video uploads, and they are even more effective at spreading information from person to person. The nature of social networking websites, and indeed of the Internet itself, is to share, and the loss of any one community is detrimental to their purpose. On the other hand, the communal properties of online content suggest that, even if a government should cut off access to all major social networking websites, new sites with similar purposes would quickly emerge. While the prohibition of web access by any group works against one of the key aspects of the Internet, freedom of information, China's attempts to conceal YouTube videos have, in fact, attracted international attention to both the government's censorship and to the political aspects of YouTube videos.

10       Beyond active control and prohibition of social networking websites, Internet users also have to address issues of access. Brad Stone and Miguel Helft reported in "In Developing Countries, Web Grows Without Profit" that Internet users in developing countries are using increasing amounts of bandwidth (particularly with photos and video), while providing the website owners with little return from advertisements. Companies are forced to consider such tactics as limiting access in specific countries or compromising the quality of web access (pars. 4, 13–19). These financial issues further complicate expansion of the Internet

and social networking. The lack of equality in Internet access, when access is even available, is a large part of what has been termed the "digital divide."

The digital divide, a discrepancy in access to technology, is one of the major difficulties facing Internet growth. In developing countries, few people have access to computers, and fewer still have their own. According to Shapiro, only about one out of nine Egyptian citizens has access to the Internet, even with Internet cafés and public computer access (par. 3). In "Trends in Media Use," however, Donald F. Roberts and Ulla G. Foehr note that (depending on familial income) 29 to 93 percent of American families have access to the Internet in their own homes, in addition to a variety of out-of-home options. This trend of accessibility variance across economic and location factors is also echoed in Hiroshi Ono and Madeline Zavodny's study, "Digital Inequality: A Five Country Comparison Using Microdata," where the authors state,

> In spite of the tremendous increase in [information technology] use in recent years, a pattern of "digital inequality," or differences in IT access and usage, persists both across countries and across certain socioeconomic and demographic groups within countries. In 2000, the 29 OECD member states contained 90% of all Internet users in the world, and there were more Internet users in Sweden than in the entire continent of Africa. (1135–36)

While there is no single factor in the digital divide, Internet access can, like many opportunities, be attributed to location and economic status. Computers and service providers are expensive; developing nations may not have the resources, while people in rural environments lack chances to connect to the Internet, and to then learn to use it. In *Digital Divide: Civic Engagement, Information Poverty, and the Internet Worldwide*, Pippa Norris goes further and separates the digital divide into the "global divide," inequality between nations in different stages of development, "social divide," a division between those rich and those lacking in information within countries, and a "democratic divide," a gap which depends on how one does (or does not) use the Internet (4–3). The attention of the general media is often on the first two of Norris's divisions—global and social, and more often than not is concentrated on rural and race groups in the United States, such as in Michael Marriott's "Digital Divide Closing as Blacks Turn to Internet," in which Marriott states that the "falling price of laptops, more computers in public schools and libraries and the newest generation of cellphones and hand-held devices that connect to the Internet have all contributed to closing the divide" (par. 3). In both developed and developing nations, however, it is vital to decrease the digital divide, not only to allow citizens in such communities equal access to information, but also for their contributions to the available, user-generated content of social networking websites in the World Wide Web.

## CONCLUSION

Social networking websites are the virtual locations of activities from gossip and photo sharing to revolution and job searching. Their functions are determined by the actions of those who use the sites—users who also contribute to the online content. It is, indeed, a "gift culture," and as the Internet continues to evolve, social networking sites become more and more centered on the user-created and member-contributed aspects of their content. Uses of popular networking websites can take the form of classified ads, job offers, and virtual employee background checks, as well as support and discussion in groups for young political activists in Egypt, Moldova, and other countries across the world. Users generate the sites' contents, and they can therefore shape the sites to suit their needs.

Some countries, however, see the freedom of the Internet as a risk, and take actions to prevent the spread of information—such as the Chinese government's ban of YouTube. This censorship, combined with social, economic, and location factors, contributes to the digital divide. It is important to overcome the digital divide not just to provide everyone with equal access to information and opportunities, but also to enhance the information that is available by allowing more individuals to contribute to the user-created content that defines social networking websites. Online social networking has been utilized in a variety of innovative ways, from marketing research to protest-planning, and it is vital that the Internet be allowed to grow so that users worldwide will be able to not only access, but also contribute to the content of social networking websites.

## WORKS CITED

Applebaum, Anne. "The Twitter Revolution that Wasn't." *Slate*. Slate.com, 20 Apr. 2009. Web. 23 Apr. 2009.

Barry, Ellen. "Protests in Moldova Explode, With Help of Twitter." *New York Times*. New York Times, 7 Apr. 2009. Web. 18 Apr. 2009.

Bennet, Daniel. "The Myth of the Moldova Twitter Revolution." *Frontline*. Washington Post, 8 Apr. 2009. Web. 20 Apr. 2009.

EUXTV. "Protesters Storm Parliament in Chisinau: Realitatea TV." *YouTube.com*. YouTube, 7 Apr. 2009. Web. 20 Apr. 2009.

"Facebook Statistics." *Facebook*. Facebook, 2009. Web. 24 Apr. 2009.

Helft, Miguel. "YouTube Blocked in China, Google Says." *New York Times*. New York Times, 24 Mar. 2009. Web. 23 Apr. 2009.

Kiss, Jemima. "Facebook. It's Just Gone Crazy." *Organ Grinder Blog*. The Guardian, 6 June 2007. Web. 19 Apr. 2009.

Laughlin, Lauren Silva, Rob Cox, and Jeff Segal. "Shine of My Space May Fade a Bit." *New York Times*. New York Times, 27 Apr. 2009. Web. 28 Apr. 2009.

Mason, Robin, and Frank Rennie. *E-Learning and Social Networking Handbook: Resources for Higher Education*. New York: Routledge, 2008. Print.

Marriott, Michael. "Digital Divide Closing as Blacks Turn to Internet." *New York Times*. New York Times, 31 Mar. 2006 Web. 22 Apr. 2009.

Marusarz, Mike. "Finding a Job Through Social Media." *NBC Action News*. NBC, 6 May 2009. Web. 6 May 2009.

One Writer's Process: Three Drafts

Massimino, Mike. "Astro_Mike on Twitter." *Twitter.com*. Twitter, 4 May 2009.
  Web. 4 May 2009.

Moscovici, Mihai. "Moscovici on Twitter" *Twitter.com*. Twitter, 26 Apr. 2009.
  Web. 26 Apr. 2009.

Norris, Pippa. *Digital Divide: Civic Engagement, Information Poverty, and the
  Internet Worldwide*. New York: Cambridge UP, 2001. Print.

Ono, Hiroshi, and Madeline Zavodny. "Digital Inequality: A Five-Country
  Comparison Using Microdata." *Social Science Research* 36 (2007):
  1135–155. *ProQuest*.Web. 22 Apr. 2009.

Roberts, Donald F., and Ulla G. Foehr. "Trends in Media Use." *The Future of
  Children* 18.1 (2008): 11–37. *JSTOR*. Web. 23 Apr. 2009.

Shapiro, Samantha M. "Revolution, Facebook Style." *New York Times*. New
  York Times, 22 Jan. 2009. Web. 20 Apr. 2009.

Stone, Brad, and Miguel Helft. "In Developing Countries, Web Grows Without Profit." *New York Times*. New York Times, 26 Apr. 2009. Web.
  27 Apr. 2009.

## RESEARCH PAPER GRADE SHEET, COMPOSITION II

Name: K. Foley

**This research paper, worth 150 points (15% of final grade), has been divided into six categories.**

**I. Ability to follow all directions related to number of sources, formatting, drafts submitted: 25/25**

*As usual, excellent work!*

**II. The quality of the thesis in regards to its scope, feasibility, assertion: 19/25**

*Your paper is more like an informative research paper than an argument.*

*The thesis is still buried or not apparent enough, and should you decide to continue work on the topic, you might offer readers careful consideration of what seems to be one of your buried assumptions: the internet and social networking as a good thing. Why should people be drawn together internationally? Do governments have good reason to fear the added impetus to mass democracy—along with the added impetus to anarchy, rebellion, terrorism—that the Internet via social networking sites brings? Your section, ¶ 8–11 really raise such questions, because in this section your assumption that the Internet is such a good thing is most prevalent.*

*Related, your thesis could easily be the last sentence of your paper's body in ¶ 11. You could argue that "it is vital to decrease the digital divide" and give reasons why, as well as articulate opposing viewpoints and rebut them.*

### III. The quality of the research in regards to its bearing on helping the writer support the thesis: 20/25

*You come at the topic of social networking from so many excellent angles, but again the thesis is more factual—a statement of what you see around you—than it is an argument.*

### IV. The writer's ability to control the argument, ensuring that his/her voice is never lost, that research is supported with writer's analysis and interpretation: 25/25

*You do a particularly fine job helping readers understand the various quotations and paraphrases that you use throughout.*

### V. The quality of documentation, including parenthetical, in-text, and Works Cited: 25/25

*Excellent!*

### VI. Grammatical and mechanical accuracy: 24/25

*Excellent!*

**Grade: 138/150 = 92 (A-)**

## Social Networking and the Digital Divide:
## Why Internet Access Is Vital
## to Worldwide Communication

Communication has advanced dramatically over the past few decades, perhaps most notably with the advent of personal computers and the Internet. Email, instant messaging, webcams, and social networking websites allow Internet users worldwide to connect in seconds. For much of the world, however, access to information technology is limited, due to financial, political, and geographical discrepancies termed the "digital divide." The existence of the divide harms users because those without access to information technology are unable to utilize its social, economic, and political benefits. Decreasing the digital divide is vital not only to enhance the right of individuals to access information, but also to allow users across the world to actively contribute to the increasingly user-generated content of the Internet.

The importance of lessening the digital divide is twofold: first, the Internet is a vast source of easily accessible information, and the social aspects of online communication have become as prominent as telephone calls. Internet access is widespread in many developed nations, where one is able to correspond, manage finances, and find entertainment on the Web, through both personal and public computers. In less-developed nations where information technology is more limited, however, citizens still deserve equal access to the benefits of the Web. Increased Internet availability will provide users worldwide with equal opportunities for knowledge and networking. Second, in addition to the right of obtaining information, decreasing the digital divide will also permit the global user base to become more than a passive audience to online information. With the prevalence of websites based on user-generated content (from YouTube and Flickr to Wikipedia and Facebook), the Internet is already a massive resource—and as Internet use grows, these websites continue to develop and expand, providing more content. In order to allow worldwide utilization of and contribution to information technology, it is imperative to decrease the digital divide.

## THE DIGITAL DIVIDE

The digital divide is, essentially, a discrepancy in access to information technology on both local and worldwide scales. While few people in developing countries have access to computers and fewer still have their own, inequality also persists in more developed nations. In "Trends in Media Use," Donald F. Roberts and Ulla G. Foehr note that, when grouped by familial income, the percentage of American families who have access to the Internet in their own homes ranges from 29 to 93 percent—wealthier families can afford more access, while less-advantaged and rural-dwelling groups have less. This trend of accessibility variance across economic and location factors is also echoed on a global scale in Hiroshi Ono and Madeline Zavodny's study, "Digital Inequality: A Five Country Comparison Using Microdata," where the authors state,

> In spite of the tremendous increase in [information technology] use in recent years, a pattern of "digital inequality," or differences in IT access and usage, persists both across countries and across certain socioeconomic and demographic groups within countries. In 2000, the 29 OECD member states contained 90 percent of all Internet users in the world, and there were more Internet users in Sweden than in the entire continent of Africa. (1135–36)

While there is no single factor in the digital divide, Internet access can, like many opportunities, be attributed to location and economic status. In *Digital Divide: Civic Engagement, Information Poverty, and the Internet Worldwide*, Pippa Norris goes further and separates the digital divide into a "global divide," the inequality between nations in different stages of development, a "social divide," a division between those rich and those lacking information technology within countries, and a "democratic divide," a gap depending on the uses to which one puts Internet access (4–13). Mainstream media attention is often on the first two of Norris's divisions, global and social, and in the United States, coverage is often concentrated on rural and race groups, such as Michael Marriott's "Digital Divide Closing as Blacks Turn to Internet," in which Marriott states that "falling price of laptops, more computers in public schools and libraries and the newest generation of cellphones and hand-held devices that connect to the Internet have all contributed to closing the divide" (par. 3). Simply having the tools necessary to access online content is clearly a large part of reducing discrepancies in the divide. He also notes the challenges facing African Americans and information technology—again, strongly rooted in finances and locations. In both developed and developing nations, within individual countries and on a worldwide level, it is vital to decrease the digital divide, not only to allow citizens in such communities equal access to information, but also to allow their contributions to content in the World Wide Web.

One reason behind the digital divide is that of costs—in countries where citizens lack access even to clean drinking water, computers are rarely affordable. In developing nations where many people do have access to the Internet, however, website owners are struggling to provide these new users with equal site contents. Brad Stone and Miguel Helft reported in "In Developing Countries, Web Grows Without Profit," that Internet users in Asia, Africa, Latin America, and Eastern Europe are using increasing amounts of bandwidth (particularly for photos and video), while at the same time providing the website owners with little monetary return from advertisements aimed at wealthier viewers. Stone and Helft quote Dmitry Shapiro, the executive of a video-sharing site called Veoh. "I believe in free, open communications," said Shapiro. "But these people are so hungry for content. They sit and they watch and watch and watch. The problem is they are eating up bandwidth, and it's very difficult to derive revenue from it." Veoh has stopped allowing Internet users in Asia, Africa, Eastern Europe, and Latin America access to the site, while other companies are also forced to consider tactics such as limiting access or compromising the quality of their online media in developing countries (pars. 4–7, 13–19). Financial issues on both sides of the divide complicate the expansion of Internet availability because, while many potential Internet users have no way of accessing computers, those who do receive inferior quality. By working with advertisers to develop planning for the new user demographics, website owners will gradually be able to equalize access to their sites, and increasing the availability of computer systems and Internet access is necessary to reduce both global and social digital divides.

Internet users in many countries also face the issue of government censorship. For example, in "YouTube Being Blocked in China, Google Says," Miguel Helft reports that the Chinese government disallowed all access to YouTube, a video-sharing website, possibly in response to a video allegedly showing Tibetans being beaten by Chinese officers (pars. 2–4, 9). "China routinely filters Internet content and blocks material that is critical of its policies," writes Helft. "It also frequently blocks individual videos on YouTube" (par. 7). In an article published three days later, "China: YouTube Again Accessible," Edward Wong noted that the government's ban was lifted. Before the block was removed, however, Chinese citizens were still able to access the site by using special software, a "common way of getting around Internet walls put up by the government" (par. 1). The block and its subsequent removal illustrates several points—that governments such as China's can feel threatened by the consequences of Internet access, that the governments themselves contribute to the digital divide by deceasing said access, and that Internet users are still able to find ways around specific website bans, as long as they are still able to connect to the Internet. Government bans are a hurdle that must be confronted to mend the digital divide and, while solutions to censorship remain more political than technological, it is clear that censorship potentially prevents individuals from accessing information important to making informed decisions while also inhibiting their contributions to online content.

5

One Writer's Process: Three Drafts

## THE BENEFITS OF ACCESS TO INFORMATION TECHNOLOGY

The Internet provides users with millions of pages of information. Free and subscriber-based services offer articles from newspapers, scholarly journals, and trade magazines, while exclusively online content exists for nearly every imaginable subject. Websites such as WorldCat, the World Digital Library, and local library websites allow users to determine the availability of printed books and, in some cases, to actually read digitalized versions of books. Beyond academic offerings, however, the Internet is home to a wide variety of social networking websites. As Robin Manson and Frank Rennie note in the *E-Learning and Social Networking Handbook*, a key value of social networking is the "gift culture"—an intrinsic feature of online communities where users both provide and partake in the site's content. They add that "the primary focus in social networking is participation rather than publication . . . the essence of social networking is that users generate the content" (Manson and Rennie 3–4). One might add to this definition that the utilization of these websites can range from personal to professional, and that the sites vary greatly in purpose. Facebook, for example, is primarily a social website where users connect and share personal information, news, photos, and videos. The site, which is run as a business, has over 200 million users, about 70 percent of whom reside outside of the United States ("Facebook"). On YouTube, viewers watch videos uploaded by users across the world and share their responses with each other in the form of text comments below each video. Another website, Twitter, is also unique, being a "microblogging" website where members send Tweets, or short messages of under 141 characters, to answer the question "What are you doing?" Users follow each other's posts and can then reply back, while a system of keywords, or "tags," sorts the updates into a searchable database. Varied as these websites are, they remain alike in their central purpose, which is to provide interpersonal connections based on user-contributed content.

In addition to providing information and entertainment for Internet users, users of social networking websites also offer support. In her article "Revolution, Facebook Style," Samantha M. Shapiro explores a series of protests led by young men and women in Egypt. These protests, she says, began as demonstrations against Israeli attacks on Hamas and evolved into larger protests against the Egyptian government and President Mubarak (pars. 1–3). Focusing on the ways in which these demonstrations grew from Facebook groups (online clubs that users create to support causes or interests), Shapiro writes,

> Although there are countless political Facebook groups in Egypt, many of which flare up and fall into disuse in a matter of days, the one with the most dynamic debates is that of the April 6 Youth Movement, a group of 70,000 mostly young and educated Egyptians, most of whom had never been involved with politics before joining the group . . . they have tried to organize street protests to free jailed journalists, and this month, hundreds of young people from the April 6 group participated in demonstrations about Gaza, some of which were coordinated on Facebook, and at least eight members of the group were detained by police. (par. 5)

In some ways, the Egyptians' use of social networking websites to organize protests is similar to Chinese users posting videos of violence on YouTube—information and support in both cases threatened the government's influence on its citizens. In the case of the young men and women in Egypt, however, the young citizens who Shapiro describes as previously being almost politically apathetic discovered an uncensored environment for discussions of political interest and, moreover, expanded their virtual community into physical displays of activism.

Another example of social networking websites spreading awareness and creating real-life results occurred in Moldova, after the April 5 election in 2009. Groups protesting the Communist Moldovan government used the Internet to coordinate gatherings at Chisinau. While Ellen Barry reported in "Protests in Moldova Explode, With Help of Twitter" that the 10,000 young Moldovan men and women used Twitter to organize their April 7 protest, other news sources quickly pointed out that Twitter users were not the sole coordinators of the demonstrations. In fact, the majority of the organization was done via blogs and Faceboook (Bennet pars. 21–22). As violence escalated, protesters such as Mihai Moscovici reported the events on Twitter, even as the Moldovan government began cutting off local Internet and cell phone services. "Presidency building is broken. The door is unlocked. Police use gas to resist protesters. Chisinau, Moldova," he Tweeted on April 7. Moscovici's succinct updates remain online for anyone to view, as are violent videos uploaded onto YouTube by individuals and news stations, such as "Protesters Storm Parliament in Chisinau" (EUXTV). "Once again," Moscovici wrote on April 12, "Twitter didn't generate any revolution in Moldova. It was used as a tool to report about the protest in Chisinau, Moldova." In this case, the electronic documentation of the protests is a key point, for it was the combination of multiple social networking sites that created power and publicity for the protesters. Social networking was used to coordinate the demonstrations, and then to share the resulting consequences with Internet users worldwide—and as news reporters latched onto the idea of Twitter as a means of rebellion, the protest's audience increased further. Information technology led not only to the initiation of protests in Moldova, but also to protester-created online content available to users worldwide.

Within the fields of information technology and the Internet, social networking websites are beginning to form complex interconnectivity for users. While reading an article on the website of the *New York Times*, for example, one can instantly share the story with others via outside sites, including MySpace and Facebook. Further links allow readers to contact the reporter and visit his or her own blog. The *Times* also has a Twitter feed with over one million followers, a Facebook page with 400,000 fans, and a YouTube stream, which features dozens of videos related to current news articles. Not only do these networking websites allow the *Times* to provide readers with up-to-date information, but readers are able to actively respond to the news. Viewers of the paper's YouTube stream can converse in the "Comments" section as Facebook users debate in public forums, and all are able to post their thoughts about breaking news without fear of repercussion. Social networking websites that have previously been viewed as virtual hangouts for adolescents are gaining a more professional appeal as businesspeople take advantage of networking opportunities and MySpace services, such as pages for bands, classified ads, and job listings. NASA astronaut Mike Massimino Tweeted from orbit on a recent mission, while surgeons at the Henry Ford Hospital have posted minute-by-minute Twitter updates during surgeries. The uses of social networking have become widespread in nations of all stages of online development, providing users with information, support, and opportunities to share their own insight, and increasing the accessibility of these sites will benefit user-contributors worldwide.

## MENDING THE DIGITAL DIVIDE

The primary arguments against diminishing the digital divide concern 10
politics and practicality: does providing Internet access to the citizens of developing countries conflict with the roles of governments in such nations, and if it does not, how is it possible to provide millions of people with access to computers and the Internet? To the first question, answers are subjective and prey to personal beliefs. In most developed countries, freedom of speech and information is a given right, as are the abilities to challenge and question authority without repercussion. The Internet as a whole (and social networking in particular) facilitates debate, which as the Egyptian and Moldovan examples illustrate, can lead to real-world revolts. The benefits of information technology extend beyond political activism, however. Communities with Internet access possess a wealth of information, from educational and medicinal aid to entertainment, maps, weather reports, and worldwide news. While information freedom can lead to rebellion, it will also benefit nations as citizens are able to answer their own questions and achieve new objectives.

Attaining Internet connections is a more straightforward problem. As the technology behind computers and software advances, prices drop and more people can afford to purchase the hardware. In areas and nations where citizens do not have enough resources for even basic needs, however, technology can be subsidized. Internet access for individuals will benefit the community as a whole—farms benefit with access to accurate weather forecasts, while other workers can improve their own skills, contributing to the overall economy and better individual quality of life. Website owners struggling to pay for bandwidth can work with local advertisers in new target demographics, and can also develop lower-bandwidth versions of their sites—MySpace, for instance, is reported by Stone and Helft to be testing an alternative version of the website called "Profile Lite" (par. 13). As communities and website owners make the Internet available to the masses, however, it bears mentioning that numbers alone will not necessarily enhance the information available online. Rather, the unique thoughts and experiences of each user, their contributions to advocacy and support groups, and the expansion of worldwide social circles will make access to user-generated social networking websites a beneficial development.

Marriott writes that minority groups are increasingly using the Internet, in part because of "the explosive evolution of the Internet itself, once mostly a tool used by researchers, which has become a cultural crossroad of work, play, and social interaction" (par. 4). Indeed, the Internet is a venue for entertainment, education, and socialization. Simply by being a part of the gift culture in social networking, one augments the available online content. The Internet allows unrestrained access to information, as well as opportunities to respond, connect, and create real-world changes. Decreasing the digital divide both globally and locally will not only improve individuals' right to information, but will also augment the information available to Internet users worldwide.

## WORKS CITED

Barry, Ellen. "Protests in Moldova Explode, With Help of Twitter." *New York Times.* New York Times, 7 Apr. 2009. Web. 18 Apr. 2009.

Bennet, Daniel. "The Myth of the Moldova Twitter Revolution." *Frontline.* Washington Post, 8 Apr. 2009. Web. 20 Apr. 2009.

EUXTV. "Protesters Storm Parliament in Chisinau: Realitatea TV." *YouTube.com.* YouTube, 7 Apr. 2009. Web. 20 Apr. 2009.

"Facebook Statistics." *Facebook.* Facebook, 2009. Web. 24 Apr. 2009.

Helft, Miguel. "YouTube Blocked in China, Google Says." *New York Times.* New York Times, 24 Mar. 2009. Web. 23 Apr. 2009.

Mason, Robin, and Frank Rennie. *E-Learning and Social Networking Handbook: Resources for Higher Education.* New York: Routledge, 2008. Print.

Marriott, Michael. "Digital Divide Closing as Blacks Turn to Internet." *New York Times.* New York Times, 31 Mar. 2006 Web. 22 Apr. 2009.

Massimino, Mike. "Astro_Mike on Twitter." *Twitter.com.* Twitter, 4 May 2009. Web. 4 May 2009.

Moscovici, Mihai. "Moscovici on Twitter." *Twitter.com.* Twitter, 26 Apr. 2009. Web. 26 Apr. 2009.

Norris, Pippa. *Digital Divide: Civic Engagement, Information Poverty, and the Internet Worldwide.* New York: Cambridge UP, 2001. Print.

Ono, Hiroshi, and Madeline Zavodny. "Digital Inequality: A Five-Country Comparison Using Microdata." *Social Science Research* 36 (2007): 1135–155. *ProQuest. Web.* 22 Apr. 2009.

Roberts, Donald F., and Ulla G. Foehr. "Trends in Media Use." *The Future of Children* 18.1 (2008): 11–37. *JSTOR.* Web. 23 Apr. 2009.

Shapiro, Samantha M. "Revolution, Facebook Style." *New York Times.* New York Times, 22 Jan. 2009. Web. 20 Apr. 2009.

Stone, Brad, and Miguel Helft. "In Developing Countries, Web Grows Without Profit." *New York Times.* New York Times, 26 Apr. 2009. Web. 27 Apr. 2009.

Wong, Edward. "China: YouTube Again Accessible." *New York Times.* New York Times, 27 Mar. 2009. Web. 2 Jun. 2009.

# Permissions Acknowledgments

Submitting Papers for Publication by W. W. Norton & Company

We are interested in receiving writing from college students to consider including in our textbooks as examples of student writing. Please send this form with the work that you would like us to consider to Marilyn Moller, Student Writing, W. W. Norton & Company, 500 Fifth Avenue, New York NY 10110.

**Text Submission Form**

Student's name _____

School _____

Address _____

Department _____

Course _____

Writing assignment the text responds to _____

_____

_____

_____

Instructor's name _____

*(continued next page)*

Please write a few sentences about what your primary purposes were for writing this text. Also, if you wish, tell us what you think you learned about writing from the experience of writing it.

_____

_____

_____

_____

_____

_____

_____

## Contact Information

*Please provide the information below so that we can contact you if your work is selected for publication.*

Name _____

Permanent Address _____

Email _____

Phone _____